PRIMITIVE, ARCHAIC, AND
MODERN ECONOMIES

KARL POLANYI (1886–1964), studied law and philosophy, and was called to the bar in Budapest in 1912. He served as a cavalry officer in the war of 1914–18. From 1924 to 1933 he was foreign affairs editor of *Der Oesterreichische Volkswirt* in Vienna. He emigrated to England in 1933, and lectured for the Workers Educational Association and for the extra-mural departments of the universities of Oxford and London. He was joint editor of *Christianity and the Social Revolution* (1935), to which he contributed a chapter, "The Essence of Fascism."

His work in economic history was done in the United States, from 1940 to 1943 as resident scholar at Bennington College, and from 1947 until his retirement in 1953, as Professor of Economics at Columbia University. From 1953 to 1958 he and Professor Conrad M. Arensberg were joint directors of a research project on the economic aspects of institutional growth.

The first of Polanyi's three principal works, *The Great Transformation* (1944), was concerned with the structure of nineteenth century capitalism and the enormity of its social consequences. His second book, *Trade and Market in the Early Empires* (1957), edited with Conrad M. Arensberg and Harry W. Pearson, created a theoretical framework for the study of economies which were neither industrialized nor organized by market institutions. His last work, published posthumously — *Dahomey and the Slave Trade* (1966) — analyzed the internal economic organization of the eighteenth century West African kingdom, and the economic organization of its external trade in slaves with Europeans.

GEORGE DALTON is Professor of Economics and Anthropology at Northwestern University and a staff member of its Program of African Studies. He received his B.A. degree from Indiana University, M.A. from Columbia University, and, in 1959, his Ph.D. from the University of Oregon. In 1961–62 he spent fifteen months in West Africa, and is co-author of a volume on the Liberian economy, *Growth without Development: An Economic Survey of Liberia* (1966). With Paul Bohannan, he edited *Markets in Africa* (1962). He has published articles on economic anthropology, comparative economy, and economic development, and has edited a volume of readings in economic anthropology, *Tribal and Peasant Economies* (1967).

Karl Polanyi, 1947

PRIMITIVE, ARCHAIC, AND MODERN ECONOMIES

Essays of Karl Polanyi

EDITED BY GEORGE DALTON

ANCHOR BOOKS
DOUBLEDAY & COMPANY, INC.
GARDEN CITY, NEW YORK
1968

To
Ilona Duczyńska Polanyi

Contents

Editor's Note

The essays in this volume originally appeared between 1944 and 1966 as chapters of four books and articles in four journals. The purpose of bringing them together is to make them easily accessible to students of economic anthropology, economic history, and comparative economic systems along with an expository Introduction to Polanyi's work. The appendices to Essays 6 and 8 are compiled from unpublished memoranda Polanyi distributed to his students.

The essays are reprinted here with slight changes in punctuation, and, in a few instances, deletion or substitution of a word to make the meaning clearer. There are also occasional editorial insertions [in square brackets] to add an explanatory word, to comment on difficult matters, or to refer the reader to related writings. The place and date of original publication appear at the beginning of each essay. (The editor regrets his inability to track down the sources of several of the brief quotations Polanyi cites without reference.)

Introduction[1]

BY GEORGE DALTON

It is only our Western societies that quite recently turned man into an economic animal.—MARCEL MAUSS

Karl Polanyi was a warm, generous, and committed man whose enormous range of interests spanned all the social sciences and beyond.[2] His was an original mind although he never claimed excessive originality. In his lectures at Columbia and in print he emphasized his indebtedness to Marx, Maine, Bücher, Weber, Thurnwald, Pirenne, Menger, Malinowski, and others. His concept of "redistribution" as an integrative mode of economic organization, and much that he said about money, external trade, market places, ports of trade, operational devices, and the birth and reform of industrial capitalism, was, I believe, original with him. His forceful presentation and keen insight made us aware of economies of record in ways different from the distinguished writers from whom he learned much.

The qualities that made him a brilliant lecturer also made him a difficult writer. His passionate commitment and enormous learning drew large numbers of students to

[1] This Introduction is an expanded and revised version of a paper given at the Annual Spring Meetings of the American Ethnological Society, 1965 [20]. I am grateful to Joseph S. Berliner, Paul Bohannan, Edward Budd, Robert Campbell, Helen Codere, J. R. T. Hughes, Walter Neale, and Ilona Polanyi for their critical comments.

[2] Karl Polanyi died in April 1964.

his lectures, several of whom made his research interests their own [13, 59, 65].[3] But what was forceful, lucid, and articulate in the lecture hall sometimes became hyperbole and polemic in print. A friend sympathetic to his work describes Polanyi's writing style as a stiletto set in the far end of a battering ram. Academics do not always like to be lectured at in print [79, 85].

Polanyi's substance is also difficult. To discuss Ricardo's England, Malinowski's Trobriand Islands, and Hitler's Germany in the same book (*The Great Transformation*) is to demand much of the reader; but to expect the reader to follow him into Hammurabi's Babylonia, Aristotle's Greece, and eighteenth-century Dahomey (*Trade and Market in the Early Empires*) is to expect altogether too much.

However, in the very range of economies he analyzes and draws from, lies one of his principal contributions: that a theory of economic anthropology becomes possible only when primitive and archaic economies are regarded as part of comparative economic systems. To understand what is special to the economies anthropologists deal with and what they share with all other economies requires comparative analysis of the kind Polanyi provides. In order for anthropologists to see what is analytically important in Trobriands' economy they must first understand the structure of industrial capitalism [15, 16]; to understand the special usage of pig-tusk and cowrie money, they must first understand the organization and usage of dollars and francs [19]. One reason why theory in economic anthropology remains underdeveloped is that anthropologists have not brought to the economic branch of their subject the same comparative grounding they bring to kinship, law, politics, and religion.

[3] The numbers and citations in brackets refer to bibliographical references listed at the end of this Introduction.

The message is reversible. The farther back one goes into European or Asian history, the more closely do economies resemble those studied by anthropologists [63, 87, 34]. The historians concerned with pre-industrial economies and the economists concerned with comparative economic systems have much to learn from economic anthropology. Firsthand accounts of primitive economy are as close to a laboratory as economic historians and those concerned with comparative economy can get [49, 50, 51, 57].

This should not come as a surprise. The economic historians today are teaching us about African and Asian economic development by pointing out what was special to European and American development [31, 78]. So, too, can we learn about modern communistic and welfare state economies by contrasting them with the pre-industrial systems we call primitive, peasant, and archaic. Polanyi's work provides a corrective to one of the shortcomings in the field of comparative economic systems: its almost exclusive concern with recent and contemporary industrial economies. The field is too narrowly confined to comparisons of industrial capitalism—the laissez-faire, welfare state, and fascist varieties—and industrial communism. The areas of fruitful comparison can be widened. The specialized subjects that are economic anthropology and economic history should be treated as part of comparative economy.

Any writer of consequence in the social sciences—Adam Smith, Karl Marx, J. M. Keynes—can be regarded as presenting a number of leading ideas and also an analytical system of concepts, causal analysis, and application of these to real world processes and problems. Intelligent laymen come to know his leading ideas; the experts concentrate on his analytical system. In what follows, I will describe Polanyi's leading ideas and the analytical system he designed to examine two broad problems that absorbed him:

(1) The origin, growth, and transformation of nineteenth-century capitalism;

(2) The relation of economy to society in primitive and archaic systems.

Laissez-faire Capitalism Contrasted with Primitive and Archaic Economies

The subject of *The Great Transformation* (1944) and "Our Obsolete Market Mentality" (1947) is the birth of laissez-faire capitalism in England between 1750 and 1850, and its death in Europe and America during the 1930s and 1940s.[4] Polanyi's principal concern is to show the uniqueness, historically, of uncontrolled market exchange as the integrating transactional mode of nineteenth-century national and international economy, and to show why the structure and performance of market economy were socially divisive and inevitably led to extensive social control (the New Deal, the welfare state, fascism).

One of his themes is that the pursuit of material self-gain as the *institutionally enforced* incentive to participate in economic life, eroded social and community life and induced protective measures throughout the nineteenth century.[5] Here Polanyi brings economic anthropology to bear to show that the attempt to create a self-regulating market economy was a radical departure from the past.

His political economy of contrast shows that in primitive and archaic economies, the institutions through which goods were produced and distributed were "embedded" in —a subordinate part of—social institutions: that the "economy" functioned as a by-product of kinship, political, and religious obligation.

[4] For an expository account of Polanyi's leading ideas—inexplicably unacknowledged—see Heilbroner [39]. A detailed analysis of *The Great Transformation* is the subject of Sievers [84].

[5] For similar conclusions about the social and cultural implications of capitalism arrived at from a different analytical viewpoint, see the work of Erich Fromm, especially [27, 28].

We must rid ourselves of the ingrained notion that the economy is a field of experience of which human beings have necessarily always been conscious [Polanyi, Arensberg, and Pearson 1957: 242].

Where markets existed, they were most frequently confined to a few produced items the sale of which did not contribute appreciably to the livelihood of producers or sellers [66]. Markets were contained, and nowhere created an economy-wide system. Typically in primitive and early economies, land and labor were allocated in accordance with kinship, political, or tribal rights and obligations, and not as commodities to be bought and sold.

In primitive and archaic economies subsistence livelihood in effect was guaranteed as a moral right of membership in a human community. It is the social right to receive land, labor, and produce in ordinary times, and emergency support from kin, friends, leaders, and rulers, that Polanyi also meant by the "embeddedness" of economy in society. Fear of hunger—the "economic whip" of nineteenth-century capitalism [11]—and the quest for material self-gain were not structured as incentives to participate in economic activity.[6] In short, Polanyi analyzes the institutional substance underlying Tönnies' point that primitive and archaic societies are *Gemeinschaft* rather than *Gesellschaft,* and Maine's point that they are organized by status rather than contract.

. . . ranging over human societies we find hunger and gain not appealed to as incentives to production, and

---

[6] To suggest that primitive economy and society provide material and psychological security is to risk being accused of ethnic nostalgia—the modern equivalent of belief in the noble savage. Frequently in primitive societies, material life is poor and physical life is nasty and short: poverty, disease, death, and pain are the common lot. But social life is meaningful, and social relationships immediate and crucial to one's well-being. Undoubtedly, the facts of illiteracy and of isolation contribute to the intensity and inwardness of personal relations within community life.

where so appealed to, they are fused with other powerful motives [Polanyi 1947: 112].

Political, religious, and familial organizations arrange production and distribution in various ways [81], but the specific institutions express variants of two broad transactional modes ("patterns of integration") that Polanyi called reciprocity (obligatory gift-giving between kin and friends), and redistribution (obligatory payments to central political or religious authority, which uses the receipts for its own maintenance, to provide community services, and as an emergency stock in case of individual or community disaster).[7] Reciprocity and redistribution are best regarded as socio-economic transactional modes because they describe internal and external appropriations, allocations, and exchanges; movements of goods, employment of specialist services and labor; and the control and use of land—induced by specific social obligation. Market exchange transactions differ because they are not expressions of social

| | *Transactional Mode* | | |
	Reciprocity	*Redistribution*	*Market Exchange*
Underlying social relationship which is expressed by the transaction	Friendship, Kinship, Status, Hierarchy	Political or Religious Affiliation	None

[7] Polanyi calls reciprocity, redistribution, and [market] exchange, "patterns of integration." Just as market exchange is integrative in U.S. economy because land and labor as well as products are transacted through purchase and sale (i.e., production entails purchasing factors and selling products), and because most people depend for their livelihood on income got from production for sale, so too, are reciprocity and redistribution integrative in primitive economies. In Malinowski's Trobriands, for example, the bulk of one's staple food (yams) comes through reciprocity—gifts from wife's brother expressed as an obligation of kinship; land also is allocated as a matter of lineage affiliation.

obligation, which makes them seem especially "economic."

Polanyi used economic anthropology and early economic history to jar us loose from ideas and generalizations about man and society implanted by the Industrial Revolution. (Classical economics and the ideology of laissez faire, as well as Marxian socialism came out of the English Industrial Revolution [41].) He was particularly concerned to dislodge the notion—so widely and implicitly held—that markets are the ubiquitous and invariable form of economic organization; that any economy can be *translated* into market terms [33, 79], and the further notion that economic organization determines social organization and culture in all societies. These he regarded as wrong generalizations from the one very special case (laissez-faire capitalism) for which they are true. He argued that these generalizations must be disproved and disbelieved if we are ever to make industrial technology serve the needs of human community [28], and indeed if we are to understand the nature of economic organization in early and primitive economies.

Man does not have an innate propensity to truck, barter, and exchange, if by this is meant to buy and sell:

. . . Adam Smith's suggestions about the economic psychology of early man were as false as Rousseau's were on the political psychology of the savage. Division of labor, a phenomenon as old as society, springs from differences inherent in the facts of sex, geography, and individual endowment; and the alleged propensity of man to barter, truck, and exchange is almost entirely apocryphal [Polanyi 1944: 44].

There is a semantic difficulty here. All communities institutionalize exchanges of material items and services, and make systematic the allocation of rights to land and other natural resources (there are no Robinson Crusoe economies). But it is not a commercial gene that makes it so. Rather it is the need for all communities—whatever their size and technology—to organize material life so as to assure the sustained, repetitive provision of food, shelter, and the items necessary for community life. (This is what Polanyi meant by the "substantive" definition of economic, universally applicable to all societies.)

Exchanges, allocations, transfers, and appropriations of resources, labor, produce, and services occur in all economies not only because of the need to structure material provision, but also because division of labor, if only according to sex and age, is universal, which itself necessitates "exchanges" of some sort. That one finds exchanges in U.S., Soviet, and Trobriand economy, does not tell us very much: it is how resources are directed to specific uses, how production is organized, and how goods are disposed of—in short, how the economy is instituted—that gives us insight into similarities and differences among U.S., Soviet, and Trobriand economy.

Polanyi's use of economic anthropology and early economic history forces us to unlearn the simplistic notion of the economic determination of history and social change, so widely shared by the left and the right [37].

The market mechanism . . . created the delusion of economic determinism as a general law for all human society [Polanyi 1947: 114].

With regard to the primacy of economy in social structure, Polanyi argues that Marx was right for laissez-faire industrial capitalism.

A market economy can only exist in a market society . . . a market economy must comprise all the elements of industry, including labor, land, and money . . . But labor and land are no other than the human beings themselves of which every society consists and the natural surroundings in which it exists. To include them in the market mechanism means to subordinate the substance of society itself to the laws of the market [Polanyi 1944: 71].

But Marx was wrong in generalizing economic determination of social organization to early and primitive societies.[8] Indeed, the lesson of economic anthropology is the unimportance of economic organization in primitive society as *the* determinative influence on social organization or culture. Rather, it is kinship, tribal affiliation, political rule, and religious obligation that control, direct, and are expressed by the economic in primitive societies (i.e., where market dependence is absent).

> The exchanges of archaic societies which he [Mauss] examines are total social movements or activities. They are at the same time economic, juridical, moral, aesthetic, religious, mythological, and socio-morphological phenomena. Their meaning can therefore only be grasped if they are viewed as a complex concrete reality [Evans-Pritchard 1954: vii].

Hayek's *Road to Serfdom* may be taken as a forward extrapolation of economic determinism. Published in the same year as Polanyi's *The Great Transformation*, it argues exactly that thesis which Polanyi's work was designed to disprove: that departures from the self-regulating market system must erode political democracy and personal freedom; that Hitler's Germany was the inevitable consequence of governmental regulation of the economy.[9]

[8] Some anthropologists seem to retain the general idea of economic determination of society and history. See the economic "surplus" controversy [65, 36, 14, 17].

[9] Polanyi [1947: 117] points out that even during World War II, the extensive governmental controls over economy in Great Britain and the United States did not abrogate essential freedoms. Nor should we forget that the fiscal policies and market controls used by fascist Germany, although geared to purposes of war preparation, are not inevitably so geared; with a few exceptions, such as governmental prohibitions of strikes and special foreign trade devices, they are the same fiscal techniques and market controls which the democracies have now institutionalized for purposes of providing welfare services, full employment, and growth. See Walker [90].

This is not the place to consider Hayek's argument, see [24,

The Social and Cultural Consequences of the Industrial Revolution

Polanyi's views on the social and cultural consequences of uncontrolled industrial capitalism in Great Britain during the first half of the nineteenth century [67, 68] are relevant to three issues: (i) The debate between the radical and the conservative economic historians who interpret in different ways the "impact" of early British industrial capitalism. (ii) The reasons for the growth of market controls and governmental regulation especially after 1860, culminating in the radical departures from the system in the 1930s and 1940s. (iii) The present concern with social and cultural consequences of economic development in the former colonies in Africa and Asia.

From Toynbee's *Lectures on the Industrial Revolution* (1884) to Carr's *The New Society* (1951), radical historians have pictured the early phase of the English Industrial Revolution in terms of misery and degradation heaped upon the mass of the populace. Conservative historians have challenged this view [38] by arguing two points: that even during the early period the real income of a substantial portion of the industrial labor force was rising. (It was displaced handicraft workers and others in

---

91]. However, in passing one might point out that in the generation since Hayek's book was published, the United States and Great Britain have become welfare states through the extension of market controls and the application of Keynesian fiscal policies. Great Britain, of course, has gone further in nationalization of industry and in the provision of some welfare services. Aside from Goldwater and his followers, there seems to be no serious concern in either country that the steady departure from the unregulated market system is destroying political democracy and personal freedoms. The evidence is to the contrary, e.g., civil rights for American Negroes, and less inequality of job opportunities in Great Britain (because of educational reforms).

rural areas whose real income had fallen.) And that the evil conditions, misery, and harshness of life depicted were vastly exaggerated because the radical writers had nostalgic and fanciful notions about the attractions of rural life in agricultural villages—Merrie England; and because harsh conditions of urban and rural working class life, which long had gone unremarked, received publicity for the first time. They were made to appear as new consequences of the factory system due to a heightened sociological awareness. In brief, the growth of cities and factory employment exposed conditions of life which long had remained nasty and unnoticed.

Polanyi argues that the conservative position misses the point. Here again, anthropological and historical comparisons are brought to bear. Rising real income for a portion of the working class no more mitigated the social and cultural consequences of the Industrial Revolution than a higher real income for slaves in the southern United States mitigated the social and cultural catastrophe of their forced migration from Africa. It is the tenacity of nineteenth-century materialism that makes some economic historians still regard real income as the sole criterion of "welfare."[10] It was the fabric of personal and community life that was changed by the industrial factory system and by reliance for livelihood upon uncontrolled labor, land, and product markets. In Polanyi's terms it was socially divisive to make the fear of hunger and the quest for profits the *socially enforced* incentives to participate in economic activity. To make livelihood depend on the uncertain sale of labor, and profits the necessary condition for entrepreneurial survival, was to divorce economy from the expression of social relationships and social obligations.

The general diffusion of manufactures throughout a country generates a new character in its inhabitants;

[10] What economists call "psychic income" deserves much more analysis than it has ever been given.

and as this character is formed upon a principle quite unfavourable to individual or general happiness, it will produce the most lamentable and permanent evils, unless its tendency be counteracted by legislative interference and direction.

. . . the governing principle of trade, manufactures, and commerce is immediate pecuniary gain, to which on the great scale every other is made to give way [Owen 1815: 121, 123].

Although real income for many industrial workers may have risen, material insecurity had also increased, because of the threat of industrial unemployment and the disappearance of subsistence guarantees for the unfortunate that characterize rural societies in which kinship and village ties remain in force [1].

With his anthropological base, Polanyi was quick to see the similarity between the social consequences of the English Industrial Revolution and the disintegration of traditional societies when forced to change by colonial domination. *The Great Transformation* has things to say to those presently concerned with the social and cultural implications of economic and technological change in underdeveloped areas [18].

Not economic exploitation, as often assumed, but the disintegration of the cultural environment of the victim is then the cause of degradation. The economic process may, naturally, supply the vehicle of destruction, and almost invariably economic inferiority will make the weaker yield, but the immediate cause of his undoing is not for that reason economic; it lies in the lethal injury to the institutions in which his social existence is embodied. The result is loss of self-respect and standards, whether the unit is a people or a class, whether the process springs from so-called "culture conflict" or from a change in the position of a class within the confines of a society [Polanyi 1944: 157, see also 290–294].

But if the organized states of Europe could protect themselves against the backwash of international free trade, the politically unorganized colonial peoples could not. The revolt against imperialism was mainly an attempt on the part of exotic peoples to achieve the political status necessary to shelter themselves from the social dislocations caused by European trade policies. The protection that the white man could easily secure for himself, through the sovereign status of his communities was out of reach of the colored man as long as he lacked the prerequisite, political government [Polanyi 1944: 182–183. See also Singer 1950 and Myrdal 1957].

Humanistic Reform: Socially Controlled Industrial Economies

There are two main streams of modern socialism—Marxism, and Democratic Socialism—and one small tributary, utopian socialism (e.g., Owen, Fourier, *kibbutzim*). All socialisms have two features in common. They are reactions against laissez-faire industrial capitalism, movements and doctrines of criticism and protest. They are also movements of reform, blueprints for improvement, models claiming superiority over capitalism. And in their reforms, blueprints, and claims for superiority are interwoven two themes: the need for higher income and material security widely diffused, and something much different, the need to create a new society in which industrial technology and economic organization are made subordinate to the needs of human community—the economy to be embedded in society.[11] The idea of a new society expresses the ethical aspiration of socialisms: the family writ large, social communion and social responsibility expressed in everyday economic activities. Although the idea is part of all socialisms, its clearest example was the small-scale, face-to-face uto-

[11] For an extended treatment of these themes, see [13, 28, 56].

pian communities created in the nineteenth and twentieth centuries [13, 7, 8, 61, 86].

The tragedy of contemporary socialism is that only the first theme is being realized: both the welfare state and Soviet communism are creating higher incomes and material security widely diffused. This is all to the good. But neither has begun to create a new society in which industrial technology is deliberately organized to express social relationships and ethical norms. Affluence and material security are lamentably compatible with materialism and individualism.[12]

> I plead for the restoration of that unity of motives which should inform man in his everyday activity as a producer, for the reabsorption of the economic system in society, for the creative adaptation of our ways of life to an industrial environment [Polanyi 1947: 115–116].

Polanyi phrased these matters as "the place of economy in society." One could restate some of his principal themes in these terms: typically, primitive and archaic economies were small-scale, non-industrial, and organized as part of political and kinship structure.[13] The economy was socially controlled in the sense that natural resource and labor allocation, the organization of work within produc-

---

[12] Sweden, perhaps, is an exception, see [56]. Lewis [1955: 68–69] may be right about the impossibility of infusing a sense of personal participation and enmeshment in large-scale organizations. The organization of factory work is constrained not only by the requirements of machine technology, e.g., the pace of assembly lines, but also by market economy and efficiency constraints: the need to produce competitively at minimum costs.

[13] Large-scale archaic and primitive societies—the Inca, the Nupe, the eighteenth-century kingdom of Dahomey, the archaic empires of the middle east—are described less frequently than the small-scale society (the Nuer, the Trobriands, the Tiv) with which the literature of economic anthropology abounds. Two good accounts of large-scale systems are Nadel [57] and Polanyi [73].

tion processes, and the disposition of produce were expressions of kinship or political obligation or some other social relationships [16, 59]. (In economies where reciprocity and redistribution are the dominant transactional modes, it is impossible to analyze economic transactions apart from the kinship, political, and religious institutions of which they form an inextricable part.[14] Therefore analysis of primitive and archaic economies is socio-economic or institutional analysis—political economy rather than economics.)

In England, the Industrial Revolution followed the expansion of commercial agriculture (through enclosures and the application of improved technology), and the expansion of external commercial trade with the New World and exotic continents (e.g., Africa). Briefly, the expansion of agricultural and foreign trade capitalism preceded industrial capitalism. So too did Mercantilism, the extension of market controls to the entire nation-state.

The Industrial Revolution was also an institutional revolution. A condition for the profitable use of expensive, long-lasting machinery, was that entrepreneurs be assured of uninterrupted supplies of labor and other resource inputs

[14] There is a kernel of truth in the notion of "primitive communism." Socialism and communism are meant to apply to large-scale, industrialized economies whose decentralized market organization is to be either controlled, or superseded by central planning. Primitive economies are not large-scale, industrialized, nor capitalist (i.e., integrated by market exchange). The local face-to-face communal ties of family, neighborhood, common ancestry, and language—frequently together with isolation from other groups—account for the organization of production and distribution being controlled by social institutions. To those who define things in such a way that if a system is not capitalist, it must be communist, primitive economies appear communistic. If so, they more nearly resemble the communalism of small utopian communities whose economic arrangements express a community ethos, than the kinds of socialism we associate with modern Russia and the welfare states. See [62].

to work the machines as well as internal and external markets to effectively demand the outputs of the machines [Polanyi 1944: 74–75]. Laissez-faire capitalism was created in response to the needs of machine technology. By acts of government, national labor, land, and other resource markets were de-controlled, and financial markets (money and capital markets) were created or enlarged.

In Polanyi's terms, the institutional structure of laissez-faire industrial capitalism separated out economy from society and polity by turning labor, land, and other natural resources into commodities—organizing their supply as though they were items produced for sale, and by allowing the price mechanism working through interdependent national and international markets to determine their allocation and the income of their owners. One consequence of this great institutional transformation was that classical and then neo-classical economics could be created: the analysis of this separate and autonomous sphere of uncontrolled resource and product markets. With Adam Smith, political economy ended; with David Ricardo, economics began.

One of Polanyi's most perceptive and telling arguments concerning the social divisiveness of uncontrolled market economy emphasizes the spontaneity with which social control of labor, land, money, and some product markets was imposed in England and the continent, especially after 1860 [Polanyi 1944: Chapters 11, 12, 13]. Not only were similar controls in different countries instituted to protect workers, farmers, and businessmen, but the sponsors and supporters of the market controls varied radically in politics and ideology.

> When men who think differently behave alike, is it not probable that they are both responding to forces that are stronger than their conscious beliefs? [Lippman 1949: 35].

It was not only the stability or amount of income of specific groups that was protected, but community life also was protected, in response to conditions created by *industrialism* and *urbanism*, as well as uncontrolled markets. Governmental intervention was not solely in the form of protective tariffs, but also in the form of anti-child labor laws, safety requirements for hazardous occupations, zoning laws, building codes, industrial accident insurance, etc.[15]

It is manifestly impracticable to separate the humane, the political, the economic, and the religious objectives of these interventions . . . The one common characteristic is the consistent readiness of interested groups to use the state for collective ends [Brebner 1952: 509; see also Robinson 1954].

Most of *The Great Transformation* is devoted to a detailed analysis of what Polanyi calls the double movement in the nineteenth century: the growth of free market transactions of produced goods throughout the world while market controls were imposed in Europe, and later America, on transactions of labor, land, and money in response to elementary needs of community stability and cohesion. His analysis of unions, factory acts, agricultural tariffs, and central banking, as devices to prevent free market forces from allocating labor and other factor resources in accordance with the model of pure competition, is extremely illuminating. So too is his analysis of the crises of the 1920s and 1930s in which German fascism and the American

[15] I believe Polanyi overstates one of his important arguments. He asserts that the socially intolerable results of uncontrolled markets induced governmental controls and policy which, in preventing the equilibrating forces of markets from working, hampered the economic system fatally [Polanyi 1944: Chapters 18, 19]. But surely a decisive feature of laissez-faire capitalism was its chronic inability to generate full employment for Keynesian reasons. Even without the pre-1930 market controls, the system would have created chronic depression and so induced fiscal intervention of the kinds now used. Uncontrolled market economy was not viable for economic as well as social reasons.

New Deal transformed market economies that had failed to function.

> In order to comprehend German fascism we must revert to Ricardian England [Polanyi 1944: 30].

The ideology of laissez faire outlived the structural reforms that changed uncontrolled market economy. Indeed, the discrepancy between what some think we ought to do—laissez faire—and what we in fact are doing—creating a welfare state—has not yet entirely disappeared in the United States. Balanced budgets and the gold standard are not yet regarded as costly anachronisms, even by all economists.

In Polanyi's terms, the welfare state is a movement toward "re-embedding" economy in society by controlling markets, assuring a minimum level of income to all as a matter of political right, and enlarging the redistributive sphere of the economy by allocating medical and some other social services on non-market criteria. (The Soviet system represents the first example of an industrial economy in which redistribution, as the dominant transactional mode, has displaced market exchange.)

The Reality of Society

> But he who is unable to live in society, or who has no need, because he is sufficient for himself, must be either a beast or a god . . .   —ARISTOTLE

Keynes' *General Theory* and Galbraith's *Affluent Society* contain a theme that Polanyi returned to repeatedly: that deeply ingrained beliefs about man, society, and economy, fashioned in the very special setting of early industrial capitalism inhibit understanding and further reform of the changed economy of the present day. This is the theme of Polanyi's "Our Obsolete Market Mentality." But Polanyi goes further. He asserts that the conventional wisdom about economy and society we inherit from nineteenth-century capitalism and economic theory is also a barrier

to the economic analysis of primitive and archaic economies studied by anthropologists and historians. Economic
anthropology still suffers from the inability of anthropologists to perceive primitive economies in ways different from
those instilled by Marshallian market theory and Marxian
analysis. But the grand theoretical scheme of conventional
economics created from David Ricardo to Maynard
Keynes was designed to analyze industrial capitalism of
Western Europe and the United States. Marxian economics, the other grand theoretical scheme, was designed also
to analyze the very same set of capitalist economies. (Until
recently, when the underdeveloped world of primitive and
peasant economies became a subject of analytical interest,
we perceived all economies through one or the other of
these theoretical frameworks. Rostow, Gershenkron, Ha-
gen, Lewis, Myrdal, and others are now creating a political
economy of development, one by-product of which is to
point up how very special were the economies and societies
of nineteenth-century Europe and America.)

It is not with the success or failure of conventional or
Marxian economic theory to analyze industrial capitalism
that Polanyi takes issue, but rather with the leading ideas
associated with these analytical systems; ideas that have
become fossilized, as it were, as permanent and general
truths. The pursuit of material gain compelled by laissez-
faire market rules is still not seen as behavior forced on
people as the only way to earn livelihood in a market system, but as an expression of their inner being; individualism
is regarded as a norm, and society remains invisible as a
cluster of individual persons who happen to live together
without responsibility for anyone other than kin; economic
improvement is assumed to be more important than any
social dislocations that accompany it; *man* is seen as a
utilitarian atom having an innate propensity to truck, barter, and exchange; material maximization and the primacy
of material self-interest are assumed to be constants in all
human societies.

The general conception which Bentham had is one that is widely prevalent today . . . The bulk of orthodox economic theory . . . rests upon a conception of *human nature* which is not very different from that which Jeremy Bentham drew up in such formal shape [Mitchell 1949: 92; italics added].

The elements of scarcity and choice, which are the outstanding factors in human experience that give economic science its reason for being, rest *psychologically* on firm ground . . . Our primary concern in these pages is to understand the cross-cultural implications of the process of economizing [Herskovits 1952: 3, 4; italics added].

The aim of this book is to show that the concepts of economic theory must be taken as having universal validity . . . the proposition that there should be more than one body of economic theory is absurd. If modern economic analysis with its instrumental concepts cannot cope equally with the Aborigine and with the Londoner, not only economic theory but the whole of the social sciences may be considerably discredited . . . if [economic theory] does not apply to the whole of humanity then it is meaningless [Goodfellow 1939: 3, 4, 5].

But this makes conventional economic theory into a Holy Ghost: everywhere present but often unseen. It is gross ethnocentrism to assume that the monk, the feudal lord, the Inca priest-king, the commissar, and the Trobriander are directed in their material lives to abide by the same market rules that drive the London stockbroker and the Iowa wheat farmer.

The powerful engine of nineteenth-century industrial capitalism and the powerful theoretical analysis by economists of its market structure and performance so permeate our thinking as to make it extremely difficult for us to understand economies markedly different from our own. The leading ideas of economics improve our vision of our own economy, but become blinders when we look at primitive and archaic economies—economies that are neither industrialized nor organized by market exchange. The differences between primitive and archaic economies and our own have been remarked on by many before Polanyi (and since). Maine's distinction between status and contract societies, and Tönnies' between *Gemeinschaft* and *Gesellschaft* point up a fundamental distinction of the same sort that Polanyi makes in contrasting market economies with the organic nature of primitive and archaic economies. Indeed, the same point has been stated succinctly by contemporary anthropologists and economists.

> In primitive communities, the individual as an economic factor is personalized, not anonymous. He tends to hold his economic position in virtue of his social position. Hence to displace him economically means a social disturbance [Firth 1951: 137].

> . . . the economist who studies the non-market economy has to abandon most of what he has learnt, and adopts the techniques of the anthropologist [Lewis 1962: vii].

Polanyi's work gives us more than occasional insights into the structure of exotic economies. His is an attempt to create a system of analysis designed to show how social organization institutes labor, land, product, and service transactions in primitive and archaic economies. He created a theory of social and economic organization which gives us new insights into a large number of economies described by anthropologists and historians. His special concern was the way in which economy relates to social organization and culture. It is a strength of Polanyi's analytical work that the concepts he uses—reciprocity, redistribution, administered trade, gift-trade, special purpose money, ports of trade—are at the same time social and economic categories.

xxix

> [We do not yet have] . . . those conceptual tools required to penetrate the maze of social relationships in which economy was embedded. This is the task of what we will here call institutional analysis [Polanyi, Arensberg, and Pearson 1957: 242].

The insights gained from examining exotic economies in systematic fashion are of more than antiquarian interest. Polanyi's analysis of the redistributive sphere of eighteenth-century Dahomey confers a perspective of use in understanding the redistributive spheres of Soviet Russia and welfare state Sweden. To see the exact ways in which economy is embedded in Trobriand society helps us understand those features of nineteenth-century industrial capitalism that Robert Owen and other socialists were reacting against in trying to create similarly embedded economies.

Several times Polanyi uses the phrase "the reality of society" by which he means the opposite of "man as a utilitarian atom." Rather, man is a social animal whose arrangements for the production and distribution of goods in many societies are an indistinguishable part of congruent arrangements for family, political, and religious life. This leading idea—an idea abundantly illustrated by economic anthropology—should make us view our continuing departure from the model of laissez-faire capitalism as an unremarkable occurrence. When contrasted with earlier and later economies, laissez-faire capitalism can be seen to be a unique and transitory event. The attempt to approximate an automatically functioning economy whose autonomous market rules required the fracturing of community, created material abundance at the expense of community integration. It was the "atomistic individualism" and the social disunity and insecurity engendered by the laissez-faire rules of the game that Polanyi pointed up. That controlled markets are an efficient allocative mechanism (compared to any known alternative) is not in doubt, as is shown by the experience of Western Europe and the United States since

World War II, and by the continual enlargement of the controlled market sphere in the communist economies since the mid 1950s.

> . . . the end of [laissez-faire] market society means in no way the absence of markets. These continue, in various fashions, to ensure the freedom of the consumer, to indicate the shifting of demand, to influence producers' income, and to serve as an instrument of accountancy, while ceasing altogether to be an organ of economic self-regulation [Polanyi 1944: 252].

Those reforms of laissez-faire capitalism that we call the welfare state are designed primarily to strengthen the economic performance of capitalism (to create full employment and higher growth rates) and, at the same time, to control markets by political decisions and politically decided compensators where the results of laissez faire were squalor, material insecurity, and abject poverty. Polanyi is not alone in applying insights from early and simple communities to reforms of our own day.

> Hence we should return to the old and elemental. Once again we shall discover those motives of action still remembered by many societies and classes: the joy of giving in public, the delight in generous artistic expenditure, the pleasure of hospitality in the public or private feast. Social insurance, solicitude in mutuality or co-operation, in the professional group and all those moral persons called Friendly Societies, are better than the mere personal security guaranteed by the nobleman to his tenant, better than the mean life afforded by the daily wage handed out by managements, and better even than the uncertainty of capitalist savings [Mauss 1954: 67].

The Economy as Instituted Process

In English, we used the word "economic" to mean "material" and also to mean "economizing." Polanyi's conceptual scheme insists on keeping these meanings separate. All societies must have some sort of economic organization in the first sense—structured arrangements for providing material goods and services—but whether or not the arrangements resemble the economizing rules of market exchange is a matter for empirical investigation. It is a further indicator of the deep penetration of the market model into our modes of thinking that the issue is a point of theoretical contention. We seem to accept readily the idea that other peoples can have markedly different religious, political, and marriage arrangements from our own—but somehow not economic arrangements.

> Does this economistic postulate allow us to infer the generality of a market system in the realms of empirical fact? The claim of formal economics to an historically universal applicability answers in the affirmative. In effect this argues the virtual presence of a market system in every society, whether such a system is empirically present or not. All human economy might then be regarded as a potential supply-demand price mechanism, and the actual processes, whatever they are, explained in terms of this hypostatization [Polanyi 1957: 240].

What some economists, anthropologists, and historians assume is either the universal presence of market institutions, or the presence of functional equivalents that compel the same economizing actions as a market system because, it is further assumed, that "scarcity" in the economist's sense is universally present. These writers simply *translate* whatever primitive and archaic economic institutions and activities they find into market terms [79, 26].

One may perhaps restate Polanyi's distinction between the "substantive" and "formal" definitions of "economic" in the following way: every society studied by anthropologists, historians, and economists has an economy of some sort because personal and community life require the structured provision of material goods and services.

This is a minimal definition of economy which calls attention to similarities among economies otherwise as different as those of the Trobriand Islands, an Israeli *kibbutz,* a twelfth-century feudal manor, nineteenth-century Britain, and the present-day economy of the Soviet Union. These very different economies have in common that they make use of natural resources, technology, division of labor and, frequently, practices such as external trade with foreigners, the use of markets, and some form of money. But the specific institutionalization of these features may vary radically among economies. Polanyi's substantive definitions of "economy," "money," and "external trade" point up what is generally true for all economies regardless of size, technology, etc., and what features money and external trade have in common regardless of which economy one examines. His formal definition relates to the special case of economy, money, foreign trade, as these are organized in a national economy integrated by market exchange.

If we are to investigate in systematic fashion the large number of pre-industrial economies studied by anthropologists and historians, we need a conceptual approach that does not commit us to the view that whatever we find may be regarded merely as some variant of our own market system. In a word we have to approach exotic economies in the same way that anthropologists approach exotic religions and polities:

> . . . most anthropologists have ceased to take their bearings in the study of religion from any religion practiced in their own society [Lienhardt 1956: 310].

> One important discovery made in . . . [*African Political Systems*] was that the institutions through which a society organized politically need not necessarily look like the kinds of political institutions with which we have long been familiar in the Western world, and in the great nations of Asia [Gluckman and Cunnison 1962: vi].

xxxiii

And so too for economies:

> . . . the anthropologist, the sociologist, or the historian
> each in his study of the place occupied by the economy
> in human society, was faced with a great variety of
> institutions other than markets, in which man's liveli-
> hood was embedded. Its problems could not be at-
> tacked with the help of an analytical method devised
> for a special form of the economy, which was de-
> pendent upon the presence of specific market elements
> [Polanyi 1957: 245].

Reciprocity, Redistribution, and [Market] Exchange: Dominance and Integration

In our own economy, market exchange is the *dominant*
transactional mode. Basic resources that enter many lines
of production—labor and land—are organized for market
sale; most people depend on the market sale of what they
produce for their primary source of income. Indeed, the
income categories conventionally used to analyze our economy are chosen to indicate what item or service is being
sold to provide the income: wage and salary, rent, interest, profit. Note that market exchange dominates not only
as the transactional mode used in the final disposition of
products (e.g., the retailing of cars to final users), but
also in production processes, since natural resources and
labor are also transacted through purchase at market price
stated in money.

Market exchange *integrates* capitalist economy in a
strictly economic sense. Labor and natural resources are
brought together, moved, allocated to specific lines of production in response to profitability as measured by money
cost and money price. The integrative function of markets
remains basic to that reformed variety of capitalism we
call the welfare state. What has changed is the extent of
autonomy we allow to market forces alone.

The main branches of conventional economic theory—price, distribution, aggregate income, and growth theory—selectively analyze those features of industrial capitalism that are relatively independent of kinship, politics, religion, and other aspects of society and culture. The same economic analysis is used in the United States, Sweden, Germany, and Japan. This systematic exclusion from their analyses of what economists call institutions does not mean that kinship, religion, etc., do not have economic consequences—a Japanese factory is different from an American factory in interesting ways attributable to cultural differences—but rather that the structural facts of market integration, the use of similar monetary systems and machine technology allow economists to analyze an important range of matters—prices, incomes, growth, international trade, etc.—without reference to those local cultural matters that differentiate Sweden from Japan from the United States.

Not all transactions in capitalist economy are market exchanges. Let us, following Polanyi, call those payments to, and disbursements by, central political authority "redistributive" transactions. Immediately a social dimension appears that is absent in market exchange transactions. Redistributive payments to government are an expression of politically defined obligation and redistributive disbursements by government are determined by political decision. A third transactional mode is what Polanyi calls "reciprocity," a general category of socially obligatory gift-giving. Perhaps it is correct to say that in welfare state capitalist economies of the present day reciprocal and redistributive transactions are in some degree socially "integrative." Gift-giving is simply a material expression of those socially cohesive relationships that we call friendship and kinship. With us, however, the quantitative importance of gift-giving is small, and our prime sources of livelihood are not connected with gift receipts.

Polanyi's categories of reciprocity, redistribution, and

market exchange and his analytical distinctions between
kinds of money, markets, and foreign trade allow us to
describe our own economy so as to make its important
aspects directly comparable with economies studied by anthropologists and historians, thereby, allowing a systematic
comparison of similarities and differences using our own
economy as a base. Moreover, they allow us to analyze the
structural features of primitive economies without perceiv-
ing them through the theoretical spectacles designed for
our own economy. The value of the approach is shown, I
believe, by what it is possible to say about forms of money,
external trade, and markets in primitive and archaic economies; and by what one can point out about the structured
relationships between economy and political, religious, and
kinship organization in all societies.

*Money, External Trade, and Markets in Primitive and Ar-
chaic Economies*

When we say that market exchange is the dominant
and integrative transactional mode (but not the exclusive
mode) of modern capitalism, we are using the category of
"market exchange" in a broad sense. For their purposes of
analyzing price determination, economists differentiate
among specific types of market exchange (pure competition, oligopoly). So too with reciprocity and redistribution
as broad categories to describe primitive and archaic economies. There are many varieties of socially obligatory gift
and counter-gift giving and of obligatory payments to political and religious authority. Moreover, as with our own
economy, more than one transactional mode typically is
present in any pre-industrial economy.

In the same sense that we can say that market exchange
integrates capitalist economy, we can also say that reciprocity and redistribution integrate primitive and archaic
economies. They are the transactional modes through
which resource allocation, work organization, and product

disposition are arranged. But one can go further here and say that reciprocity and redistribution are *socially* integrative, as well, and indicate in specific fashion for economies such as the Trobriands where exactly its *Gemeinschaft* aspects are that link the economic to the social.

> . . . *the whole tribal life is permeated by a constant give and take;* that every ceremony, every legal and customary act is done to the accompaniment of material gift and counter-gift; that wealth, given and taken, is one of the main instruments of social organization, of the power of the chief, of the bonds of kinship, and of relationships in law [Malinowski 1922: 167].

In primitive and archaic economies foreign trade, money, and markets are organized in ways different from those we are so familiar with in capitalism. (Even without further examination, one may say that the use of foreign trade, money, and markets in the Soviet economy indicates that devices and practices familiar to capitalism can be incorporated within economies differently organized.) As always, there are similarities and differences in the organization and functioning of, say, foreign trade, in the U.S.S.R. and the United States. But note that the differences are direct expressions of more fundamental differences in economic structure.

Anthropological and historical literature indicate that many kinds of external trade, money uses, and market places existed in primitive and archaic economies: kula gift trade, silent trade, the use of cattle to make status payments (bridewealth, bloodwealth), petty markets in ninth-century Europe—are a few among hundreds of ascertained practices. Polanyi's schema attempts to make analytical sense of these by suggesting that foreign trade, money, and markets took only a few characteristic organizational forms in these economies, depending upon which of the transactional modes ("patterns of integration") dominated.

Economic Anthropology and Comparative Economy

In *The Great Transformation* (Chapter 4) and "Our Obsolete Market Mentality," Polanyi touched on the economic organization of primitive and archaic economies simply to provide a contrast to nineteenth-century market economy, which was his main concern. In his later writings [69, 70, 71, 72, 73] he analyzed the origins of modern economic institutions and created a conceptual framework with which to analyze primitive and archaic economies. His work is of interest to economic anthropology, economic history, the history of economic thought,[16] and comparative economy.

Rather than give a more detailed account of his work on transactional modes, special purpose money, external trade, ports of trade, markets, and operational devices, I shall indicate the kinds of questions and problems to which Polanyi's conceptual framework is designed to apply.

Economic Anthropology

One of the peculiarities of economic anthropology is that neither the facts nor the folk views of primitive economic life are in doubt. The ethnographic record is large and detailed. What is in doubt is the most useful theoretical approach to organize the many descriptive accounts and the most fruitful concepts to use in order to make

[16] On three matters Polanyi's work should be of interest to those concerned with the history of economic thought: (i) Early writers considering economic matters in pre-industrial economies in which markets were not important, e.g., "Aristotle Discovers the Economy" [69], and Polanyi's remarks on "just price" in medieval economy. (ii) Most important is Polanyi's analysis of the English transition period from Mercantilism, and the institutional structure which crucially influenced the classical economics of Bentham, Ricardo, and Malthus [67]. (iii) The socio-cultural economics (institutionalism) of Veblen and Galbraith.

statements of importance about economic life in primitive and peasant[17] communities. The methodological and theoretical disputes seem to be various expressions of one unsettled problem: should anthropologists use economic concepts and categories from our own economy, or are special categories of analysis necessary? This question will remain unsettled as long as the similarities and the differences between industrial capitalism, primitive, and peasant economies are insufficiently described.

Polanyi believed that in order to understand the relation of economic to social organization the differences between primitive economies and industrial capitalism had to be analyzed, and so he contrived conceptual categories to delineate these structural differences. To indicate why some of us find his approach useful requires some preliminary remarks about different approaches to economic anthropology.

A disturbing feature of anthropology is that some practitioners display a sort of nervous inferiority toward physical science and economics. Perhaps it is because more laymen can understand a book on anthropology than a book on physics or economics that some anthropologists seem to feel naked before their mathematically padded colleagues [5]. They grab for fig leaves by using what they regard as scientific words, such as "hypothesis" or "behavior"—as though behavior meant something more than what people do. Others, believing that science is concerned exclusively with uniformities and laws of Parsonian generality—and above all wanting to be scientists—search for similarities between primitive and Western societies, even where differences provide greater insight into social structure and process.

[17] Polanyi said little about the organization of peasant economies. He used the phrase "primitive economy" to mean one in which market exchange is absent or only of minor importance, such as the economy of the Trobriand Islands. See [18, 9].

One way anthropologists think they find similarities be
tween primitive economies and our own is by translating
primitive economy into the categories of industrial capital
ism and conventional economic theory. By describing the
potlatch as an investment yielding 100% interest, and bride
wealth as the price one pays for sexual and domestic serv
ices, primitive economies inevitably are made to appear
merely as simpler and bizarre versions of our own—capi
talism writ small [74]. But if it is true that the similarities
between primitive economies and American capitalism are
so striking, and that primitive economies differ from ou
own only in degree, not in kind [4, 82, 40], why do econo
mists have so much difficulty developing primitive econo
mies [55, 80, 22]? And if the similarities between small
scale, non-industrial subsistence economies and large-scale
industrial market economies are so striking, why can't an
thropologists find use for that powerful corpus of pure
and applied economics—price, distribution, aggregate in
come, and growth theory; national income accounting—
invented for our own economy, to analyze economies such
as the Trobriand or the Nuer?

> The fact that the attention of economists has been
> focused so exclusively on just those aspects of our
> economy least likely to be found among non-literate
> folk has thus confused anthropologists who turned to
> economic treatises for clarification of problems and
> methods in the study of the economic systems of non-
> literate societies [Herskovits 1952: 53].

> An attempt to examine the structure and problems of
> a primitive community in the light of the existing body
> of economic thought raises fundamental conceptual
> issues. Economic analysis and its framework of gen-
> eralization are characteristically described in terms
> appropriate to the modern exchange economy. It is by
> no means certain that the existing tools of analysis can
> usefully be applied to material other than that for
> which they have been developed. In particular it is not

clear what light, if any, is thrown on subsistence economies by a science which seems to regard the use of money and specialization of labor as axiomatic. The jargon of the market place seems remote, on the face of it, from the problems of an African village where most individuals spend the greater part of their lives in satisfying their own or their families' needs and desires, where money and [commercial] trade play a subordinate role in motivating productive activity [Deane 1953: 115–116].

The differences between primitive economies and our own are of some importance in answering the questions anthropologists put to their data. Indeed, the fact that anthropologists put different questions to their economic data from those asked by economists for our own economy, is itself an indicator of structural differences between primitive economies and our own [15].

Economic anthropology deals primarily with the economic aspects of the social relations of persons [Firth 1951: 138].

One must be clear about similarities and differences among economies. All economies—the United States, the Soviet Union, the Trobriand Islands—share three basic features and in this sense are similar: (1) Whatever the human grouping is called, tribe, village, nation, society, it consists of people who must eat to stay alive, and acquire or produce material items and specialist services to sustain social and community life (i.e., goods and services for religion, defense, *rites de passage*, etc.) The acquisition or production of these material items and services necessary for physical and social existence are never left to chance because deprivation means death. All societies therefore have an "economy" of some sort, i.e., structured arrangements and enforced rules for the acquisition or production of material items and services.

(2) A second basic similarity among economies is that

they all make use of natural resources (land), human co-operation (division of labor), and technology (tools and knowledge). Again, this is true for the U.S., Soviet, and Trobriand economies. What we call *economic* organization, or *economic* structure, or *economic* institutions are the rules in force through which natural resources, human co-operation, and technology are brought together to provide material items and services, in sustained, repetitive fashion. (One need hardly point out that the rules are somewhat different in U.S., Soviet, and Trobriand economies.)

(3) A third similarity—if not universal, then extremely frequent—is that superficially similar economic devices are used: market places (peasant markets and retail stores in the U.S.S.R., retail stores in the United States, *gimwali* in the Trobriands); monetary objects (rubles, dollars, shell necklaces); accounting devices (double-entry bookkeeping, *quipu* strings, pebble counts in Dahomey); and external trade (exports and imports in the United States, U.S.S.R., and kula and *wasi* in the Trobriands).

If it would be rash to conclude that because the United States and the U.S.S.R. both use money, market places, accounting devices, and foreign trade they have basically similar economic organization (rules, structure, transactional modes, institutions), then I suggest it would be even more egregious to conclude that because the United States and Malinowski's Trobriand Islands both use some form of money and foreign trade they have basically similar economic organization.

One of Polanyi's contributions to economic anthropology and comparative economy is to have shown how similar economic devices (money, external trade) play different economic and social roles where economies are organized differently. Moreover, not only do economies differ with regard to structure (transactional modes) and economic devices, but also with regard to technology, size, physical environment, and the range of items and services produced or acquired. And since economies function within societies and cultures there are economic differences among them because there are differences in social relationships (kinship and political systems) and culture (literacy, religion).

It is a task of economic anthropology (and comparative economy) to show the distinguishing characteristics of different types of economy by considering similarities and differences and relating these to social organization and culture. To do so requires categories of analysis that are meaningful for economies markedly different from our own. The analytical categories of modern economics were designed exclusively for the special case of industrialized market economy [15].

> English economists, from Ricardo to Keynes, have been accustomed to assume as a tacitly accepted background the institutions and problems of the England each of his own day; when their works are studied in other climes and other periods by readers who import other assumptions, a great deal of confusion and argument at cross-purposes arises in consequence [Robinson 1961: xvii].

If we are to understand economies which are neither industrialized nor integrated by market exchange, then different analytical categories are necessary to reveal their structural characteristics. Polanyi invented several such analytical categories and used them to indicate the distinguishing characteristics of primitive and archaic economies.

Polanyi's analysis is designed to answer two sets of questions of interest to economic anthropology and comparative economy: For any economy of record, what is the place of the economy in the society? How are the arrangements for acquiring or producing goods related to kinship, politics, religion, and other forms of social organization and culture? Since all human communities require the sustained provision of goods and services and all make use of natural resources, human co-operation, and technique, what are the structured rules for combining resources, co-operation, and technique to provide material items and services in repetitive fashion? What are the institutionally imposed incentives to participate in economic activity?[18]

The second set of questions Polanyi's analysis is designed to answer concerns the ways in which economic devices function—money, market places, external trade, accounting devices, ports of trade, equivalency ratios—in non-industrial economies in which reciprocity and redistribution are the dominant transactional modes [15, 16, 19]. His distinctions between gift-trade, politically administered trade, and market trade, and between special-purpose money and our own kind, open up promising lines of investigation into systematic types of economic organization. And his work on ports of trade and sortings is an important addition to our scanty knowledge of economic devices of culture contact

18 To summarize Polanyi's analytical answers to this first set of questions: three modes of transaction are employed widely in primitive and archaic economies, the socio-economic modes of reciprocity and redistribution, and the economic mode of market exchange. These are not mutually exclusive, but, typically, one mode is integrative, i.e., it organizes basic production—it is the mode which allocates labor and land, and through which the bulk of produce for livelihood is obtained. Reciprocity and redistribution take a variety of specific forms [81] which have in common that underlying social relationships are the impetus for labor, land, and produce transactions. Reciprocity and redistribution express the ways in which social organization relates the economy to its contextual society. In non-industrial economies studied by historians and anthropologists, reciprocity and redistribution are more frequently found to be dominant and integrative than is market exchange. Where they are dominant (the Trobriands, the Tiv, the Nuer), the economy is "embedded" in society in the sense of having no separate existence apart from its controlling social integument: transactional dispositions of natural resources, labor, produce, and services, are expressions of socially defined obligation and relationships.

—devices like silent trade, used to facilitate material transactions between peoples of different cultures.

Comparative Economic Systems

These matters should be as much the concern of comparative economic systems as of economic anthropology. For example, there is not (to my knowledge) any work that systematically compares similarities and differences between the organization and usage of money in Soviet compared to capitalist economies, and relates these similarities and differences to economic structure (transactional modes), as Polanyi's work allows us to do for money in primitive compared to capitalist economies [19]. Similarly, I do not know of any work that sets out to answer the question, what exactly is the relevance of orthodox economic theory—invented for industrial capitalism—to the problems and processes of Soviet economy.[19] Obviously the similarities between the two systems allow the application of familiar measurement devices (suitably amended), such as national income accounting. Obviously the differences between the two systems do not allow the application of branches of price theory, because some Soviet prices are determined differently and perform some different functions from capitalist prices [35, 60]. But how about other areas of relevance or non-relevance of formal economic theory to the Soviet system?

So too for comparisons relating to welfare states and the underdeveloped countries. Galbraith [30] and Myrdal [55, 56] are right to raise new questions and create new socio-economic analyses to answer them. But they have not exhausted the field. The American welfare state has some special characteristics that seem to go unremarked.

[19] Professor Berliner has kindly told me that specialists in Soviet economy have begun to consider these matters in recent years. See Berliner [6] and his references cited, also Grossman [35a].

Training for the Ph.D. has become socialized in that an increasing proportion of graduate students are subsidized. And philanthropic foundations (Ford, Rockefeller, Carnegie, Guggenheim) have become a device of private redistribution (something like *leiturgy* in ancient Greece, when noble families were obliged to provide public services).

One final word. Economics at present is stretching at both of its methodological extremes. Mathematics and statistics have opened whole new areas of fruitful application of economics to real problems and processes, to the benefit of the Russians as well as ourselves [43]. But those problems and processes wherein economics becomes intertwined with politics, sociology, anthropology, and history—areas traditionally swept under the rug of "institutionalism" —are also getting increased attention. The analysis of "meaningfulness in work," which Bell [2, 3], Galbraith [30], and Crosland [12] give us, add to the brilliant insights of Tawney [88] two generations ago. The remarkable fact that socialist doctrines and policies designed for industrialized Europe are being embraced by underdeveloped Africa [83, 4, 29] surely is worth investigation. These are important matters. Polanyi's analysis has much to teach us in these areas of economy and society.

REFERENCES

ARENSBERG, CONRAD M.

[1] 1937 *The Irish Countryman.* London: Macmillan.

BELL, DANIEL

[2] 1956 *Work and Its Discontents.* Boston: Beacon Press.

[3] 1959 "Meaning in Work." *Dissent,* summer issue.

BERG, ELLIOT J.

[4] 1964 "Socialism and Economic Development in Tropical Africa." *The Quarterly Journal of Economics* 78: 549–573.

BERLINER, JOSEPH S.

[5] 1962 "The Feet of the Natives Are Large: An Essay on Anthropology by an Economist." *Current Anthropology* 3: 47–76.

[6] 1964 "Marxism and the Soviet Economy." *Problems of Communism*, issue of September–October.

BESTOR, A. E.

[7] 1950 *Backwoods Utopias*. Philadelphia: University of Pennsylvania Press.

BISHIP, CLAIRE

[8] 1950 *All Things Common*. New York: Harper.

BOHANNAN, PAUL

[9] 1959 "The Impact of Money on an African Subsistence Economy." *The Journal of Economic History* 19: 491–503. Reprinted in [20a].

BREBNER, J. B.

[10] 1952 "Laissez-faire and State Intervention in Nineteenth-century Britain." R. L. Schuyler and H. Ausubel (eds.). *The Making of English History*. New York: Dryden Press.

CARR, E. H.

[11] 1951 *The New Society*. London: Macmillan.

CROSLAND, C. A. R.

[12] 1962 "Industrial Democracy and Workers' Control." *The Conservative Enemy*. London: Jonathan Cape.

DALTON, GEORGE

[13] 1959 "Robert Owen and Karl Polanyi as Socioeconomic Critics and Reformers of Industrial Capitalism." Unpublished Ph.D. dissertation, University of Oregon.

[14] 1960 "A Note of Clarification on Economic Surplus." *American Anthropologist* 62: 483–490.

[15] 1961 "Economic Theory and Primitive Society." *American Anthropologist* 63: 1–25.

[16] 1962 "Traditional Production in Primitive African Economies." *The Quarterly Journal of Economics* 76: 360–378. Reprinted in [20a].

[17] 1963 "Economic Surplus, Once Again." *American Anthropologist* 65: 389–394.

[18] 1964 "The Development of Subsistence and Peasant Economies in Africa." *The International Social Science Journal* 16: 378–389. Reprinted in [20a].

[19] 1965 "Primitive Money." *American Anthropologist* 67: 44–65. Reprinted in [20a].

[20] 1965a "Primitive, Archaic, and Modern Economies: Karl Polanyi's Contribution to Economic Anthropology and Comparative Economy." Proceedings of the American Ethnological Society.

[20a] 1967 *Tribal and Peasant Economies: Readings in Economic Anthropology.* New York: Anchor Books, Natural History Press.

DEANE, PHYLLIS
[21] 1953 *Colonial Social Accounting.* Cambridge: Cambridge University Press.

DOUGLAS, MARY
[22] 1962 "Lele Economy Compared with the Bushong: A Study of Economic Backwardness." *Markets in Africa,* Paul Bohannan and George Dalton (eds.). Evanston: Northwestern University Press. Revised edition in paperback Natural History Press, 1965.

EVANS-PRITCHARD, E. E.
[23] 1954 "Introduction." *The Gift,* by Marcel Mauss. Glencoe: The Free Press.

FINER, HERMAN
[24] 1945 *The Road to Reaction.* Boston: Little, Brown & Co.

FIRTH, RAYMOND
[25] 1951 *The Elements of Social Organization.* London: Watts.

FRENCH, A.
[26] 1964 *The Growth of Athenian Economy.* London: Routledge and Kegan Paul.

FROMM, ERICH
[27] 1941 *Escape from Freedom.* New York: Rinehart.
[28] 1955 *The Sane Society.* New York: Rinehart.

FRIEDLAND, W. H., and ROSBERG, C. G., JR., eds.
[29] 1964 *African Socialism*. Stanford: Stanford University Press.

GALBRAITH, JOHN KENNETH
[30] 1958 *The Affluent Society*. Boston: Houghton-Mifflin.

GERSHENKRON, ALEXANDER
[31] 1952 "Economic Backwardness in Historical Perspective." *The Progress of Underdeveloped Areas*, B. Hoselitz (ed.). Chicago: University of Chicago Press.

GLUCKMAN, MAX, and I. G. CUNNISON
[32] 1962 "Foreword." *Politics of the Kula Ring*, by J. P. Singh Uberoi. Manchester: the University Press.

GOODFELLOW, D. M.
[33] 1939 *Principles of Economic Sociology*. London: Routledge.

GOODY, JACK
[34] 1963 "Feudalism in Africa?" *Journal of African History* 4: 1–18.

GROSSMAN, GREGORY
[35] 1959 "Industrial Prices in the U.S.S.R." *American Economic Review* 49: 50–64.
[35a] 1966 "Gold and the Sword: Money in the Soviet Command Economy," in H. Rosovsky (ed.). *Industrialization in Two Systems: Essays in Honor of Alexander Gershenkron*. New York: John Wiley & Sons.

HARRIS, MARVIN
[36] 1959 "The Economy Has No Surplus?" *American Anthropologist* 61: 185–199.

HAYEK, F. A.
[37] 1944 *The Road to Serfdom*. Chicago: University of Chicago Press.
[38] 1954 *Capitalism and the Historians*. Chicago: University of Chicago Press.

HEILBRONER, ROBERT L.
[39] 1962 *The Making of Economic Society*. New Jersey: Prentice-Hall.

HERSKOVITS, MELVILLE J.

[40] 1952 *Economic Anthropology*. Revised ed.; New York: Knopf.

KEYNES, JOHN MAYNARD

[41] 1926 *The End of Laissez-faire*. London: Hogarth Press.

LE CLAIR, EDWARD E.

[42] 1962 "Economic Theory and Economic Anthropology." *American Anthropologist* 64: 1179–1203.

LEONTIEV, W.

[43] 1960 "The Decline and Rise of Soviet Economic Science." *Foreign Affairs*, January: 261–272.

LEVITT, KARI

[44] 1964 "Karl Polanyi and Co-Existence." *Co-Existence* 1: 113–121.

LEWIS, W. ARTHUR

[45] 1955 *The Theory of Economic Growth*. London: Allen and Unwin.

[46] 1962 "Foreword." *Economic Development and Social Change in South India*, by T. Scarlett Epstein. Manchester: Manchester University Press.

LIENHARDT, R. GODFREY

[47] 1956 "Religion." *Man, Culture and Society*. Harry L. Shapiro (ed.). New York: Oxford University Press.

LIPPMANN, WALTER

[48] 1949 "The Permanent New Deal." *The New Deal: Revolution or Evolution?* Department of American Studies, Amherst College, ed. Boston: D. C. Heath. Reprinted from the Yale Review, June 1935.

MALINOWSKI, BRONISLAW

[49] 1921 "The Primitive Economics of the Trobriand Islanders." *Economic Journal* 31: 1–15.

[50] 1922 *Argonauts of the Western Pacific*. London: Routledge.

[51] 1935 *Coral Gardens and Their Magic*, Vol. I. New York: American Book Company.

1

MAUSS, MARCEL

[52] 1954 *The Gift: Forms and Functions of Exchange in Archaic Societies.* Glencoe: The Free Press. Translated by I. G. Cunnison from the French ed. of 1925.

MEILLASSOUX, CLAUDE

[53] 1962 "Social and Economic Factors Affecting Markets in Guroland." *Markets in Africa,* Paul Bohannan and George Dalton (eds.). Evanston: Northwestern University Press.

MITCHELL, WESLEY C.

[54] 1949 *Lecture Notes on Types of Economic Theory.* New York: Kelley.

MOORE, WILBERT E.

[55] 1955 "Labor Attitudes Toward Industrialization in Underdeveloped Countries." *American Economic Review* 45: 156–165.

MYRDAL, GUNNAR

[55] 1957 *Rich Lands and Poor.* New York: Harper.

[56] 1960 *Beyond the Welfare State.* New Haven: Yale University Press.

NADEL, S. F.

[57] 1942 *A Black Byzantium: The Kingdom of Nupe in Nigeria.* London: Oxford University Press.

NASH, MANNING

[58] 1964 "The Organization of Economic Life." *Horizons of Anthropology,* Sol Tax (ed.). Chicago: Aldine Press. Reprinted in [20a].

NEALE, WALTER C.

[59] 1957 "Reciprocity and Redistribution in the Indian Village." *Trade and Market in the Early Empires,* K. Polanyi, C. M. Arensberg, H. W. Pearson (eds.). Glencoe: The Free Press.

NOVE, ALEC

[60] 1963 "The Changing Role of Soviet Prices." *Economics of Planning* 3: 185–195.

NOYES, JOHN HUMPHREY

[61] 1870 *American Socialisms.* Philadelphia: J. B. Lippincott.

NYERERE, JULIUS
  [62] 1964 "Communitarian Socialism." *Seeds of Liberation,* Paul Goodman (ed.). New York: Brazilier. Reprinted in [29].

OPPENHEIM, A. L.
  [63] 1957 "A Bird's-eye View of Mesopotamian Economic History." *Trade and Market in the Early Empires,* K. Polanyi, C. M. Arensberg, H. W. Pearson (eds.). Glencoe: The Free Press.

OWEN, ROBERT
  [64] 1815 "Observations on the Effects of the Manufacturing System." *A New View of Society and Other Writings.* New York: Dutton, Everyman ed., 1927.

PEARSON, HARRY W.
  [65] 1957 "The Economy Has No Surplus; A Critique of a Theory of Development." *Trade and Market in the Early Empires,* K. Polanyi, C. M. Arensberg, H. W. Pearson (eds.). Glencoe: The Free Press.

PIRENNE, HENRI
  [66] 1936 *Economic and Social History of Medieval Europe.* London: Routledge.

POLANYI, KARL
  [67] 1944 *The Great Transformation.* New York: Rinehart.
  [68] 1947 "Our Obsolete Market Mentality." *Commentary* 13: 109–117.
  [69] 1957 "Marketless Trading in Hammurabi's Time." "Aristotle Discovers the Economy." "The Economy as Instituted Process." *Trade and Market in the Early Empires,* K. Polanyi, C. M. Arensberg, H. W. Pearson (eds.). Glencoe: The Free Press.
  [70] 1960 "On the Comparative Treatment of Economic Institutions in Antiquity with Illustrations from Athens, Mycenae, and Alalakh." *City Invincible.* Chicago: University of Chicago Press.

[71] 1963 "Ports of Trade in Early Societies." *The Journal of Economic History* 23: 30–45.

[72] 1964 "Sortings and 'Ounce Trade' in the West African Slave Trade." *The Journal of African History.*

[73] 1966 *Dahomey and the Slave Trade.* American Ethnological Society series; Seattle: University of Washington Press.

POLANYI, K., ARENSBERG, C. M., and PEARSON, H. W.

[73a] 1957 "The Place of Economies in Societies." *Trade and Market in the Early Empires.* Glencoe: The Free Press.

POSPISIL, LEOPOLD

[74] 1963 *Kapauku Papuan Economy.* Yale University Publications in Anthropology, No. 67.

ROBINSON, JOAN

[75] 1954 "The Impossibility of Competition." *Monopoly and Competition and Their Regulation*, E. H. Chamberlin (ed.). London: Macmillan.

[76] 1955 "Marx, Marshall, and Keynes." Occasional paper No. 9, Delhi School of Economics, University of Delhi.

[77] 1962 *Economic Philosophy.* London: Watts.

[77a] 1961 *Exercises in Economic Analysis.* London: Macmillan.

ROSTOW, W. W.

[78] 1960 *The Stages of Economic Growth.* Cambridge: Cambridge University Press.

ROTTENBERG, SIMON

[79] 1958 "Review of *Trade and Market in the Early Empires*." *American Economic Review* 48: 675–678.

SADIE, J. L.

[80] 1960 "The Social Anthropology of Economic Development." *Economic Journal* 70: 294–303.

SAHLINS, MARSHALL

[81] 1965 "On the Sociology of Primitive Exchange." M. Banton (ed.). *The Relevance of Models in Social Anthropology.* London: Tavistock.

SCHNEIDER, HAROLD K.

[82] 1964 "Economics in East African Aboriginal Societies." *Economic Transition in Africa,* Melville J. Herskovits and Mitchell Harwitz (eds.). Evanston: Northwestern University Press.

SENGHOR, LEOPOLD S.

[83] 1964 *On African Socialism.* New York: Praeger.

SIEVERS, ALLEN MORRIS

[84] 1949 *Has Market Capitalism Collapsed? A Critique of Karl Polanyi's New Economics.* New York: Columbia University Press.

SINGER, HANS

[84a] 1950 "The Distribution of Gains between Investing and Borrowing Countries." *American Economic Review,* Papers and Proceedings.

SMELSER, NEIL J.

[85] 1959 "A Comparative View of Exchange Systems." *Economic Development and Cultural Change* 7: 173–182.

SPIRO, M. E.

[86] 1956 *Kibbutz: Venture in Utopia.* Cambridge: Harvard University Press.

SWEET, R. F. G.

[87] 1959 "On Prices, Moneys, and Money-uses in the Old Babylonian Period." Unpublished Ph.D. dissertation, Oriental Institute, University of Chicago.

TAWNEY, R. H.

[88] 1920 *The Acquisitive Society.* New York: Harcourt, Brace.

TOYNBEE, A.

[89] 1884 *Lectures on the Industrial Revolution in England.* Paper ed.; Boston: Beacon Press, 1956.

WALKER, GILBERT

[90] 1957 *Economic Planning by Program and Control in Great Britain.* New York: Macmillan.

WOOTTON, BARBARA

[91] 1945 *Freedom under Planning.* Chapel Hill: University of North Carolina Press.

PART I

ECONOMY AND SOCIETY

1

Societies and Economic Systems

Before we can proceed to the discussion of the laws
governing a market economy, such as the nineteenth century was trying to establish, we must first have a firm grip
on the extraordinary assumptions underlying such a system.

Market economy implies a self-regulating system of markets; in slightly more technical terms, it is an economy
directed by market prices and nothing but market prices.
Such a system capable of organizing the whole of economic life without outside help or interference would certainly deserve to be called self-regulating. These rough indications should suffice to show the entirely unprecedented
nature of such a venture in the history of the race.

Let us make our meaning more precise. No society
could, naturally, live for any length of time unless it possessed an economy of some sort; but prior to our time no
economy has ever existed that, even in principle, was controlled by markets. In spite of the chorus of academic in-
cantations so persistent in the nineteenth century, gain and
profit made on exchange never before played an important part in human economy. Though the institution of the
market was fairly common since the later Stone Age, its
role was no more than incidental to economic life.

We have good reason to insist on this point with all the
emphasis at our command. No less a thinker than Adam
Smith suggested that the division of labor in society was

FROM Chapter 4, "Societies and Economic Systems," pp. 43–
55, 269–273, of Karl Polanyi, *The Great Transformation*, New
York: Rinehart, 1944. Reprinted by permission of the publisher.

dependent upon the existence of markets, or, as he put it, upon man's "propensity to barter, truck, and exchange one thing for another." This phrase was later to yield the concept of the Economic Man. In retrospect it can be said that no misreading of the past ever proved more prophetic of the future. For while up to Adam Smith's time that propensity had hardly shown up on a considerable scale in the life of any observed community, and had remained, at best, a subordinate feature of economic life, a hundred years later an industrial system was in full swing over the major part of the planet which, practically and theoretically, implied that the human race was swayed in all its economic activities, if not also in its political, intellectual, and spiritual pursuits, by that one particular propensity. Herbert Spencer, in the second half of the nineteenth century, could, without more than a cursory acquaintance with economics, equate the principle of the division of labor with barter and exchange, and another fifty years later, Ludwig von Mises and Walter Lippmann could repeat this same fallacy. By that time there was no need for argument. A host of writers on political economy, social history, political philosophy, and general sociology had followed in Smith's wake and established his paradigm of the bartering savage as an axiom of their respective sciences. In point of fact, Adam Smith's suggestions about the economic psychology of early man were as false as Rousseau's were on the political psychology of the savage. Division of labor, a phenomenon as old as society, springs from differences inherent in the facts of sex, geography, and individual endowment; and the alleged propensity of man to barter, truck, and exchange is almost entirely apocryphal. While history and ethnography know of various kinds of economies, most of them comprising the institution of markets, they know of no economy prior to our own, even approximately controlled and regulated by markets. This will become abundantly clear from a bird's-eye view of the history of economic systems and of markets, presented

4

separately. The role played by markets in the internal economy of the various countries, it will appear, was insignificant up to recent times, and the changeover to an economy dominated by the market pattern will stand out all the more clearly.

To start with, we must discard some nineteenth-century prejudices that underlay Adam Smith's hypothesis about primitive man's alleged predilection for gainful occupations. Since his axiom was much more relevant to the immediate future than to the dim past, it induced in his followers a strange attitude toward man's early history. On the face of it, the evidence seemed to indicate that primitive man, far from having a capitalistic psychology, had, in effect, a communistic one (later this also proved to be mistaken). Consequently, economic historians tended to confine their interest to that comparatively recent period of history in which truck and exchange were found on any considerable scale, and primitive economics was relegated to prehistory. Unconsciously, this led to a weighting of the scales in favor of a marketing psychology, for within the relatively short period of the last few centuries everything might be taken to tend toward the establishment of that which was eventually established, i.e., a market system, irrespective of other tendencies which were temporarily submerged. The corrective of such a "short-run" perspective would obviously have been the linking up of economic history with social anthropology, a course which was consistently avoided.

We cannot continue today on these lines. The habit of looking at the last ten thousand years as well as at the array of early societies as a mere prelude to the true history of our civilization, which started approximately with the publication of the *Wealth of Nations* in 1776, is, to say the least, out of date. It is this episode which has come to a close in our days, and in trying to gauge the alternatives of the future, we should subdue our natural proneness to follow the proclivities of our fathers. But the same bias which made Adam Smith's generation view primeval man as bent on barter and truck induced their successors to disavow all interest in early man, as he was now known *not* to have indulged in those laudable passions. The tradition of the classical economists, who attempted to base the law of the market on the alleged propensities of man in the state of nature, was replaced by an abandonment of all interest in the cultures of "uncivilized" man as irrelevant to an understanding of the problems of our age.

Such an attitude of subjectivism in regard to earlier civilizations should make no appeal to the scientific mind. The differences existing between civilized and "uncivilized" peoples have been vastly exaggerated, especially in the economic sphere. According to the historians, the forms of industrial life in agricultural Europe were, until recently, not much different from what they had been several thousand years earlier. Ever since the introduction of the plow —essentially a large hoe drawn by animals—the methods of agriculture remained substantially unaltered over the major part of Western and Central Europe until the beginning of the modern age. Indeed, the progress of civilization was, in these regions, mainly political, intellectual, and spiritual; in respect to material conditions, the Western Europe of 1100 A.D. had hardly caught up with the Roman world of a thousand years before. Even later, change flowed more easily in the channels of statecraft, literature, and the arts, but particularly in those of religion and learning, than in those of industry. In its economics, medieval Europe was largely on a level with ancient Persia, India, or China, and certainly could not rival in riches and culture the New Kingdom of Egypt, two thousand years before. Max Weber was the first among modern economic historians to protest against the brushing aside of primitive economics as irrelevant to the question of the motives and mechanisms of civilized societies. The subsequent work of social anthropology proved him emphatically right. For, if one conclusion stands out more clearly than another from the recent

6

study of early societies, it is the changelessness of man as a social being. His natural endowments reappear with a remarkable constancy in societies of all times and places; and the necessary preconditions of the survival of human society appear to be immutably the same.

The outstanding discovery of recent historical and anthropological research is that man's economy, as a rule, is submerged in his social relationships. He does not act so as to safeguard his individual interest in the possession of material goods; he acts so as to safeguard his social standing, his social claims, his social assets. He values material goods only insofar as they serve this end. Neither the process of production nor that of distribution is linked to specific economic interests attached to the possession of goods; but every single step in that process is geared to a number of social interests which eventually ensure that the required step be taken. These interests will be very different in a small hunting or fishing community from those in a vast despotic society, but in either case the economic system will be run on non-economic motives.

The explanation, in terms of survival, is simple. Take the case of a tribal society. The individual's economic interest is rarely paramount, for the community keeps all its members from starving unless it is itself borne down by catastrophe, in which case interests are again threatened collectively, not individually. The maintenance of social ties, on the other hand, is crucial. First, because by disregarding the accepted code of honor, or generosity, the individual cuts himself off from the community and becomes an outcast; second, because, in the long run, all social obligations are reciprocal, and their fulfillment serves also the individual's give-and-take interests best. Such a situation must exert a continuous pressure on the individual to eliminate economic self-interest from his consciousness to the point of making him unable, in many cases (but by no means in all), even to comprehend the implications of his own actions in terms of such an interest. This attitude is reinforced by the frequency of communal activities such as partaking of food from the common catch or sharing in the results of some far-flung and dangerous tribal expedition. The premium set on generosity is so great when measured in terms of social prestige as to make any other behavior than that of utter self-forgetfulness simply not pay. Personal character has little to do with the matter. Man can be as good or evil, as social or asocial, jealous or generous, in respect to one set of values as in respect to another. Not to allow anybody reason for jealousy is, indeed, an accepted principle of ceremonial distribution, just as publicly bestowed praise is the due of the industrious, skillful, or otherwise successful gardener (unless he be *too* successful, in which case he may deservedly be allowed to wither away under the delusion of being the victim of black magic). The human passions, good or bad, are merely directed toward non-economic ends. Ceremonial display serves to spur emulation to the utmost and the custom of communal labor tends to screw up both quantitative and qualitative standards to the highest pitch. The performance of all acts of exchange as free gifts that are expected to be reciprocated though not necessarily by the same individuals—a procedure minutely articulated and perfectly safeguarded by elaborate methods of publicity, by magic rites, and by the establishment of "dualities" in which groups are linked in mutual obligations—should in itself explain the absence of the notion of gain or even of wealth other than that consisting of objects traditionally enhancing social prestige.

In this sketch of the general traits characteristic of a Western Melanesian community we took no account of its sexual and territorial organization, in reference to which custom, law, magic, and religion exert their influence, as we only intended to show the manner in which so-called economic motives spring from the context of social life. For it is on this one negative point that modern ethnographers agree: the absence of the motive of gain; the absence of the principle of laboring for remuneration; the absence of the principle of least effort; and, especially, the absence of any separate and distinct institution based on economic motives. But how, then, is order in production and distribution ensured?

The answer is provided in the main by two principles of behavior not primarily associated with economics: *reciprocity* and *redistribution*.[1] With the Trobriand Islanders of Western Melanesia, who serve as an illustration of this type of economy, reciprocity works mainly in regard to the sexual organization of society, that is, family and kinship; redistribution is mainly effective in respect to all those who are under a common chief and is, therefore, of a territorial character. Let us take these principles separately.

The sustenance of the family—the female and the children—is the obligation of their matrilineal relatives. The male, who provides for his sister and her family by delivering the finest specimens of his crop, will mainly earn the credit due to his good behavior, but will reap little immediate material benefit in exchange; if he is slack, it is first and foremost his reputation that will suffer. It is for the benefit of his wife and her children that the principle of reciprocity will work, and thus compensate him economically for his acts of civic virtue. Ceremonial display of food both in his own garden and before the recipient's storehouse will ensure that the high quality of his gardening be known to all. It is apparent that the economy of garden and household here forms part of the social relations connected with good husbandry and fine citizenship. The broad principle of reciprocity helps to safeguard both production and family sustenance.

The principle of redistribution is no less effective. A substantial part of all the produce of the island is delivered

---

[1] Cf., the appendix to this chapter. The works of Malinowski and Thurnwald have been extensively used in this chapter.

by the village headmen to the chief who keeps it in storage. But as all communal activity centers around the feasts, dances, and other occasions when the islanders entertain one another as well as their neighbors from other islands (at which the results of long-distance trading are handed out, gifts are given and reciprocated according to the rules of etiquette, and the chief distributes the customary presents to all), the overwhelming importance of the storage system becomes apparent. Economically, it is an essential part of the existing system of division of labor, of foreign trading, of taxation for public purposes, of defense provisions. But these functions of an economic system proper are completely absorbed by the intensely vivid experiences which offer superabundant non-economic motivation for every act performed in the frame of the social system as a whole.

However, principles of behavior such as these cannot become effective unless existing institutional patterns lend themselves to their application. Reciprocity and redistribution are able to ensure the working of an economic system without the help of written records and elaborate administration only because the organization of the societies in question meets the requirements of such a solution with the help of patterns such as *symmetry* and *centricity*.

Reciprocity is enormously facilitated by the institutional pattern of symmetry, a frequent feature of social organization among non-literate peoples. The striking "duality" which we find in tribal subdivisions lends itself to the pairing out of individual relations and thereby assists the give-and-take of goods and services in the absence of permanent records. The moieties of savage society which tend to create a "pendant" to each subdivision, turned out to result from, as well as help to perform, the acts of reciprocity on which the system rests. Little is known of the origin of "duality"; but each coastal village on the Trobriand Islands appears to have its counterpart in an inland village, so that the important exchange of breadfruits and

10

fish, though disguised as a reciprocal distribution of gifts, and actually disjoint in time, can be organized smoothly. In the Kula trade, too, each individual has his partner on another isle, thus personalizing to a remarkable extent the relationship of reciprocity. But for the frequency of the symmetrical pattern in the subdivisions of the tribe, in the location of settlements, as well as in intertribal relations, a broad reciprocity relying on the long-run working of separated acts of give-and-take would be impracticable.

The institutional pattern of centricity, again, which is present to some extent in all human groups, provides a track for the collection, storage, and redistribution of goods and services. The members of a hunting tribe usually deliver the game to the headman for redistribution. It is in the nature of hunting that the output of game is irregular, besides being the result of a collective input. Under conditions such as these, no other method of sharing is practicable if the group is not to break up after every hunt. Yet in all economies of kind a similar need exists, be the group ever so numerous. And the larger the territory and the more varied the produce, the more will redistribution result in an effective division of labor, since it must help to link up geographically differentiated groups of producers.

Symmetry and centricity will meet halfway the needs of reciprocity and redistribution; institutional patterns and principles of behavior are mutually adjusted. As long as social organization runs in its ruts, no individual economic motives need come into play; no shirking of personal effort need be feared; division of labor will automatically be ensured; economic obligations will be duly discharged; and, above all, the material means for an exuberant display of abundance at all public festivals will be provided. In such a community the idea of profit is barred; higgling and haggling is decried; giving freely is acclaimed as a virtue; the supposed propensity to barter, truck, and exchange does

11

not appear. The economic system is, in effect, a mere function of social organization.

It should by no means be inferred that socioeconomic principles of this type are restricted to primitive procedures or small communities; that a gainless and marketless economy must necessarily be simple. The Kula ring, in Western Melanesia, based on the principle of reciprocity, is one of the most elaborate trading transactions known to man; and redistribution was present on a gigantic scale in the civilization of the pyramids.

The Trobriand Islands belong to an archipelago forming roughly a circle, and an important part of the population of this archipelago spends a considerable proportion of its time in activities of the Kula trade. We describe it as trade though no profit is involved, either in money or in kind; no goods are hoarded or even possessed permanently; the goods received are enjoyed by giving them away; no higgling and haggling, no truck, barter, or exchange enters; and the whole proceedings are entirely regulated by etiquette and magic. Still, it is trade, and large expeditions are undertaken periodically by natives of this approximately ring-shaped archipelago in order to carry one kind of valuable object to peoples living on distant islands situated clockwise, while other expeditions are arranged carrying another kind of valuable object to the islands of the archipelago lying counterclockwise. In the long run, both sets of objects—white-shell armbands and red-shell necklaces of traditional make—will move round the archipelago, a traject which may take them up to ten years to complete. Moreover, there are, as a rule, individual partners in Kula who reciprocate one another's Kula gift with equally valuable armbands and necklaces, preferably such that have previously belonged to distinguished persons. Now, a systematic and organized give-and-take of valuable objects transported over long distances is justly described as trade. Yet this complex whole is exclusively run on the lines of reciprocity. An intricate time-space-person system covering

12

hundreds of miles and several decades, linking many hundreds of people in respect to thousands of strictly individual objects, is being handled here without any records or administration, but also without any motive of gain or truck. Not the propensity to barter, but reciprocity in social behavior dominates. Nevertheless, the result is a stupendous organizational achievement in the economic field. Indeed, it would be interesting to consider whether even the most-advanced modern market organization, based on exact accountancy, would be able to cope with such a task, should it care to undertake it. It is to be feared that the unfortunate dealers, faced with innumerable monopolists buying and selling individual objects with extravagant restrictions attached to each transaction, would fail to make a standard profit and might prefer to go out of business.

Redistribution also has its long and variegated history which leads up almost to modern times. The Bergdama returning from his hunting excursion, the woman coming back from her search for roots, fruit, or leaves are expected to offer the greater part of their spoil for the benefit of the community. In practice, this means that the produce of their activity is shared with the other persons who happen to be living with them. Up to this point the idea of reciprocity prevails: today's giving will be recompensed by tomorrow's taking. Among some tribes, however, there is an intermediary in the person of the headman or other prominent member of the group; it is he who receives and distributes the supplies, especially if they need to be stored. This is redistribution proper. Obviously, the social consequences of such a method of distribution may be far reaching, since not all societies are as democratic as the primitive hunters. Whether the redistributing is performed by an influential family or an outstanding individual, a ruling aristocracy or a group of bureaucrats, they will often attempt to increase their political power by the manner in which they redistribute the goods. In the *potlatch* of the Kwakiutl it is a point of honor with the chief to display his wealth of hides and to distribute them; but he does this also in order to place the recipients under an obligation, to make them his debtors, and ultimately, his retainers.

All large-scale economies in kind were run with the help of the principle of redistribution. The kingdom of Hammurabi in Babylonia and, in particular, the New Kingdom of Egypt were centralized despotisms of a bureaucratic type founded on such an economy. The household of the patriarchal family was reproduced here on an enormously enlarged scale, while its "communistic" distribution was graded, involving sharply differentiated rations. A vast number of storehouses was ready to receive the produce of the peasant's activity, whether he was cattle breeder, hunter, baker, brewer, potter, weaver, or whatever else. The produce was minutely registered and, insofar as it was not consumed locally, transferred from smaller to larger storehouses until it reached the central administration situated at the court of the Pharaoh. There were separate treasure houses for cloth, works of art, ornamental objects, cosmetics, silverware, the royal wardrobe; there were huge grain stores, arsenals, and wine cellars.

But redistribution on the scale practiced by the pyramid builders was not restricted to economies which knew not money. Indeed, all archaic kingdoms made use of metal currencies for the payment of taxes and salaries, but relied for the rest on payments in kind from granaries and warehouses of every description, from which they distributed the most varied goods for use and consumption mainly to the non-producing part of the population, that is, to the officials, the military, and the leisure class. This was the system practiced in ancient China, in the empire of the Incas, in the kingdoms of India, and also in Babylonia. In these, and many other civilizations of vast economic achievement, an elaborate division of labor was worked by the mechanism of redistribution.

Under feudal conditions also, this principle held. In the ethnically stratified societies of Africa it sometimes happens that the superior strata consist of herdsmen settled among agriculturalists who are still using the digging stick or the hoe. The gifts collected by the herdsmen are mainly agricultural—such as cereals and beer—while the gifts distributed by them may be animals, especially sheep or goats. In these cases there is division of labor, though usually an unequal one, between the various strata of society: distribution may often cover up a measure of exploitation, while at the same time the symbiosis benefits the standards of both strata owing to the advantages of an improved division of labor. Politically, such societies live under a regime of feudalism, whether cattle or land be the privileged value. There are "regular cattle fiefs in East Africa." Thurnwald, whom we follow closely on the subject of redistribution, could therefore say that feudalism implied everywhere a system of redistribution. Only under very advanced conditions and exceptional circumstances does this system become predominantly political as happened in Western Europe, where the change arose out of the vassal's need for protection, and gifts were converted into feudal tributes.[2]

These instances show that redistribution also tends to enmesh the economic system proper in social relationships. We find, as a rule, the process of redistribution forming part of the prevailing political regime, whether it be that of tribe, city-state, despotism, or feudalism of cattle or land. The production and distribution of goods is organized in the main through collection, storage, and redistribution, the pattern being focused on the chief, the temple, the despot, or the lord. Since the relations of the leading group to the led are different according to the foundation on which political power rests, the principle of redistribution will involve individual motives as different as the voluntary sharing of the game by hunters and the dread of punishment which urges the *fellaheen* to deliver his taxes in kind.

[2] [See the appendix to this Chapter, "Selected References to 'Societies and Economic Systems.'" Ed.]

We deliberately disregarded in this presentation the vital distinction between homogeneous and stratified societies, i.e., societies which are on the whole socially unified, and such as are split into rulers and ruled. Though the relative status of slaves and masters may be worlds apart from that of the free and equal members of some hunting tribes, and, consequently, motives in the two societies will differ widely, the organization of the economic system may still be based on the same principles, though accompanied by very different culture traits, according to the very different human relations with which the economic system is intertwined.

The third principle, which was destined to play a big role in history and which we will call the principle of *householding,* consists in production for one's own use. The Greeks called it *oeconomia,* the etymon of the word "economy." As far as ethnographical records are concerned, we should not assume that production for a person's or group's own sake is more ancient than reciprocity or redistribution. On the contrary, orthodox tradition as well as some more recent theories on the subject have been emphatically disproved. The individualistic savage collecting food and hunting on his own or for his family has never existed. Indeed, the practice of catering for the needs of one's household becomes a feature of economic life only on a more advanced level of agriculture; however, even then it has nothing in common either with the motive of gain or with the institution of markets. Its pattern is the closed group. Whether the very different entities of the family or the settlement or the manor formed the self-sufficient unit, the principle was invariably the same, namely, that of producing and storing for the satisfaction of the wants of the members of the group. The principle is as broad in its application as either reciprocity or redistribution. The nature of the institutional nucleus is indifferent: It may be sex as with the patriarchal family, locality as with the village settlement, or political power as with the seigneurial manor.

Nor does the internal organization of the group matter. It may be as despotic as the Roman *familia* or as democratic as the South Slav *zadruga;* as large as the great domains of the Carolingian magnates or as small as the average peasant holding of Western Europe. The need for trade or markets is no greater than in the case of reciprocity or redistribution.

It is such a condition of affairs that Aristotle tried to establish as a norm more than two thousand years ago.[3] Looking back from the rapidly declining heights of a world-wide market economy we must concede that his famous distinction of householding proper and money-making, in the introductory chapter of his *Politics,* was probably the most prophetic pointer ever made in the realm of the social sciences; it is certainly still the best analysis of the subject we possess. Aristotle insists on production for use as against production for gain as the essence of householding proper; yet accessory production for the market need not, he argues, destroy the self-sufficiency of the household as long as the cash crop would also otherwise be raised on the farm for sustenance, as cattle or grain; the sale of the surpluses need not destroy the basis of householding. Only a genius of common sense could have maintained, as he did, that gain was a motive peculiar to production for the market, and that the money factor introduced a new element into the situation, yet nevertheless, as long as markets and money were mere accessories to an otherwise self-sufficient household, the principle of production for use could operate. Undoubtedly, in this he was right, though he failed to see how impracticable it was to ignore the existence of markets at a time when Greek economy had made itself dependent upon wholesale trading and loaned capital. For this was the century when Delos and Rhodes were developing into emporia of freight insurance,

[3] [See Essay 5 of this volume, "Aristotle Discovers the Economy." Ed.]

sea-loans, and giro-banking, compared with which the Western Europe of a thousand years later was the very picture of primitivity. Yet Jowett, Master of Balliol, was grievously mistaken when he took it for granted that his Victorian England had a fairer grasp than Aristotle of the nature of the difference between householding and money-making. He excused Aristotle by conceding that the "subjects of knowledge that are concerned with man run into one another; and in the age of Aristotle were not easily distinguished." Aristotle, it is true, did not recognize clearly the implications of the division of labor and its connection with markets and money; nor did he realize the uses of money as credit and capital. So far Jowett's strictures were justified. But it was the Master of Balliol, not Aristotle, who was impervious to the human implications of money-making. He failed to see that the distinction between the principle of use and that of gain was the key to the utterly different civilization the outlines of which Aristotle accurately forecast two thousand years before its advent out of the bare rudiments of a market economy available to him, while Jowett, with the full-blown specimen before him, overlooked its existence. In denouncing the principle of production for gain "as not natural to man," as boundless and limitless, Aristotle was, in effect, aiming at the crucial point, namely the divorcedness of a separate economic motive from the social relations in which these limitations inhered.

Broadly, the proposition holds that all economic systems known to us up to the end of feudalism in Western Europe were organized either on the principles of reciprocity or redistribution, or householding, or some combination of the three. These principles were institutionalized with the help of a social organization which, *inter alia,* made use of the patterns of symmetry, centricity, and autarchy. In this framework, the orderly production and distribution of goods was secured through a great variety of individual motives disciplined by general principles of behavior. Among these motives gain was not prominent. Custom and law, magic and religion co-operated in inducing the individual to comply with rules of behavior which, eventually, ensured his functioning in the economic system.

The Greco-Roman period, in spite of its highly developed trade, represented no break in this respect; it was characterized by the grand scale on which redistribution of grain was practiced by the Roman administration in an otherwise householding economy, and it formed no exception to the rule that up to the end of the Middle Ages, markets played no important part in the economic system; other institutional patterns prevailed.

From the sixteenth century onward markets were both numerous and important. Under the mercantile system they became, in effect, a main concern of government; yet there was still no sign of the coming control of markets over human society. On the contrary. Regulation and regimentation were stricter than ever; the very idea of a self-regulating market was absent. To comprehend the sudden changeover to an utterly new type of economy in the nineteenth century, we must now turn to the history of the market, an institution we were able practically to neglect in our review of the economic systems of the past.

APPENDIX

Selected References to "Societies and Economic Systems"

The nineteenth century attempted to establish a self-regulating economic system on the motive of individual gain. We maintain that such a venture was in the very nature of things impossible. Here we are merely concerned with the distorted view of life and society implied in such an approach. Nineteenth-century thinkers assumed, for instance, that to behave like a trader in the market was "natural," any other mode of behavior being artificial economic behavior—the result of interference with human instincts; that markets would spontaneously arise, if only men were let alone; that whatever the desirability of such a society on moral grounds, its practicability, at least, was founded on the immutable characteristics of the race, and so on. Almost exactly the opposite of these assertions is implied in the testimony of modern research in various fields of social science such as social anthropology, primitive economics, the history of early civilization, and general economic history. Indeed, there is hardly an anthropological or sociological assumption—whether explicit or implicit—contained in the philosophy of economic liberalism that has not been refuted. Some citations follow.

(a) *The motive of gain is not "natural" to man.*

"The characteristic feature of primitive economics is the absence of any desire to make profits from production or exchange" (Thurnwald, *Economics in Primitive Communities,* 1932, p. xiii). "Another notion which must be exploded, once and forever, is that of the Primitive Economic Man of some current economic textbooks" (Malinowski, *Argonauts of the Western Pacific,* 1922, p. 60). "We must reject the *Idealtypen* of Manchester liberalism, which are not only theoretically, but also historically misleading" (Brinkmann, "Das soziale System des Kapitalismus." In *Grundriss der Sozialökonomik,* Abt. IV, p. 11).

(b) *To expect payment for labor is not "natural" to man.*

"Gain, such as is often the stimulus for work in more civilized communities, never acts as an impulse to work under the original native conditions" (Malinowski, op. cit., p. 156). "Nowhere in uninfluenced primitive society do we find labor associated with the idea of payment" (Lowie, "Social Organization," *Encyclopedia of the Social Sciences,* Vol. XIV, p. 14). "*Nowhere* is labor being leased or sold" (Thurnwald, *Die menschliche Gesellschaft,* Bk. III, 1932,

p. 169). "The treatment of labor as an obligation, not requiring indemnification . . ." is general (Firth, *Primitive Economics of the New Zealand Maori*, 1929). "Even in the Middle Ages payment for work for strangers is something unheard of." "The stranger has no *personal* tie of duty, and, therefore, he should work for honor and recognition." Minstrels, while being strangers, "accepted payment, and were consequently despised" (Lowie, op. cit.).

(c) *To restrict labor to the unavoidable minimum is not "natural" to man.*

"We cannot fail to observe that work is never limited to the unavoidable minimum but exceeds the absolutely necessary amount, owing to a natural or acquired functional urge to activity" (Thurnwald, *Economics*, p. 209). "Labor always tends beyond that which is strictly necessary" (Thurnwald, *Die menschliche Gesellschaft*, p. 163).

(d) *The usual incentives to labor are not gain but reciprocity, competition, joy of work, and social approbation.*

Reciprocity: "Most, if not all economic acts are found to belong to some chain of reciprocal gifts and counter-gifts, which in the long run balance, benefiting both sides equally. . . . The man who would persistently disobey the rulings of law in his economic dealings would soon find himself outside the social and economic order—and he is perfectly well aware of it" (Malinowski, *Crime and Custom in Savage Society*, 1926, pp. 40–41).

Competition: "Competition is keen, performance, though uniform in aim, is varied in excellence. . . . A scramble for excellence in reproducing patterns" (Goldenweiser, "Loose Ends of Theory on the Individual, Pattern, and Involution in Primitive Society." In *Essays in Anthropology*, 1936, p. 99). "Men vie with one another in their speed, in their thoroughness, and in the weights they can lift, when bringing big poles to the garden, or in carrying away the harvested yams" (Malinowski, *Argonauts,* p. 61).

Joy of work: "Work for its own sake is a constant characteristic of Maori industry" (Firth, "Some Features of Primitive Industry," *Economic Journal,* 1926, p. 17). "Much time and labor is given up to aesthetic purposes, to making the gardens tidy, clean, cleared of all debris; to building fine, solid fences, to providing specially strong and big yam-poles. All these things are, to some extent, required for the growth of the plant; but there can be no doubt that the natives push their conscientiousness far beyond the limit of the purely necessary" (Malinowski, *Argonauts,* pp. 58–59).

Social approbation: "Perfection in gardening is the general index to the social value of a person" (Malinowski, *Coral Gardens and Their Magic,* Vol. II, 1935, p. 124). "Every person in the community is expected to show a normal measure of application" (Firth, *Primitive Polynesian Economy,* 1939, p. 161). "The Andaman Islanders regard laziness as an antisocial behavior" (Radcliffe-Brown, *The Andaman Islanders*). "To put one's labor at the command of another is a social service, not merely an economic service" (Firth, op. cit., p. 303).

(e) *Man the same down the ages.*

Linton in his *Study of Man* advises caution against the psychological theories of personality determination, and asserts that "general observations lead to the conclusion that the total range of these types is much the same in all societies. . . . In other words, as soon as he [the observer] penetrates the screen of cultural difference, he finds that these people are fundamentally like ourselves" (p. 484). Thurnwald stresses the similarity of men at all stages of their development: "Primitive economics as studied in the preceding pages is not distinguished from any other form of economics, as far as human relations are concerned, and rests on the same general principles of social life" (*Eco-*

nomics, p. 288). "Some collective emotions of an elemental nature are essentially the same with all human beings and account for the recurrence of similar configurations in their social existence" ("Sozialpsychische Abläufe im Völkerleben." In *Essays in Anthropology,* p. 383). Ruth Benedict's *Patterns of Culture* ultimately is based on a similar assumption: "I have spoken as if human temperament were fairly constant in the world, as if in every society a roughly similar distribution were potentially available, and, as if the culture selected from these, according to its traditional patterns, had moulded the vast majority of individuals into conformity. Trance experience, for example, according to this interpretation, is a potentiality of a certain number of individuals in any population. When it is honored and rewarded, a considerable proportion will achieve or simulate it . . ." (p. 233). Malinowski consistently maintained the same position in his works.

(f) *Economic systems, as a rule, are embedded in social relations; distribution of material goods is ensured by non-economic motives.*

Primitive economy is "a social affair, dealing with a number of persons as parts of an interlocking whole" (Thurnwald, *Economics,* p. xii). This is equally true of wealth, work, and barter. "Primitive wealth is not of an economic but of a social nature" (ibid.). Labor is capable of "effective work," because it is *"integrated into an organized effort by social forces"* (Malinowski, *Argonauts,* p. 157). "Barter of goods and services is carried on mostly within a standing partnership, or associated with definite social ties or coupled with a mutuality in non-economic matters" (Malinowski, *Crime and Custom,* p. 39).

The two main principles which govern economic behavior appear to be reciprocity and *storage-cum-redistribution:*

"The whole tribal life is permeated by a constant give and take" (Malinowski, *Argonauts,* p. 167). "Today's giv-

ing will be recompensed by tomorrow's taking. This is the outcome of the principle of reciprocity which pervades every relation of primitive life . . ." (Thurnwald, *Economics*, p. 106). In order to make such reciprocity possible, a certain "duality" of institutions or "symmetry of structure will be found in every savage society, as the indispensable basis of reciprocal obligations" (Malinowski, *Crime and Custom*, p. 25). "The symmetrical partition of their chambers of spirits is based with the Banaro on the structure of their society, which is similarly symmetrical" (Thurnwald, *Die Gemeinde der Bánaro*, 1921, p. 378).

Thurnwald discovered that apart from, and sometimes combined with, such reciprocating behavior, the practice of storage and redistribution was of the most general application from the primitive hunting tribe to the largest of empires. Goods were centrally collected and then distributed to the members of the community, in a great variety of ways. Among Micronesian and Polynesian peoples, for instance, "the kings as the representatives of the first clan, receive the revenue, redistributing it later in the form of largesse among the population" (Thurnwald, *Economics*, p. xii). This distributive function is a prime source of the political power of central agencies (ibid., p. 107).

(g) *Individual food collection for the use of his own person and family does not form part of early man's life.*

The classics assumed the pre-economic man had to take care of himself and his family. This assumption was revived by Carl Buecher in his pioneering work around the turn of the century [*Industrial Evolution*, 1901] and gained wide currency. Recent research has unanimously corrected Buecher on this point. (Firth, *Primitive Economics of the New Zealand Maori*, pp. 12, 206, 350; Thurnwald, *Economics*, pp. 170, 268, and *Die menschliche Gesellschaft*, Vol. III, p. 146; Herskovits, *The Economic*

24

Life of Primitive Peoples, 1940, p. 34; Malinowski, *Argonauts,* p. 167, footnote).

(h) *Reciprocity and redistribution are principles of economic organization which apply not only to small primitive communities, but also to large and wealthy empires.*

"Distribution has its own particular history, starting from the most primitive life of the hunting tribes. . . . The case is different with societies with a more recent and more pronounced stratification. . . . The most impressive example is furnished by the contact of herdsmen with agricultural people. . . . The conditions in these societies differ considerably. But the distributive function increases with the growing political power of a few families and the rise of despots. The chief receives the gifts of the peasant, which have now become 'taxes,' and distributes them among his officials, especially those attached to his court."

"This development involved more complicated systems of distribution. . . . All archaic states—ancient China, the Empire of the Incas, the Indian kingdoms, Egypt, Babylonia—made use of a metal currency for taxes and salaries but relied mainly on payments in kind stored in granaries and warehouses . . . and distributed to officials, warriors, and the leisured classes, that is, to the non-producing part of the population. In this case distribution fulfills an essentially economic function" (Thurnwald, *Economics,* pp. 106–8).

"When we speak of feudalism, we are usually thinking of the Middle Ages in Europe. . . . However, it is an institution, which very soon makes its appearance in stratified communities. The fact that most transactions are in kind and that the upper stratum claims all the land or cattle, are the economic causes of feudalism . . ." (ibid., p. 195).

2

The Self-regulating Market and the Fictitious Commodities: Labor, Land, and Money

This cursory outline of the economic system and mar kets, taken separately, shows that never before our own time were markets more than accessories of economic life As a rule, the economic system was absorbed in the socia system, and whatever principle of behavior predominated in the economy, the presence of the market pattern wa found to be compatible with it. The principle of barter o exchange, which underlies this pattern, revealed no tend ency to expand at the expense of the rest. Where market were most highly developed, as under the mercantile sys tem, they throve under the control of a centralized ad ministration which fostered autarchy both in the house holds of the peasantry and in respect to national life Regulation and markets, in effect, grew up together. Th self-regulating market was unknown; indeed the emergenc of the idea of self-regulation was a complete reversal o the trend of development. It is in the light of these fact that the extraordinary assumptions underlying a marke economy can alone be fully comprehended.

A market economy is an economic system controlled regulated, and directed by markets alone; order in the pro duction and distribution of goods is entrusted to this self regulating mechanism. An economy of this kind derive from the expectation that human beings behave in such a

FROM Chapter 6, "The Self-regulating Market and the Fic titious Commodities: Labor, Land, and Money," pp. 68–76, o Karl Polanyi, *The Great Transformation*, New York: Rinehart 1944. Reprinted by permission of the publisher.

way as to achieve maximum money gains. It assumes markets in which the supply of goods (including services) available at a definite price will equal the demand at that price. It assumes the presence of money, which functions as purchasing power in the hands of its owners. Production will then be controlled by prices, for the profits of those who direct production will depend upon them; the distribution of the goods also will depend upon prices, for prices form incomes, and it is with the help of these incomes that the goods produced are distributed amongst the members of society. Under these assumptions order in the production and distribution of goods is ensured by prices alone.

Self-regulation implies that all production is for sale on the market and that all incomes derive from such sales. Accordingly, there are markets for all elements of industry, not only for goods (always including services) but also for labor, land, and money, their prices being called respectively commodity prices, wages, rent, and interest. The very terms indicate that prices form incomes: interest is the price for the use of money and forms the income of those who are in the position to provide it; rent is the price for the use of land and forms the income of those who supply it; wages are the price for the use of labor power, and form the income of those who sell it; commodity prices, finally, contribute to the incomes of those who sell their entrepreneurial services, the income called profit being actually the difference between two sets of prices, the price of the goods produced and their costs, i.e., the price of the goods necessary to produce them. If these conditions are fulfilled, all incomes will derive from sales on the market, and incomes will be just sufficient to buy all the goods produced.

A further group of assumptions follows in respect to the state and its policy. Nothing must be allowed to inhibit the formation of markets, nor must incomes be permitted to be formed otherwise than through sales. Neither must there

27

be any interference with the adjustment of prices to changed market conditions—whether the prices are those of goods, labor, land, or money. Hence there must not only be markets for all elements of industry,[1] but no measure or policy must be countenanced that would influence the action of these markets. Neither price, nor supply, nor demand must be fixed or regulated; only such policies and measures are in order that help to ensure the self-regulation of the market by creating conditions which make the market the only organizing power in the economic sphere.

To realize fully what this means, let us return for a moment to the mercantile system and the national markets which it did so much to develop. Under feudalism and the guild system, land and labor formed part of the social organization itself (money had as yet hardly developed into a major element of industry). Land, the pivotal element in the feudal order, was the basis of the military, judicial, administrative, and political system; its status and function were determined by legal and customary rules. Whether its possession was transferable or not, and if so, to whom and under what restrictions; what the rights of property entailed; to what uses some types of land might be put—all these questions were removed from the organization of buying and selling, and subjected to an entirely different set of institutional regulations.

The same was true of the organization of labor. Under the guild system, as under every other economic system in previous history, the motives and circumstances of productive activities were embedded in the general organization of society. The relations of master, journeyman, and apprentice; the terms of the craft; the number of apprentices; the wages of the workers were all regulated by the custom and rule of the guild and the town. What the mer-

---

[1] Henderson, H. D., *Supply and Demand*, 1922. The practice of the market is twofold: the apportionment of factors between different uses, and the organizing of the forces influencing aggregate supplies of factors.

cantile system did was merely to unify these conditions either through statute as in England, or through the "nationalization" of the guilds as in France. As to land, its feudal status was abolished only insofar as it was linked with provincial privileges; for the rest, land remained *extra commercium,* in England as in France. Up to the time of the Great Revolution of 1789, landed estate remained the source of social privilege in France, and even after that time in England, Common Law on land was essentially medieval. Mercantilism, with all its tendency toward commercialization, never attacked the safeguards that protected these two basic elements of production—labor and land—from becoming the objects of commerce. In England the "nationalization" of labor legislation through the Statute of Artificers (1563) and the Poor Law (1601), removed labor from the danger zone, and the anti-enclosure policy of the Tudors and early Stuarts was one consistent protest against the principle of the gainful use of landed property.

That mercantilism, however emphatically it insisted on commercialization as a national policy, thought of markets in a way exactly contrary to market economy, is best shown by its vast extension of state intervention in industry. On this point there was no difference between mercantilists and feudalists, between crowned planners and vested interests, between centralizing bureaucrats and conservative particularists. They disagreed only on the methods of regulation: guilds, towns, and provinces appealed to the force of custom and tradition, while the new state authority favored statute and ordinance. But they were all equally averse to the idea of commercializing labor and land—the precondition of market economy. Craft guilds and feudal privileges were abolished in France only in 1790; in England the Statute of Artificers was repealed only in 1813–14, the Elizabethan Poor Law in 1834. Not before the last decade of the eighteenth century was, in either country, the establishment of a free labor market even discussed; and the idea of the self-regulation of economic life was utterly beyond the horizon of the age. The mercantilist was concerned with the development of the resources of the country, including full employment, through trade and commerce; the traditional organization of land and labor he took for granted. He was in this respect as far removed from modern concepts as he was in the realm of politics, where his belief in the absolute powers of an enlightened despot was tempered by no intimations of democracy. And just as the transition to a democratic system and representative politics involved a complete reversal of the trend of the age, the change from regulated to self-regulating markets at the end of the eighteenth century represented a complete transformation in the structure of society.

A self-regulating market demands nothing less than the institutional separation of society into an economic and political sphere. Such a dichotomy is, in effect, merely the restatement, from the point of view of society as a whole, of the existence of a self-regulating market. It might be argued that the separateness of the two spheres obtains in every type of society at all times. Such an inference, however, would be based on a fallacy. True, no society can exist without a system of some kind that ensures order in the production and distribution of goods. But that does not imply the existence of separate economic institutions; normally, the economic order is merely a function of the social, in which it is contained. Neither under tribal, nor feudal, nor mercantile conditions was there, as we have shown, a separate economic system in society. Nineteenth-century society, in which economic activity was isolated and imputed to a distinctive economic motive, was, indeed, a singular departure.

Such an institutional pattern could not function unless society was somehow subordinated to its requirements. A market economy can exist only in a market society. We reached this conclusion on general grounds in our analysis of the market pattern. We can now specify the reasons for his assertion. A market economy must comprise all elements of industry, including labor, land, and money. (In a market economy the last also is an essential element of industrial life and its inclusion in the market mechanism was, as we will see, far-reaching institutional consequences.) But labor and land are no other than the human beings themselves of which every society consists and the natural surroundings in which it exists. To include them in the market mechanism means to subordinate the substance of society itself to the laws of the market.

We are now in the position to develop in a more concrete form the institutional nature of a market economy, and the perils to society which it involves. We will, first, describe the methods by which the market mechanism is enabled to control and direct the actual elements of industrial life; second, we will try to gauge the nature of the effects of such a mechanism on the society that is subjected to its action.

It is with the help of the commodity concept that the mechanism of the market is geared to the various elements of industrial life. Commodities are here empirically defined as objects produced for sale on the market; markets, again, are empirically defined as actual contacts between buyers and sellers. Accordingly, every element of industry is regarded as having been produced for sale, as then and then only will it be subject to the supply-and-demand mechanism interacting with price. In practice this means that there must be markets for every element of industry; that in these markets each of these elements is organized into a supply and a demand group; and that each element has a price, which interacts with demand and supply. These markets—and they are numberless—are interconnected and form One Big Market.[2]

The crucial point is this: labor, land, and money are

[2] Hawtrey, G. R., *The Economic Problem,* 1925. Its function is seen by Hawtrey in making "the relative market values of all commodities mutually consistent."

31

essential elements of industry; they also must be organized in markets; in fact, these markets form an absolutely vital part of the economic system. But labor, land, and money are obviously *not* commodities; the postulate that anything that is bought and sold must have been produced for sale is emphatically untrue in regard to them. In other words, according to the empirical definition of a commodity they are not commodities. Labor is only another name for a human activity that goes with life itself, which in its turn is not produced for sale but for entirely different reasons, nor can that activity be detached from the rest of life, be stored or mobilized; land is only another name for nature, which is not produced by man; actual money, finally, is merely a token of purchasing power which, as a rule, is not produced at all, but comes into being through the mechanism of banking or state finance. None of them is produced for sale. The commodity description of labor, land, and money is entirely fictitious.

Nevertheless, it is with the help of this fiction that the actual markets for labor, land, and money are organized; they are being actually bought and sold on the market; their demand and supply are real magnitudes; and any measures or policies that would inhibit the formation of such markets would *ipso facto* endanger the self-regulation of the system. The commodity fiction, therefore, supplies a vital organizing principle in regard to the whole of society affecting almost all its institutions in the most varied way namely, the principle according to which no arrangement or behavior should be allowed to exist that might prevent the actual functioning of the market mechanism on the lines of the commodity fiction.

Now, in regard to labor, land, and money such a postulate cannot be upheld. To allow the market mechanism to

---

[3] Marx's assertion of the fetish character of the value of commodities refers to the exchange value of genuine commodities and has nothing in common with the fictitious commodities mentioned in the text.

e sole director of the fate of human beings and their natural environment, indeed, even of the amount and use of purchasing power, would result in the demolition of society. For the alleged commodity "labor power" cannot be shoved about, used indiscriminately, or even left unused, without affecting also the human individual who happens to be the bearer of this peculiar commodity. In disposing of a man's labor power the system would, incidentally, dispose of the physical, psychological, and moral entity "man" attached to that tag. Robbed of the protective covering of cultural institutions, human beings would perish from the effects of social exposure; they would die as the victims of acute social dislocation through vice, perversion, crime, and starvation. Nature would be reduced to its elements, neighborhoods and landscapes defiled, rivers polluted, military safety jeopardized, the power to produce food and raw materials destroyed. Finally, the market administration of purchasing power would periodically liquidate business enterprise, for shortages and surfeits of money would prove as disastrous to business as floods and droughts in primitive society. Undoubtedly, labor, land, and money markets *are* essential to a market economy. But no society could stand the effects of such a system of crude fictions even for the shortest stretch of time unless its human and natural substance, as well as its business organization was protected against the ravages of this satanic mill.

The extreme artificiality of market economy is rooted in the fact that the process of production itself is here organized in the form of buying and selling.[4] No other way of organizing production for the market is possible in a commercial society. During the late Middle Ages industrial production for export was organized by wealthy burgesses, and carried on under their direct supervision in the home town. Later, in the mercantile society, production was or-

[4] Cunningham, W., "Economic Change," *Cambridge Modern History*, Vol. I.

ganized by merchants and was not restricted any more to
the towns; this was the age of "putting out" when domestic
industry was provided with raw materials by the merchant
capitalist, who controlled the process of production as a
purely commercial enterprise. It was then that industrial
production was definitely and on a large scale put under the
organizing leadership of the merchant. He knew the market, the volume as well as the quality of the demand; and
he could vouch also for the supplies which, incidentally
consisted merely of wool, woad, and, sometimes, the looms
or the knitting frames used by the cottage industry. If supplies failed, it was the cottager who was worst hit, for his
employment was gone for the time; but no expensive plant
was involved and the merchant incurred no serious risk in
shouldering the responsibility for production. For centuries
this system grew in power and scope until in a country like
England the wool industry, the national staple, covered
large sectors of the country where production was organized by the clothier. He who bought and sold, incidentally
provided for production—no separate motive was required.
The creation of goods involved neither the reciprocating
attitudes of mutual aid; nor the concern of the householder
for those whose needs are left to his care; nor the craftsman's pride in the exercise of his trade; nor the satisfaction
of public praise—nothing but the plain motive of gain so
familiar to the man whose profession is buying and selling.
Up to the end of the eighteenth century, industrial production in Western Europe was a mere accessory to commerce.

As long as the machine was an inexpensive and unspe-
cific tool, there was no change in this position. The mere
fact that the cottager could produce larger amounts than
before within the same time might induce him to use machines to increase earnings, but this fact in itself did not
necessarily affect the organization of production. Whether
the cheap machinery was owned by the worker or by the
merchant made some difference in the social position of
the parties, and it almost certainly made a difference in the

earnings of the worker, who was better off as long as he owned his tools; but it did not force the merchant to become an industrial capitalist, or to restrict himself to lending his money to such persons as were. The vent of goods rarely gave out; the greater difficulty continued to be on the side of supply of raw materials, which was sometimes unavoidably interrupted. But, even in such cases, the loss to the merchant who owned the machines was not substantial. It was not the coming of the machine as such, but the invention of elaborate and therefore specific machinery and plant that completely changed the relationship of the merchant to production. Although the new productive organization was introduced by the merchant—a fact that determined the whole course of the transformation—the use of elaborate machinery and plant involved the development of the factory system and therewith a decisive shift in the relative importance of commerce and industry in favor of the latter. Industrial production ceased to be an accessory of commerce organized by the merchant as a buying and selling proposition; it now involved long-term investment with corresponding risks. Unless the continuance of production was reasonably assured, such a risk was not bearable.

But the more complicated industrial production became, the more numerous were the elements of industry the supply of which had to be safeguarded. Three of these, of course, were of outstanding importance: labor, land, and money. In a commercial society their supply could be organized in one way only: by being made available for purchase. Hence, they would have to be organized for sale on the market—in other words, as commodities. The extension of the market mechanism to the elements of industry—labor, land, and money—was the inevitable consequence of the introduction of the factory system in a commercial society. The elements of industry had to be on sale.

This was synonymous with the demand for a market system. We know that profits are ensured under such a

35

system only if self-regulation is safeguarded through inter-dependent competitive markets. As the development of the factory system had been organized as part of a process of buying and selling, therefore labor, land, and money had to be transformed into commodities in order to keep production going. They could, of course, not be really transformed into commodities, as actually they were not produced for sale on the market. But the fiction of their being so produced became the organizing principle of society. Of the three, one stands out: labor is the technical term used for human beings, insofar as they are not employers but employed; it follows that henceforth the organization of labor would change concurrently with the organization of the market system. But as the organization of labor is only another word for the forms of life of the common people, this means that the development of the market system would be accompanied by a change in the organization of society itself. All along the line, human society had become an accessory of the economic system.

We recall our parallel between the ravages of the enclosures in English history and the social catastrophe that followed the Industrial Revolution.[5] Improvements, we said, are, as a rule, bought at the price of social dislocation. If the rate of dislocation is too great, the community must succumb in the process. The Tudors and early Stuarts saved England from the fate of Spain by regulating the course of change so that it became bearable, and its effects could be canalized into less destructive avenues. But nothing saved the common people of England from the impact of the Industrial Revolution. A blind faith in spontaneous progress had taken hold of people's minds, and with the fanaticism of sectarians, the most enlightened pressed forward for boundless and unregulated change in society. The effects on the lives of the people were awful beyond

[5] [See Chapter 3, "Habitation versus Improvement," pp. 33-42, of The Great Transformation, New York: Rinehart, 1944 Ed.]

description. Indeed, human society would have been an-
nihilated but for protective countermoves that blunted the
action of this self-destructive mechanism.

Social history in the nineteenth century was thus the result of a double movement: the extension of the market
organization in respect to genuine commodities was accompanied by its restriction in respect to fictitious ones.
While on the one hand markets spread all over the face of
the globe and the amount of goods involved grew to un-
believable proportions, on the other hand a network of
measures and policies was integrated into powerful institutions designed to check the action of the market relative to
labor, land, and money. While the organization of world
commodity markets, world capital markets, and world currency markets under the aegis of the gold standard gave
an unparalleled momentum to the mechanism of markets,
a deep-seated movement sprang into being to resist the
pernicious effects of a market-controlled economy. Society protected itself against the perils inherent in a self-
regulating market system—this was the one comprehensive
feature in the history of the age.

3

Class Interest and Social Change

The liberal myth of the collectivist conspiracy must be completely dissipated before the true basis of nineteenth-century policies can be laid bare. This legend has it that protectionism was merely the result of sinister interest of agrarians, manufacturers, and trade unionists, who selfishly wrecked the automatic machinery of the market. In another form, and, of course, with an opposite political tendency, Marxian parties argued in equally sectional terms. (That the essential philosophy of Marx centered on the totality of society and the non-economic nature of man is irrelevant here.[1]) Marx himself followed Ricardo in defining classes in economic terms, and economic exploitation was undoubtedly a feature of the bourgeois age.

In popular Marxism this led to a crude class theory of social development. Pressure for markets and zones of influence was simply ascribed to the profit motive of a handful of financiers. Imperialism was explained as a capitalist conspiracy to induce governments to launch wars in the interests of big business. Wars were held to be caused by these interests in combination with armament firms who miraculously gained the capacity to drive whole nations into fatal policies, contrary to their vital interests. Liberals and Marxists agreed, in effect, in deducing the protectionist

FROM Chapter 13, "Birth of the Liberal Creed: Class Interest and Social Change," pp. 151–162, 290–294, of Karl Polanyi *The Great Transformation*, New York: Rinehart, 1944. Reprinted by permission of the publisher.

[1] Marx, K., *Nationalökonomie und Philosophie*. In "De Historische Materialismus," 1932.

movement from the force of sectional interests; in accounting for agrarian tariffs by the political pull of reactionary
landlords; in making the profit hunger of industrial magnates accountable for the growth of monopolistic forms of
enterprise; in presenting war as the result of business
rampant.

The liberal economic outlook thus found powerful support in a narrow class theory. Upholding the viewpoint of
opposing classes, liberals and Marxists stood for identical
propositions. They established a watertight case for the assertion that nineteenth-century protectionism was the result
of class action, and that such action must have primarily
served the economic interests of the members of the classes
concerned. Between them they all but completely obstructed an over-all view of market society, and of the
function of protectionism in such a society.

Actually, class interests offer only a limited explanation
of long-run movements in society. The fate of classes is
much more often determined by the needs of society than
the fate of society is determined by the needs of classes.
Given a definite structure of society, the class theory works;
but what if that structure itself undergoes change? A class
that has become functionless may disintegrate and be sup-
planted overnight by a new class or classes. Also, the
chances of classes in a struggle will depend upon their
ability to win support from outside their own membership,
which again will depend upon their fulfillment of tasks set
by interests wider than their own. Thus, neither the birth
nor the death of classes, neither their aims nor the degree
to which they attain them; neither their co-operations nor
their antagonisms can be understood apart from the situation of society as a whole.

Now, this situation is created, as a rule, by external
causes, such as a change in climate, in the yield of crops,
a new foe, a new weapon used by an old foe, the emergence
of new communal ends, or, for that matter, the discovery
of new methods of achieving the traditional ends. To such

a total situation must sectional interests be ultimately related if their function in social development should become clear.

The essential role played by class interests in social change is in the nature of things. For any widespread form of change must affect the various parts of the community in different fashions, if for no other reason than that of differences of geographical location, and of economic and cultural equipment. Sectional interests are thus the natural vehicle of social and political change. Whether the source of the change be war or trade, startling inventions or shifts in natural conditions, the various sections in society will stand for different methods of adjustment (including forcible ones) and adjust their interests in a different way from those of other groups to whom they may seek to give a lead; hence only when one can point to the group or groups that effected a change is it explained *how* that change has taken place. Yet the ultimate cause is set by external forces, and it is for the mechanism of the change only that society relies on internal forces. The "challenge" is to society as a whole; the "response" comes through groups, sections, and classes.

Mere class interests cannot offer, therefore, a satisfactory explanation for any long-run social process. First, because the process in question may decide about the existence of the class itself; second, because the interests of given classes determine only the aims and purposes toward which those classes are striving, not also the success or failure of such endeavors. There is no magic in class interests that would secure to members of one class the support of members of other classes. Yet such support is an everyday occurrence. Protectionism, in fact, is an instance. The problem here was not so much why agrarians, manufacturers, or trade unionists wished to increase their incomes through protectionist action, but why they succeeded in doing so; not why businessmen and workers wished to establish monopolies for their wares, but why they attained their end; not why some groups wished to act in a similar fashion in a number of Continental countries, but why such groups existed in these otherwise dissimilar countries and equally achieved their aims everywhere; not why those who grew corn attempted to sell it dear, but why they regularly succeeded in persuading those who bought the corn to help to raise its price.

Second, there is the equally mistaken doctrine of the essentially economic nature of class interests. Though human society is naturally conditioned by economic factors, the motives of human individuals are only exceptionally determined by the needs of material want-satisfaction. That nineteenth-century society was organized on the assumption that such a motivation could be made universal was a peculiarity of the age. It was therefore appropriate to allow a comparatively wide scope to the play of economic motives when analyzing that society. But we must guard against prejudging the issue, which is precisely to what extent such an unusual motivation could be made effective.

Purely economic matters such as affect want-satisfaction are incomparably less relevant to class behavior than questions of social recognition. Want-satisfaction may be, of course, the result of such recognition, especially as its outward sign or prize. But the interests of a class most directly refer to standing and rank, to status and security, that is, they are primarily not economic but social.

The classes and groups that intermittently took part in the general movement toward protectionism after 1870 did not do so primarily on account of their economic interests. The "collectivist" measures enacted in the critical years reveal that only exceptionally was the interest of any single class involved, and if so, that interest could be rarely described as economic. Assuredly no "shortsighted economic interests" were served by an Act authorizing town authorities to take over neglected ornamental spaces; by regulations requiring the cleaning of bakehouses with hot water and soap at least once in six months; or an Act making compulsory the testing of cables and anchors. Such measures simply responded to the needs of an industrial civilization with which market methods were unable to cope. The great majority of these interventions had no direct, and hardly more than an indirect, bearing on incomes. This was true practically of all laws relating to health and homesteads, public amenities and libraries, factory conditions, and social insurance. No less was it true of public utilities, education, transportation, and numberless other matters. But even where money values were involved, they were secondary to other interests. Almost invariably professional status, safety and security, the form of a man's life, the breadth of his existence, the stability of his environment were in question. The monetary importance of some typical interventions, such as customs tariffs, or workmen's compensation, should in no way be minimized. But even in these cases non-monetary interests were inseparable from monetary ones. Customs tariffs, which implied profits for capitalists and wages for workers, meant, ultimately, security against unemployment, stabilization of regional conditions, assurance against liquidation of industries, and, perhaps most of all, the avoidance of that painful loss of status which inevitably accompanies transference to a job at which a man is less skilled and experienced than at his own.

Once we are rid of the obsession that only sectional, never general, interests can become effective, as well as of the twin prejudice of restricting the interests of human groups to their monetary income, the breadth and comprehensiveness of the protectionist movement lose their mystery. While monetary interests are necessarily voiced solely by the persons to whom they pertain, other interests have a wider constituency. They affect individuals in innumerable ways as neighbors, professional persons, consumers, pedestrians, commuters, sportsmen, hikers, gardeners, patients, mothers, or lovers—and are accordingly capable of representation by almost any type of territorial or functional association such as churches, townships, fraternal lodges, clubs, trade unions, or, most commonly, political parties based on broad principles of adherence. An all too narrow conception of interest must in effect lead to a warped vision of social and political history, and no purely monetary definition of interests can leave room for that vital need for social protection, the representation of which commonly falls to the persons in charge of the general interests of the community—under modern conditions, the governments of the day. Precisely because not the economic but the social interests of different cross sections of the population were threatened by the market, persons belonging to various economic strata unconsciously joined forces to meet the danger.

The spread of the market was thus both advanced and obstructed by the action of class forces. Given the need of machine production for the establishment of a market system, the trading classes alone were in the position to take the lead in that early transformation. A new class of entrepreneurs came into being out of the remnants of older classes, in order to take charge of a development that was consonant with the interests of the community as a whole. But if the rise of the industrialists, entrepreneurs, and capitalists was the result of their leading role in the expansionist movement, the defense fell to the traditional landed classes and the nascent working class. And if among the trading community it was the capitalists' lot to stand for the structural principles of the market system, the role of the die-hard defender of the social fabric was the portion of the feudal aristocracy on the one hand, the rising industrial proletariat on the other. But while the landed classes would naturally seek the solution for all evils in the maintenance of the past, the workers were, up to a point, in the position to transcend the limits of a market society and to borrow solutions from the future. This does not imply that the return to feudalism or the proclamation of socialism was amongst the possible lines of action; but it does indicate

43

the entirely different directions in which agrarians and urban working-class forces tended to seek for relief in an emergency. If market economy broke down, as in every major crisis it threatened to do, the landed classes might attempt a return to a military or feudal regime of paternalism, while the factory workers would see the need for the establishment of a co-operative commonwealth of labor. In a crisis "responses" might point toward mutually exclusive solutions. A mere clash of class interests, which otherwise would have been met by compromise, was invested with a fatal significance.

All this should warn us against relying too much on the economic interests of given classes in the explanation of history. Such an approach would tacitly imply the givenness of those classes in a sense in which this is possible only in an indestructible society. It leaves outside its range those critical phases of history, when a civilization has broken down or is passing through a transformation, when as a rule new classes are formed, sometimes within the briefest space of time, out of the ruins of older classes, or even out of extraneous elements like foreign adventurers or outcasts. Frequently, at a historical juncture new classes have been called into being simply by virtue of the demands of the hour. Ultimately, therefore, it is the relation of a class to society as a whole that maps out its part in the drama; and its success is determined by the breadth and variety of the interests, other than its own, which it is able to serve. Indeed, no policy of a narrow class interest can safeguard even that interest well—a rule which allows of but few exceptions. Unless the alternative to the social setup is a plunge into utter destruction, no crudely selfish class can maintain itself in the lead.

In order to fix safely the blame on the alleged collectivist conspiracy, economic liberals must ultimately deny that any need for the protection of society had arisen. Recently, they acclaimed views of some scholars who had rejected the traditional doctrine of the Industrial Revolution according to which a catastrophe broke in upon the unfortunate laboring classes of England about the 1790s. Nothing in the nature of a sudden deterioration of standards, according to these writers, ever overwhelmed the common people. They were, on the average, substantially better off after than before the introduction of the factory system, and, as to numbers, nobody could deny their rapid increase. By the accepted yardsticks of economic welfare—real wages and population figures—the Inferno of early capitalism, they maintained, never existed; the working classes, far from being exploited, were economically the gainers, and to argue the need for social protection against a system that benefited all was obviously impossible.[2]

Critics of liberal capitalism were baffled. For some seventy years, scholars and Royal Commissions alike had denounced the horrors of the Industrial Revolution, and a galaxy of poets, thinkers, and writers had branded its cruelties. It was deemed an established fact that the masses were being sweated and starved by the callous exploiters of their helplessness; that enclosures had deprived the country folk of their homes and plots, and thrown them on the labor market created by the Poor Law Reform; and that the authenticated tragedies of the small children, who were sometimes worked to death in mines and factories, offered ghastly proof of the destitution of the masses. Indeed, the familiar explanation of the Industrial Revolution rested on the degree of exploitation made possible by eighteenth-century enclosures; on the low wages offered to homeless workers, which accounted for the high profits of the cotton industry as well as the rapid accumulation of capital in the hands of the early manufacturers. And the charge against them was exploitation, a boundless exploitation of their fellow citizens that was the root cause of so much misery

[2] [See F. A. Hayek (ed.), *Capitalism and the Historians*, Chicago: University of Chicago Press, 1954. Ed.]

and debasement. All this was now apparently refuted. Economic historians proclaimed the message that the black shadow that overcast the early decades of the factory system had been dispelled. For how could there be social catastrophe where there was undoubtedly economic improvement?

Actually, of course, a social calamity is primarily a cultural not an economic phenomenon that can be measured by income figures or population statistics. Cultural catastrophes involving broad strata of the common people can naturally not be frequent; but neither are cataclysmic events like the Industrial Revolution—an economic earthquake which transformed within less than half a century vast masses of the inhabitants of the English countryside from settled folk into shiftless migrants. But if such destructive landslides are exceptional in the history of classes, they are a common occurrence in the sphere of culture contacts between peoples of various races. Intrinsically, the conditions are the same. The difference is mainly that a social class forms part of a society inhabiting the same geographical area, while culture contact occurs usually between societies settled in different geographical regions. In both cases the contact may have a devastating effect on the weaker part. Not economic exploitation, as often assumed, but the disintegration of the cultural environment of the victim is then the cause of the degradation. The economic process may, naturally, supply the vehicle of the destruction, and almost invariably economic inferiority will make the weaker yield, but the immediate cause of his undoing is not for that reason economic; it lies in the lethal injury to the institutions in which his social existence is embodied. The result is loss of self-respect and standards, whether the unit is a people or a class, whether the process springs from so-called "culture conflict" or from a change in the position of a class within the confines of a society.

To the student of early capitalism the parallel is highly significant. The condition of some native tribes in Africa

46

today carries an unmistakable resemblance to that of the English laboring classes during the early years of the nineteenth century. The Kaffir of South Africa, a noble savage, than whom none felt socially more secure in his native *kraal,* has been transformed into a human variety of half-domesticated animal dressed in the "unrelated, the filthy, the unsightly rags that not the most degenerated white man would wear,"[3] a nondescript being, without self-respect or standards, veritable human refuse. The description recalls the portrait Robert Owen drew of his own work people, when addressing them in New Lanark, telling them to their faces, coolly and objectively as a social researcher might record the facts, why they had become the degraded rabble which they were;[4] and the true cause of their degradation could not be more aptly described than by their existing in a "cultural vacuum"—the term used by an anthropologist[5] to describe the cause of the cultural debasement of some of the valiant black tribes of Africa under the influence of contact with white civilization. Their crafts have decayed, the political and social conditions of their existence have been destroyed, they are dying from boredom, in Rivers' famous phrase, or wasting their lives and substance in dissipation. While their own culture offers them no longer any objectives worthy of effort or sacrifice, racial snobbishness and prejudice bar the way to their adequate participation in the culture of the white intruders.[6] Substitute social bar for color bar and the Two Nations of the 1840s emerge, the Kaffir having been appropriately replaced by the shambling slum dweller of Kingsley's novels.

[3] Millin, Mrs. S. G., *The South Africans,* 1926.
[4] [Robert Owen, "An Address Delivered to the Inhabitants of New Lanark on the 1st of January, 1816, at the opening of the Institution for the Formation of Character," in *A New View of Society, and Other Essays,* New York: E. P. Dutton & Co., 1927. Everyman's Library. Ed.]
[5] Goldenweiser, A., *Anthropology,* 1937.
[6] Ibid.

Some who would readily agree that life in a cultural void is no life at all nevertheless seem to expect that economic needs would automatically fill that void and make life appear livable under whatever conditions. This assumption is sharply contradicted by the result of anthropological research. "The goals for which individuals will work are culturally determined, and are not a response of the organism to an external culturally undefined situation, like a simple scarcity of food," says Dr. Mead. "The process by which a group of savages is converted into gold miners or ship's crew or merely robbed of all incentive to effort and left to die painlessly beside streams still filled with fish, may seem so bizarre, so alien to the nature of society and its normal functioning as to be pathological," yet, she adds, "precisely this will, as a rule, happen to a people in the midst of violent externally introduced, or at least externally produced change. . . ." She concludes: "This rude contact, this uprooting of simple peoples from their *mores,* is too frequent to be undeserving of serious attention on the part of the social historian."

However, the social historian fails to take the hint. He still refuses to see that the elemental force of culture contact, which is now revolutionizing the colonial world, is the same which, a century ago, created the dismal scenes of early capitalism. An anthropologist[7] drew the general inference: "In spite of numerous divergencies there are at the bottom the same predicaments among the exotic peoples today as there were among us decades or centuries ago. The new technical devices, the new knowledge, the new forms of wealth and power enhanced the social mobility, i.e., migration of individuals, rise and fall of families, differentiation of groups, new forms of leadership, new models of life, different valuations." Thurnwald's penetrating mind recognized that the cultural catastrophe of black

[7] Thurnwald, R. C., *Black and White in East Africa; The Fabric of a New Civilization,* 1935.

society today is closely analogous to that of a large part of white society in the early days of capitalism. The social historian alone still misses the point of the analogy.

Nothing obscures our social vision as effectively as the economistic prejudice. So persistently has exploitation been put into the forefront of the colonial problem that the point deserves special attention. Also, exploitation in a humanly obvious sense has been perpetrated so often, so persistently, and with such ruthlessness on the backward peoples of the world by the white man that it would seem to argue utter insensibility not to accord it pride of place in any discussion of the colonial problem. Yet, it is precisely this emphasis put on exploitation that tends to hide from our view the even greater issue of cultural degeneration. If exploitation is defined in strictly economic terms as a permanent inadequacy of ratios of exchange, it is doubtful whether, as a matter of fact, there was exploitation. The catastrophe of the native community is a direct result of the rapid and violent disruption of the basic institutions of the victim (whether force is used in the process or not does not seem altogether relevant). These institutions are disrupted by the very fact that a market economy is foisted upon an entirely differently organized community; labor and land are made into commodities, which, again, is only a short formula for the liquidation of every and any cultural institution in an organic society. Changes in income and population figures are evidently incommensurable with such a process. Who, for instance, would care to deny that a formerly free people dragged into slavery was exploited, though their standard of life, in some artificial sense, may have been improved in the country to which they were sold as compared with what it was in their native bush? And yet nothing would be altered if we assumed that the conquered natives had been left free and not even been made to overpay the cheap cotton goods thrust upon them, and that their starvation was "merely" caused by the disruption of their social institutions.

To cite the famous instance of India. Indian masses in the second half of the nineteenth century did not die of hunger because they were exploited by Lancashire; they perished in large numbers because the Indian village community had been demolished. That this was brought about by forces of economic competition, namely, the permanent underselling of hand-woven *chaddar* by machine-made piece goods, is doubtless true; but it proves the opposite of economic exploitation, since dumping implies the reverse of surcharge. The actual source of famines in the last fifty years was the free marketing of grain combined with local failure of incomes. Failure of crops was, of course, part of the picture, but despatch of grain by rail made it possible to send relief to the threatened areas; the trouble was that the people were unable to buy the corn at rocketing prices, which on a free but incompletely organized market were bound to be the reaction to a shortage. In former times small local stores had been held against harvest failure, but these had been now discontinued or swept away into the big market. Famine prevention for this reason now usually took the form of public works to enable the population to buy at enhanced prices. The three or four large famines that decimated India under British rule since the Rebellion were thus neither a consequence of the elements, nor of exploitation, but simply of the new market organization of labor and land, which broke up the old village without actually resolving its problems. While under the regime of feudalism and of the village community, *noblesse oblige,* clan solidarity, and regulation of the corn market checked famines, under the rule of the market the people could not be prevented from starving according to the rules of the game. The term "exploitation" describes but ill a situation that became really grave only after the East India Company's ruthless monopoly was abolished and free trade was introduced into India. Under the monopolists the situation had been fairly kept in hand with the help of the archaic organization of the countryside, including free distribution of corn, while under free and equal exchange Indians perished by the millions. Economically, India may have been —and, in the long run, certainly was—benefited, but socially she was disorganized and thus thrown a prey to misery and degradation.

In some cases at least, the opposite of exploitation, if we may say so, started the disintegrating culture contact. The forced land allotment to the North American Indians, in 1887, benefited them individually, according to our financial scale of reckoning. Yet the measure all but destroyed the race in its physical existence—the outstanding case of cultural degeneration on record. The moral genius of a John Collier retrieved the position almost half a century later by insisting on the need for a return to tribal land-holdings: today the North American Indian's is in some places, at least, a live community again—and not economic betterment, but *social restoration* wrought the miracle. The shock of a devastating culture contact was recorded by the pathetic birth of the famous Ghost Dance version of the Pawnee Hand Game about 1890, exactly at the time when improving economic conditions made the aboriginal culture of these Red Indians anachronistic.[8] Furthermore, the fact that not even an increasing population—the other economic index—need exclude a cultural catastrophe is equally borne out by anthropological research. Natural rates of increase of population may actually be an index either of cultural vitality or of cultural degradation. The original meaning of the word "proletarian," linking fertility and mendicity, is a striking expression of this ambivalence.

Economistic prejudice was the source both of the crude exploitation theory of early capitalism and of the no less

---

[8] [See the reference to Lesser in the appendix to this Chapter. Also, James Mooney, *The Ghost-Dance Religion and the Sioux Outbreak of 1890,* Chicago: University of Chicago Press, 1965. Ed.]

crude, though more scholarly, misapprehension, which later denied the existence of a social catastrophe. The significant implication of this latter and more recent interpretation of history was the rehabilitation of laissez-faire economy. For if liberal economics did *not* cause disaster, then protectionism, which robbed the world of the benefits of free markets, was a wanton crime. The very term "Industrial Revolution" was now frowned upon as conveying an exaggerated idea of what was essentially a slow process of change. No more had happened, these scholars insisted, than that a gradual unfolding of the forces of technological progress transformed the lives of the people; undoubtedly, many suffered in the course of the change, but on the whole the story was one of continuous improvement. This happy outcome was the result of the almost unconscious working of economic forces which did their beneficial work in spite of the interference of impatient parties who exaggerated the unavoidable difficulties of the time. The inference was no less than a denial that danger had threatened society from the new economy. Had the revised history of the Industrial Revolution been true to fact, the protectionist movement would have lacked all objective justification and laissez faire would have been vindicated. The materialistic fallacy in regard to the nature of social and cultural catastrophe thus bolstered the legend that all the ills of the time had been caused by our lapse from economic liberalism.

Briefly, not single groups or classes were the source of the so-called collectivist movement, though the outcome was decisively influenced by the character of the class interests involved. Ultimately, what made things happen were the interests of society as a whole, though their defense fell primarily to one section of the population in preference to another. It appears reasonable to group our account of the protective movement not around class interests but around the social substances imperiled by the market.

The danger points were given by the main directions of the attack. The competitive labor market hit the bearer of labor power, namely, man. International free trade was primarily a threat to the largest industry dependent upon nature, namely, agriculture. The gold standard imperiled productive organizations depending for their functioning on the relative movement of prices. In each of these fields markets were developed, which implied a latent threat to society in some vital aspects of its existence.

Markets for labor, land, and money are easy to distinguish; but it is not so easy to distinguish those parts of a culture the nucleus of which is formed by human beings, their natural surroundings, and productive organizations, respectively. Man and nature are practically *one* in the cultural sphere; and the money aspect of productive enterprise enters only into one socially vital interest, namely, the unity and cohesion of the nation. Thus, while the markets for the fictitious commodities labor, land, and money were distinct and separate, the threats to society which they involved were not always strictly separable.

In spite of this an outline of the institutional development of Western society during the critical eighty years (1834–1914), might refer to each of these danger points in similar terms. For whether man, nature, or productive organization was concerned, market organization grew into a peril, and definite groups or classes pressed for protection. In each case the considerable time lag between English, Continental, and American development had important bearings, and yet by the turn of the century the protectionist countermove had created an analogous situation in all Western countries.

Accordingly, we will deal separately with the defense of man, nature, and productive organization—a movement of self-preservation as the result of which a more closely knit type of society emerged, yet one that stood in danger of total disruption.

APPENDIX

Several authors have insisted on the similarity between colonial problems and those of early capitalism. But they failed to follow up the analogy the other way, that is, to throw light on the condition of the poorer classes of England a century ago by picturing them as what they were— the detribalized, degraded natives of their time.

The reason why this obvious resemblance was missed lay in our belief in the liberalistic prejudice that gave undue prominence to the economic aspects of what were essentially non-economic processes. For neither racial degradation in some colonial areas today nor the analogous dehumanization of the laboring people a century ago was economic in essence.

(a) *Destructive culture contact is not primarily an economic phenomenon.*

Most native societies are now undergoing a process of rapid and forcible transformation comparable only to the violent changes of a revolution, says L. P. Mair. Although the invaders' motives are definitely economic, and the collapse of primitive society is certainly often caused by the destruction of its economic institutions, the salient fact is that *the new economic institutions fail to be assimilated by the native culture* which consequently disintegrates without being replaced by any other coherent value system.

First among the destructive tendencies inherent in Western institutions stands "peace over a vast area," which shatters "clan life, patriarchal authority, the military training of the youth; it is almost prohibitive to migration of clans or tribes" (Thurnwald, *Black and White in East Africa; The Fabric of a New Civilization,* 1935, p. 394). "War must have given a keenness to native life which is sadly lacking in these times of peace. . . ." The abolition of fighting decreases population, since war resulted in very few casualties, while its absence means the loss of vitalizing customs and ceremonies and a consequent unwholesome dullness and apathy of village life (F. E. Williams, *Depopulation of the Suan District*, 1933, "Anthropology" Report, No. 13, p. 43). Compare with this the "lusty, animated, excited existence" of the native in his traditional cultural environment (Goldenweiser, *Loose Ends*, p. 99).

The real danger, in Goldenweiser's words, is that of a "cultural in-between" (Goldenweiser, *Anthropology*, 1937, p. 429). On this point there is practical unanimity. "The old barriers are dwindling and no kind of new guiding lines are offered" (Thurnwald, *Black and White*, p. 111). "To maintain a community in which the accumulation of goods is regarded as anti-social and integrate the same with contemporary white culture is to try to harmonize two incompatible institutional systems" (Wissel in Introduction to M. Mead, *The Changing Culture of an Indian Tribe*, 1932). "Immigrant culture-bearers may succeed in extinguishing an aboriginal culture, but yet fail either to extinguish or to assimilate its bearers" (Pitt-Rivers, "The Effect on Native Races of Contact with European Civilization." In *Man*, Vol. XXVII, 1927). Or, in Lesser's pungent phrase of yet another victim of industrial civilization: "From cultural maturity as Pawnee they were reduced to cultural infancy as white men" (*The Pawnee Ghost Dance Hand Game*, p. 44).

This condition of living death is not due to economic exploitation in the accepted sense in which exploitation means an economic advantage of one partner at the cost of the other, though it is certainly intimately linked with changes in the economic conditions connected with land tenure, war, marriage, and so on, each of which affects a vast number of social habits, customs, and traditions of all descriptions. When a money economy is forcibly introduced into sparsely populated regions of Western Africa, it is not the insufficiency of wages that results in the fact that the natives "cannot buy food to replace that which has not been grown, for nobody else has grown a surplus of food to sell to them" (Mair, *An African People in the Twentieth Century*, 1934, p. 5). Their institutions imply a different value scale; they are both thrifty and at the same time non-market-minded. "They will ask the same price when the market is glutted as prevailed when there was great scarcity, and yet they will travel long distances at considerable cost of time and energy to save a small sum on their purchases" (Mary H. Kingsley, *West African Studies*, p. 339). A rise in wages often leads to absenteeism. Zapotec Indians in Tehuantepec were said to work half as well at 50 centavos as at 25 centavos a day. This paradox was fairly general during the early days of the Industrial Revolution in England.

The economic index of population rates serves us no better than wages. Goldenweiser confirms the famous observation Rivers made in Melanesia that culturally destitute natives may be "dying of boredom." F. E. Williams, himself a missionary working in that region, writes that the "influence of the psychological factor on the death rate" is easily understood. "Many observers have drawn attention to the remarkable ease or readiness with which a native may die." "The restriction of former interests and activities seems fatal to his spirits. The result is that the native's power of resistance is impaired, and he easily goes under to any kind of sickness" (op. cit., p. 43). This has nothing to do with the pressure of economic want. "Thus an extremely high rate of natural increase may be a symptom either of cultural vitality or cultural degradation" (Frank Lorimer, *Observations on the Trend of Indian Population in the United States*, p. 11).

Cultural degradation can be stopped only by social measures, incommensurable with economic standards of life, such as the restoration of tribal land tenure or the isolation of the community from the influence of capitalistic market methods. "Separation of the Indian from his land was the

ONE *death blow,*" writes John Collier in 1942. The General Allotment Act of 1887 "individualized" the Indian's land; the disintegration of his culture which resulted, lost him some three-quarters or ninety million acres, of this land. The Indian Reorganization Act of 1934 reintegrated tribal holdings, and saved the Indian community, *by revitalizing his culture.*

The same story comes from Africa. Forms of land tenure occupy the center of interest, because it is on them that social organization most directly depends. What appear as economic conflicts—high taxes and rents, low wages—are almost exclusively veiled forms of pressure to induce the natives to give up their traditional culture and thus compel them to adjust to the methods of market economy, i.e., to work for wages and procure their goods on the market. It was in this process that some of the native tribes, like the Kaffirs and those who had migrated to town, lost their ancestral virtues and became a shiftless crowd, "semidomesticated animals," among them loafers, thieves, and prostitutes—an institution unknown amongst them before—resembling nothing more than the mass of the pauperized population of England about 1795–1834.

(b) *The human degradation of the laboring classes under early capitalism was the result of a social catastrophe not measurable in economic terms.*

Robert Owen observed of his laborers as early as 1816 that "whatever wage they received the mass of them must be wretched. . . ." (*To the British Master Manufacturers,* p. 146).[9] It will be remembered that Adam Smith expected the land-divorced laborer to lose all intellectual interest. And M'Farlane expected "that the knowledge of writing and accounts will every day become less frequent among the common people" (*Enquiries Concerning the Poor,*

[9] [Robert Owen, *A New View of Society and Other Writings,* London: J. M. Dent & Sons, Ltd; New York: E. P. Dutton & Co., 1927. Everyman's Library. Ed.]

1782, pp. 249–50). A generation later Owen put down the laborers' degradation to "neglect in infancy" and "overwork," thus rendering them "incompetent from ignorance to make a good use of high wages when they can procure them." He himself paid them low wages and raised their status by creating for them artificially an entirely new cultural environment. The vices developed by the mass of the people were on the whole the same as characterized colored populations debased by disintegrating culture contact: dissipation, prostitution, thievishness, lack of thrift and providence, slovenliness, low productivity of labor, lack of self-respect and stamina. The spreading of market economy was destroying the traditional fabric of the rural society, the village community, the family, the old form of land tenure, the customs and standards that supported life within a cultural framework. The protection afforded by Speenhamland had made matters only worse. By the 1830s the social catastrophe of the common people was as complete as that of the Kaffir is today. One and alone, an eminent Negro sociologist, Charles S. Johnson, reversed the analogy between racial debasement and class degradation, applying it this time to the latter: "In England, where, incidentally, the Industrial Revolution was more advanced than in the rest of Europe, the social chaos which followed the drastic economic reorganization converted impoverished children into the 'pieces' that the African slaves were, later, to become. . . . The apologies for the child serf system were almost identical with those of the slave trade." ("Race Relations and Social Change." In E. Thompson, *Race Relations and the Race Problem*, 1939, p. 274).

4

Our Obsolete Market Mentality

The first century of the Machine Age is drawing to a close amid fear and trepidation. Its fabulous material success was due to the willing, indeed the enthusiastic, subordination of man to the needs of the machine. Liberal capitalism was in effect man's initial response to the challenge of the Industrial Revolution. In order to allow scope to the use of elaborate, powerful machinery, we transformed human economy into a self-adjusting system of markets, and cast our thoughts and values in the mold of this unique innovation.

Today, we begin to doubt the truth of some of these thoughts and the validity of some of these values. Outside the United States, liberal capitalism can hardly be said to exist any more. How to organize human life in a machine society is a question that confronts us anew. Behind the fading fabric of competitive capitalism there looms the portent of an industrial civilization, with its paralyzing division of labor, standardization of life, supremacy of mechanism over organism, and organization over spontaneity. Science itself is haunted by insanity. This is the abiding concern.

No mere reversion to the ideals of a past century can show us the way. We must brave the future, though this may involve us in an attempt to shift the place of industry in society so that the extraneous fact of the machine can be absorbed. The search for industrial democracy is not

FROM "Our Obsolete Market Mentality," *Commentary*, Vol. 3, February 1947, pp. 109–117. Reprinted by permission of *Commentary*, copyright 1947 by the American Jewish Committee.

merely the search for a solution to the problems of capitalism, as most people imagine. It is a search for an answer to industry itself. Here lies the concrete problem of our civilization. Such a new dispensation requires an inner freedom for which we are but ill equipped. We find ourselves stultified by the legacy of a market-economy which bequeathed us oversimplified views of the function and role of the economic system in society. If the crisis is to be overcome, we must recapture a more realistic vision of the human world and shape our common purpose in the light of that recognition.

Industrialism is a precariously grafted scion upon man's age-long existence. The outcome of the experiment is still hanging in the balance. But man is not a simple being and can die in more than one way. The question of individual freedom, so passionately raised in our generation, is only one aspect of this anxious problem. In truth, it forms part of a much wider and deeper need—the need for a new response to the total challenge of the machine.

Our condition can be described in these terms: Industrial civilization may yet undo man. But since the venture of a progressively artificial environment cannot, will not, and indeed, should not, be voluntarily discarded, the task of adapting life *in such a surrounding* to the requirements of human existence must be resolved if man is to continue on earth. No one can foretell whether such an adjustment is possible, or whether man must perish in the attempt. Hence the dark undertone of concern.

Meanwhile, the first phase of the Machine Age has run its course. It involved an organization of society that derived its name from its central institution, the market. This system is on the downgrade. Yet our practical philosophy was overwhelmingly shaped by this spectacular episode. Novel notions about man and society became current and gained the status of axioms. Here they are: As regards *man,* we were made to accept the heresy that his motives can be described as "material" and "ideal," and that the incentives on which everyday life is organized spring from the "material" motives. Both utilitarian liberalism and popular Marxism favored such views. As regards *society,* the kindred doctrine was propounded that its institutions were "determined" by the economic system. This opinion was even more popular with Marxists than with liberals.

Under a market-economy both assertions were, of course, true. *But only under such an economy.* In regard to the past, such a view was no more than an anachronism. In regard to the future, it was a mere prejudice. Yet under the influence of current schools of thought, reinforced by the authority of science and religion, politics and business, these strictly time-bound phenomena came to be regarded as timeless, as transcending the age of the market. To overcome such doctrines, which constrict our minds and souls and greatly enhance the difficulty of the life-saving adjustment, may require no less than a reform of our consciousness.

Market Society

The birth of laissez faire administered a shock to civilized man's views of himself, from the effects of which he never quite recovered. Only very gradually are we realizing what happened to us as recently as a century ago.

Liberal economy, this primary reaction of man to the machine, was a violent break with the conditions that preceded it. A chain-reaction was started—what before was merely isolated markets was transmuted into a self-regulating *system* of markets. And with the new economy, a new society sprang into being. The crucial step was this: labor and land were made into commodities, that is, they were treated *as if* produced for sale. Of course, they were not actually commodities, since they were either not produced at all (as land) or, if so, not for sale (as labor). Yet

61

no more thoroughly effective fiction was ever devised. By buying and selling labor and land freely, the mechanism of the market was made to apply to them. There was now supply of labor, and demand for it; there was supply of land, and demand for it. Accordingly, there was a market price for the use of labor power, called wages, and a market price for the use of land, called rent. Labor and land were provided with markets of their own, similar to the commodities proper that were produced with their help. The true scope of such a step can be gauged if we remember that labor is only another name for man, and land for nature. The commodity fiction handed over the fate of man and nature to the play of an automaton running in its own grooves and governed by its own laws.

Nothing similar had ever been witnessed before. Under the mercantile regime, though it deliberately pressed for the creation of markets, the converse principle still operated. Labor and land were not entrusted to the market; they formed part of the organic structure of society. Where land was marketable, only the determination of price was, as a rule, left to the parties; where labor was subject to contract, wages themselves were usually assessed by public authority. Land stood under the custom of manor, monastery, and township, under common-law limitations concerning rights of real property; labor was regulated by laws against beggary and vagrancy, statutes of laborers and artificers, poor laws, guild and municipal ordinances. In effect, all societies known to anthropologists and historians restricted markets to commodities in the proper sense of the term.

Market-economy thus created a new type of society. The economic or productive system was here entrusted to a self-acting device. An institutional mechanism controlled human beings in their everyday activities as well as the resources of nature. This instrument of material welfare was under the sole control of the incentives of hunger and gain

—or, more precisely, fear of going without the necessities of life, and expectation of profit. So long as no propertyless person could satisfy his craving for food without first selling his labor in the market, and so long as no propertied person was prevented from buying in the cheapest market and selling in the dearest, the blind mill would turn out ever-increasing amounts of commodities for the benefit of the human race. Fear of starvation with the worker, lure of profit with the employer, would keep the vast establishment running.

In this way an "economic sphere" came into existence that was sharply delimited from other institutions in society. Since no human aggregation can survive without a functioning productive apparatus, its embodiment in a distinct and separate sphere had the effect of making the "rest" of society dependent upon that sphere. This autonomous zone, again, was regulated by a mechanism that controlled its functioning. As a result, the market mechanism became determinative for the life of the body social. No wonder that the emergent human aggregation was an "economic" society to a degree previously never even approximated. "Economic motives" reigned supreme in a world of their own, and the individual was made to act on them under pain of being trodden under foot by the juggernaut market. Such a forced conversion to a utilitarian outlook fatefully warped Western man's understanding of himself.

This new world of "economic motives" was based on a fallacy. Intrinsically, hunger and gain are no more "economic" than love or hate, pride or prejudice. No human motive is per se economic. There is no such thing as a *sui generis* economic experience in the sense in which man may have a religious, aesthetic, or sexual experience. These latter give rise to motives that broadly aim at evoking similar experiences. In regard to material production these terms lack self-evident meaning.

The economic factor, which underlies all social life, no

more gives rise to definite incentives than the equally universal law of gravitation. Assuredly, if we do not eat, we must perish, as much as if we were crushed under the weight of a falling rock. But the pangs of hunger are not automatically translated into an incentive to produce. Production is not an individual, but a collective affair. If an individual is hungry, there is nothing definite for him to do. Made desperate, he might rob or steal, but such an action can hardly be called productive. With man, the political animal, everything is given not by natural, but by social circumstance. What made the nineteenth century think of hunger and gain as "economic" was simply the organization of production under a market economy.

Hunger and gain are here linked with production through the need of "earning an income." For under such a system, man, if he is to keep alive, is compelled to buy goods on the market with the help of an income derived from selling other goods on the market. The name of these incomes—wages, rent, interest—varies accordingly to what is offered for sale: use of labor power, of land, or of money; the income called profit—the remuneration of the entrepreneur—derives from the sale of goods that fetch a higher price than the goods that go into the producing of them. Thus all incomes derive from sales, and all sales—directly or indirectly—contribute to production. The latter is, in effect, *incidental to the earning of an income*. So long as an individual is "earning an income," he is, automatically, contributing to production. Obviously, the system works only so long as individuals have a reason to indulge in the activity of "earning an income." The motives of hunger and gain—separately and conjointly—provide them with such a reason. These two motives are thus geared to production and, accordingly, are termed "economic." The semblance is compelling that hunger and gain are *the* incentives on which any economic system must rest. This assumption is baseless. Ranging over human societies, we

64

find hunger and gain not appealed to as incentives to production, and where so appealed to, they are fused with other powerful motives.

Aristotle was right: man is not an economic, but a social being. He does not aim at safeguarding his individual interest in the acquisition of material possessions, but rather at ensuring social good will, social status, social assets. He values possessions primarily as a means to that end. His incentives are of that "mixed" character which we associate with the endeavor to gain social approval—productive efforts are no more than incidental to this. *Man's economy is, as a rule, submerged in his social relations.* The change from this to a society which was, on the contrary, submerged in the economic system was an entirely novel development.

The evidence of facts, I feel, should at this point be adduced. *First,* there are the discoveries of primitive economics. Two names are outstanding: Bronislaw Malinowski and Richard Thurnwald. They and some other research workers revolutionized our conceptions in this field and, by so doing, founded a new discipline. The myth of the individualistic savage had been exploded long ago. Neither the crude egotism, nor the apocryphal propensity to barter, truck, and exchange, nor even the tendency to cater to one's self was in evidence. But equally discredited was the legend of the communistic psychology of the savage, his supposed lack of appreciation for his own personal interests. (Roughly, it appeared that man was very much the same all through the ages. Taking his institutions not in isolation, but in their interrelation, he was mostly found to be behaving in a manner broadly comprehensible to us.) What appeared as "communism" was the fact that the productive or economic system was usually arranged in such a fashion as not to threaten any individual with starvation. His place at the campfire, his share in the common resources, was secure to him, whatever part he happened to have played in hunt, pasture, tillage, or gardening. Here are a few instances: Under the *kraalland* system of the Kaffirs, "destitution is impossible; whosoever needs assistance receives it unquestioningly" (L. P. Mair, *An African People in the Twentieth Century,* 1934). No Kwakiutl "ever ran the least risk of going hungry" (E. M. Loeb, *The Distribution and Function of Money in Early Society,* 1936). "There is no starvation in societies living on the subsistence margin" (M. J. Herskovits, *The Economic Life of Primitive Peoples,* 1940). In effect, the individual is not in danger of starving unless the community as a whole is in a like predicament. It is this absence of the menace of individual destitution that makes primitive society, in a sense, more humane than nineteenth-century society, and at the same time less "economic."

The same applies to the stimulus of individual gain. Again, a few quotations: "The characteristic feature of primitive economics is the absence of any desire to make profits from production and exchange" (R. Thurnwald, *Economics in Primitive Communities,* 1932). "Gain, which is often the stimulus for work in more civilized communities, never acts as an impulse to work under the original native conditions" (B. Malinowski, *Argonauts of the Western Pacific,* 1922). If so-called economic motives were natural to man, we would have to judge all early and primitive societies as thoroughly unnatural.

Secondly, there is no difference between primitive and civilized society in this regard. Whether we turn to ancient city-state, despotic empire, feudalism, thirteenth-century urban life, sixteenth-century mercantile regime, or eighteenth-century regulationism—invariably the economic system is found to be merged in the social. Incentives spring from a large variety of sources, such as custom and tradition, public duty and private commitment, religious observance and political allegiance, judicial obligation and administrative regulation as established by prince, municipality, or guild.

Rank and status, compulsion of law and threat of punishment, public praise and private reputation, insure that the individual contributes his share to production. Fear of privation or love of profit need not be altogether absent. Markets occur in all kinds of societies, and the figure of the merchant is familiar to many types of civilization. But isolated markets do not link up into an economy. The motive of gain was specific to merchants, as was valor to the knight, piety to the priest, and pride to the craftsman. The notion of making the motive of gain universal never entered the heads of our ancestors. At no time prior to the second quarter of the nineteenth century were markets more than a subordinate feature in society.

Thirdly, there was the startling abruptness of the change. Predominance of markets emerged not as a matter of degree, but of kind. Markets through which otherwise self-sufficient householders get rid of their surplus neither direct production nor provide the producer with his income.[1] This is only the case in a market-economy where *all* incomes derive from sales, and commodities are obtainable exclusively by purchase. A free market for labor was born in England only about a century ago. The ill-famed Poor Law Reform (1834) abolished the rough-and-ready provisions made for the paupers by patriarchal governments. The poorhouse was transformed from a refuge of the destitute into an abode of shame and mental torture to which even hunger and misery were preferable. Starvation or work was the alternative left to the poor. Thus was a competitive national market for labor created. Within a decade, the Bank Act (1844) established the principle of the gold standard; the making of money was removed from the hands of the government regardless of the effect upon the level of employment. Simultaneously, reform of land

[1] [On such peripheral or petty markets as they function in Africa, see Paul Bohannan and George Dalton, "Introduction," to *Markets in Africa,* New York: Natural History Press, 1965. Ed.]

laws mobilized the land, and repeal of the Corn Laws (1846) created a world pool of grain, thereby making the unprotected Continental peasant-farmer subject to the whims of the market. Thus were established the three tenets of economic liberalism, the principle on which market economy was organized: that labor should find its price on the market; that money should be supplied by a self-adjusting mechanism; that commodities should be free to flow from country to country irrespective of the consequences—in brief, a labor market, the gold standard, and free trade. A self-inflammatory process was induced, as a result of which the formerly harmless market pattern expanded into a sociological enormity.

These facts roughly outline the genealogy of an "economic" society. Under such conditions the human world must appear as determined by "economic" motives. It is easy to see why. Single out whatever motive you please, and organize production in such a manner as to make that motive the individual's incentive to produce, and you will have induced a picture of man as altogether absorbed by that particular motive. Let that motive be religious, political, or aesthetic; let it be pride, prejudice, love, or envy; and man will appear as essentially religious, political, aesthetic, proud, prejudiced, engrossed in love or envy. Other motives, in contrast, will appear distant and shadowy since they cannot be relied upon to operate in the vital business of production. The particular motive selected will represent "real" man.

As a matter of fact, human beings will labor for a large variety of reasons as long as things are arranged accordingly. Monks traded for religious reasons, and monasteries became the largest trading establishments in Europe. The Kula trade of the Trobriand Islanders, one of the most intricate barter arrangements known to man, is mainly an aesthetic pursuit. Feudal economy was run on customary lines. With the Kwakiutl, the chief aim of industry seems to be to satisfy a point of honor. Under mercantile despotism, industry was often planned so as to serve power and glory. Accordingly, we tend to think of monks or villeins, Western Melanesians, the Kwakiutl, or seventeenth-century statesmen, as ruled by religion, aesthetics, custom, honor, or politics, respectively.

Under capitalism, every individual has to earn an income. If he is a worker, he has to sell his labor at current prices; if he is an owner, he has to make as high a profit as he can, for his standing with his fellows will depend upon the level of his income. Hunger and gain—even if vicariously—make them plow and sow, spin and weave, mine coal, and pilot planes. Consequently, members of such a society will think of themselves as governed by these twin motives. In actual fact, man was never as selfish as the theory demanded. Though the market mechanism brought his dependence upon material goods to the fore, "economic" motives never formed with him the sole incentive to work. In vain was he exhorted by economists and utilitarian moralists alike to discount in business all other motives than "material" ones. On closer investigation, he was still found to be acting on remarkably "mixed" motives, not excluding those of duty toward himself and others—and maybe, secretly, even enjoying work for its own sake.

However, we are not here concerned with actual, but with assumed motives, not with the psychology, but with the ideology of business. *Not on the former, but on the latter, are views of man's nature based.* For once society expects a definite behavior on the part of its members, and prevailing institutions become roughly capable of enforcing that behavior, opinions on human nature will tend to mirror the ideal whether it resembles actuality or not. Accordingly, hunger and gain were defined as economic motives, and man was supposed to be acting on them in everyday life, while his other motives appeared more ethereal and removed from humdrum existence. Honor and pride, civic obligation and moral duty, even self-respect and common decency, were now deemed irrelevant to production, and

69

were significantly summed up in the word "ideal." Hence man was believed to consist of two components, one more akin to hunger and gain, the other to honor and power. The one was "material," the other "ideal"; the one "economic," the other "non-economic"; the one "rational," the other "non-rational." The Utilitarians went so far as to identify the two sets of terms, thus endowing the economic side of man's character with the aura of rationality. He who would have refused to imagine that he was acting for gain alone was thus considered not only immoral, but also mad.

Economic Determinism

The market mechanism, moreover, created the delusion of economic determinism as a general law for all human society. Under a market-economy, of course, this law holds good. Indeed, the working of the economic system here not only "influences" the rest of society, but determines it—as in a triangle the sides not merely influence, but determine, the angles. Take the stratification of classes. Supply and demand in the labor market were *identical* with the classes of workers and employers, respectively. The social classes of capitalists, landowners, tenants, brokers, merchants, professionals, and so on, were delimited by the respective markets for land, money, and capital and their uses, or for various services. The income of these social classes was fixed by the market, their rank and position by their income. This was a complete reversal of the secular practice. In Maine's famous phrase, "contractus" replaced "status"; or, as Tönnies preferred to put it, "society" superseded "community"; or, in terms of the present article, *instead of the economic system being embedded in social relationships, these relationships were now embedded in the economic system.*

While social classes were directly, other institutions were indirectly determined by the market mechanism. State and government, marriage and the rearing of children, the organization of science and education, of religion and the arts, the choice of profession, the forms of habitation, the shape of settlements, the very aesthetics of private life— everything had to comply with the utilitarian pattern, or at least not interfere with the working of the market mechanism. But since very few human activities can be carried on in the void; even a saint needing his pillar, the indirect effect of the market system came very near to determining the whole of society. It was almost impossible to avoid the erroneous conclusion that as "economic" man was "real" man, so the economic system was "really" society.

Yet it would be truer to say that the basic human institutions abhor unmixed motives. Just as the provisioning of the individual and his family does not commonly rely on the motive of hunger, so the institution of the family is not based on the sexual motive. Sex, like hunger, is one of the most powerful of incentives when released from the control of other incentives. That is probably why the family in all its variety of forms is never allowed to center on the sexual instinct, with its intermittences and vagaries, but on the combination of a number of effective motives that prevent sex from destroying an institution on which so much of man's happiness depends. Sex in itself will never produce anything better than a brothel, and even then it might have to draw on some incentives of the market mechanism. An economic system actually relying for its mainspring on hunger would be almost as perverse as a family system based on the bare urge of sex.

To attempt to apply economic determinism to all human societies is little short of fantastic. Nothing is more obvious to the student of social anthropology than the variety of institutions found to be compatible with practically identical instruments of production. Only since the market was permitted to grind the human fabric into the featureless uniformity of selenic erosion has man's institutional creativeness been in abeyance. No wonder that his social imagination shows signs of fatigue. It may come to a point where he will no longer be able to recover the elasticity, the imaginative wealth and power, of his savage endowment.

No protest of mine, I realize, will save me from being taken for an "idealist." For he who decries the importance of "material" motives must, it seems, be relying on the strength of "ideal" ones. Yet no worse misunderstanding is possible. Hunger and gain have nothing specifically "material" about them. Pride, honor, and power, on the other hand, are not necessarily "higher" motives than hunger and gain.

The dichotomy itself, we assert, is arbitrary. Let us once more adduce the analogy of sex. Assuredly, a significant distinction between "higher" and "lower" motives can here be drawn. Yet, whether hunger or sex, it is pernicious to *institutionalize* the separation of the "material" and "ideal" components of man's being. As regards sex, this truth, so vital to man's essential wholeness, has been recognized all along; it is at the basis of the institution of marriage. But in the equally strategic field of economy, it has been neglected. This latter field has been "separated out" of society as the realm of hunger and gain. Our animal dependence upon food has been bared and the naked fear of starvation permitted to run loose. Our humiliating enslavement to the "material," which all human culture is designed to mitigate, was deliberately made more rigorous. This is at the root of the "sickness of an acquisitive society" that Tawney warned of. And Robert Owen's genius was at its best when, a century before, he described the profit motive as "a principle entirely unfavorable to individual and public happiness."

The Reality of Society

I plead for the restoration of that unity of motives which should inform man in his everyday activity as a producer, for the reabsorption of the economic system in society, for the creative adaptation of our ways of life to an industrial environment.

On all these counts, laissez-faire philosophy, with its corollary of a marketing society, falls to the ground. It is responsible for the splitting up of man's vital unity into "real" man, bent on material values, and his "ideal" better self. It is paralyzing our social imagination by more or less unconsciously fostering the prejudice of economic determinism. It has done its service in that phase of industrial civilization which is behind us. At the price of impoverishing the individual, it enriched society. Today, we are faced with the vital task of restoring the fullness of life to the person, even though this may mean a technologically less efficient society. In different countries in different ways, classical liberalism is being discarded. On Right and Left and Middle, new avenues are being explored. British Social-Democrats, American New Dealers, and also European fascists and American anti-New Dealers of the various "managerialist" brands, reject the liberal utopia. Nor should the present political mood of rejection of everything Russian blind us to the achievement of the Russians in creative adjustment to some of the fundamental aspects of an industrial environment.

On general grounds, the Communist's expectation of the "withering away of the state" seems to me to combine elements of liberal utopianism with practical indifference to institutional freedoms. As regards the withering state, it is impossible to deny that industrial society is complex society, and no complex society can exist without organized power at the center. Yet, again, this fact is no excuse for the Communist's slurring over the question of concrete institutional freedoms. It is on this level of realism that the problem of individual freedom should be met. No human society is possible in which power and compulsion are absent, nor is a world in which force has no function. Liberal

73

philosophy gave a false direction to our ideals in seeming to promise the fulfillment of such intrinsically utopian expectations.

But under the market system, society as a whole remained invisible. Anybody could imagine himself free from responsibility for those acts of compulsion on the part of the state which he, personally, repudiated, or for unemployment and destitution from which he, personally, did not benefit. Personally, he remained unentangled in the evils of power and economic value. In good conscience, he could deny their reality in the name of his imaginary freedom. Power and economic value are, indeed, a paradigm of social reality. Neither power nor economic value spring from human volition; non-co-operation is impossible in regard to them. The function of power is to insure that measure of conformity which is needed for the survival of the group: as David Hume showed, its ultimate source is opinion—and who could help holding opinions of some sort or other? Economic value, in any society, insures the usefulness of the goods produced; it is a seal set on the division of labor. Its source is human wants—and how could we be expected not to prefer one thing to another? Any opinion or desire, no matter what society we live in, will make us participants in the creation of power and the constituting of value. No freedom to do otherwise is conceivable. An ideal that would ban power and compulsion from society is intrinsically invalid. By ignoring this limitation on man's meaningful wishes, the marketing view of society reveals its essential immaturity.

Freedom in Industrial Society

The breakdown of market-economy imperils two kinds of freedoms: some good, some bad.

That the freedom to exploit one's fellows, or the freedom to make inordinate gains without commensurable service to the community, the freedom to keep technological

74

inventions from being used for the public benefit, or the freedom to profit from public calamities secretly engineered for private advantage, may disappear, together with the free market, is all to the good. But the market economy under which these freedoms throve also produced freedoms that we prize highly. Freedom of conscience, freedom of speech, freedom of meeting, freedom of association, freedom to choose one's job—we cherish them for their own sake. Yet to a large extent they were by-products of the same economy that was also responsible for the evil freedoms.

The existence of a separate economic sphere in society created, as it were, a gap between politics and economics, between government and industry, that was in the nature of a no man's land. As division of sovereignty between pope and emperor left medieval princes in a condition of freedom sometimes bordering on anarchy, so division of sovereignty between government and industry in the nineteenth century allowed even the poor man to enjoy freedoms that partly compensated for his wretched status. Current skepticism in regard to the future of freedom largely rests on this. There are those who argue, like Hayek, that since free institutions were a product of market-economy, they must give place to serfdom once that economy disappears. There are others, like Burnham, who assert the inevitability of some new form of serfdom called "managerialism."

Arguments like these merely prove to what extent economistic prejudice is still rampant. For such determinism, as we have seen, is only another name for the market mechanism. It is hardly logical to argue the effects of its absence on the strength of an economic necessity that derives from its presence. And it is certainly contrary to Anglo-Saxon experience. Neither the freezing of labor nor selective service abrogated the essential freedoms of the American people, as anybody can witness who spent the crucial years 1940–43 in these States. Great Britain during the war introduced an all-round planned economy and did away with that separation of government and industry from which nineteenth-century freedom sprang, yet never were public liberties more securely entrenched than at the height of the emergency. In truth, we will have just as much freedom as we will desire to create and to safeguard. There is no *one* determinant in human society. Institutional guarantees of personal freedom are compatible with any economic system. In market society alone did the economic mechanism lay down the law.

What appears to our generation as the problem of capitalism is, in reality, the far greater problem of an industrial civilization. The economic liberal is blind to this fact. In defending capitalism as an economic system, he ignores the challenge of the Machine Age. Yet the dangers that make the bravest quake today transcend economy. The idyllic concerns of trust-busting and Taylorization have been superseded by Hiroshima. Scientific barbarism is dogging our footsteps. The Germans were planning a contrivance to make the sun emanate death rays. We, in fact, produced a burst of death rays that blotted out the sun. Yet the Germans had an evil philosophy, and we had a humane philosophy. In this we should learn to see the symbol of our peril.

Among those in America who are aware of the dimensions of the problem, two tendencies are discernible: some believe in elites and aristocracies, in managerialism and the corporation. They feel that the whole of society should be more intimately adjusted to the economic system which they would wish to maintain unchanged. This is the ideal of the Brave New World, where the individual is conditioned to support an order that has been designed for him by such as are wiser than he. Others, on the contrary, believe that in a truly democratic society, the problem of industry would resolve itself through the planned intervention of the producers and consumers themselves. Such conscious and responsible action is, indeed, one of the embodiments of freedom in a complex society. But, as the contents of this article suggest, such an endeavor cannot be successful unless it is disciplined by a total view of man and society very different from that which we inherited from market economy.

5

Aristotle Discovers the Economy

The contempt into which Aristotle's "Economics" has
fallen in our day is a portent. Very few thinkers have been
listened to on a greater diversity of subjects over so many
centuries as he. Yet on a matter to which he devoted a
signal effort and which happens also to be reckoned among
the issues vital to our own generation, the economy, his
teachings are judged inadequate by the leading spirits of
the time to the point of irrelevance.[1]

Aristotle's influence on medieval city economy exerted

FROM Chapter 5, "Aristotle Discovers the Economy," pp. 64–
94, of Karl Polanyi, Conrad M. Arensberg, and Harry W.
Pearson (eds.), *Trade and Market in the Early Empires*, Glencoe: The Free Press, 1957. Reprinted by permission of the
publisher. [The section of this chapter titled "The Anonymity
of the Economy in Early Society," is an especially clear statement of some of Polanyi's leading ideas and the concepts he
uses to analyze primitive and archaic economies. The first five
paragraphs of the original version of this essay are here deleted.
Ed.]

[1] J. A. Schumpeter, *History of Economic Analysis* (New
York, 1954), p. 57, "Aristotle's performance is . . . decorous,
pedestrian, slightly mediocre and more than slightly pompous
common sense." Schumpeter had no doubt that Aristotle was
engaged in "analyzing actual market mechanisms. Several passages show . . . that Aristotle tried to do so and failed" (p. 60).
The latest detailed study is no less negative on the merits of
the case. Cf. C. J. Soudek, "Aristotle's Theory of Exchange,"
Proceedings of American Philosophical Society, V, 96, NR, 1
(1952). Joseph J. Spengler's "Aristotle on Economic Imputa-
tion and Related Matters," *Southern Economics Journal*, XXI
(April, 1955), 386, fn. 59, is the lone exception: "Aristotle did
not concern himself with how prices are formed in the market."

through Thomas Aquinas was as great as later that of Adam Smith and David Ricardo on nineteenth-century world economy. Naturally, one might say, with the actual establishment of the market system and the subsequent rise of the classical schools, Aristotle's doctrines on the subject went into eclipse. But the matter does not rest here. The more outspoken among modern economists seem to feel as though almost everything he had written on questions of man's livelihood suffered from some baneful weakness. Of his two broad topics—the nature of the economy and the issues of commercial trade and just price—neither had been carried to any clear conclusion. Man, like any other animal, was presented by him as naturally self-sufficient. The human economy did not, therefore, stem from the boundlessness of man's wants and needs, or, as it is phrased today, from the fact of scarcity. As to those two policy issues, commercial trade sprang, according to Aristotle, from the unnatural urge of money-making, which was of course unlimited, while prices should conform to the rules of justice (the actual formula remaining quite obscure). There were also his illuminating, if not altogether consistent, remarks on money and that puzzling outburst against the taking of interest. This meager and fragmentary outcome was mostly attributed to an unscientific bias—the preference for that which ought to be over that which is. That prices, for instance, should depend upon the relative standing in the community of partners in the exchange seemed indeed an almost absurd view to take.

This sharply circumscribed breaking away from the body of thought inherited from classical Greece deserves more attention than it has hitherto received. The stature of the thinker and the dignity of the subject should make us hesitate to accept as final the erasing of Aristotle's teaching on the economy.

A very different appreciation of his position will be sustained here. He will be seen as attacking the problem of man's livelihood with a radicalism of which no later writer on the subject was capable—none has ever penetrated deeper into the material organization of man's life. In effect, he posed, in all its breadth, the question of the place occupied by the economy in society.

We will have to reach far back to explain why Aristotle thought as he did of what we call "the economy," or what impelled him to regard money-making in trade and the just price as the chief policy questions. Also we agree that economic theory cannot expect to benefit from Book I of *Politics* and Book V of the *Nichomachian Ethics*. Economic analysis, in the last resort, aims at elucidating the functions of the market mechanism, an institution that was still unknown to Aristotle.

To go to the root of our approach, classical antiquity was altogether wrongly placed by economic historians along the time scale which led up to market trade. In spite of intensive trading activities and fairly advanced money uses, Greek business life as a whole, was still in the very first beginnings of market trade in Aristotle's time. His occasional vagueness and obscurities, not to speak of his alleged philosopher's remoteness from life, should be put down to difficulties of expression in regard to what actually were recent developments, rather than to the supposed insufficient penetration by him of practices allegedly current in contemporary Greece and nourished by a millennial tradition of the civilizations of the East.

This leaves classical Greece, however definitely some of her eastern states were already advancing toward the market habit, still considerably below the level of commercial trading with which she was later credited. Thus the Greeks may not have been, as was so confidently assumed, simply latecomers picking up the commercial practices developed by the Oriental empires. Rather, they were latecomers in a civilized, marketless world, and compelled by circumstances to become pioneers in the development of the novel trading methods which were, at most, on the point of turning toward market trade.

All this, far from diminishing, as might superficially appear, the significance of Aristotle's thought on economic questions must, on the contrary, very greatly enhance their importance. For if our "non-market" reading of the Mesopotamian scene is true to fact, which we have no more cause to doubt, we have every reason to believe that in Aristotle's writings we possess an eye-witness account of some of the pristine features of incipient market trading at its very first appearance in the history of civilization.

The Anonymity of the Economy in Early Society

Aristotle was trying to master theoretically the elements of a new complex social phenomenon in *statu nascendi*.

The economy, when it first attracted the conscious awareness of the philosopher in the shape of commercial trading and price differentials, was already destined to run its variegated course toward its fulfilment some twenty centuries later. Aristotle divined the full-fledged specimen from the embryo.[2]

The conceptual tool with which to tackle this transition from namelessness to a separate existence we submit, is the distinction between the embedded and the disembedded condition of the economy in relation to society. The disembedded economy of the nineteenth century stood apart from the rest of society, more especially from the political and governmental system. In a market economy the production and distribution of material goods in principle is carried on through a self-regulating system of price-making markets. It is governed by laws of its own, the so-called laws of supply and demand, and motivated by fear of hunger and hope of gain. Not blood-tie, legal compul-

[2] Cf. Karl Polanyi, *The Great Transformation* (New York, 1944), p. 64.

sion, religious obligation, fealty, or magic creates the sociological situations which make individuals partake in economic life, but specifically economic institutions such as private enterprise and the wage system.

With such a state of affairs we are, of course, fairly conversant. Under a market system men's livelihood is secured by way of institutions, that are activated by economic motives and governed by laws that are specifically economic. The vast comprehensive mechanism of the economy can be conceived of working without the conscious intervention of human authority, state, or government; no other motives than dread of destitution and desire for legitimate profit need be invoked; no other juridical requirement is set than that of the protection of property and the enforcement of contract; given the distribution of resources, of purchasing power, as well as of the individual scales of preference, the result will be an optimum of want-satisfaction for all.

This, then, is the nineteenth-century version of an independent economic sphere in society. It is motivationally distinct, for it receives its impulse from the urge of monetary gain. It is institutionally separated from the political and governmental center. It attains to an autonomy that invests it with laws of its own. In it we possess that extreme case of a disembedded economy, which takes its start from the widespread use of money as a means of exchange.

In the nature of things the development from embedded to disembedded economies is a matter of degree. Nevertheless the distinction is fundamental to the understanding of modern society. Its sociological background was first mooted by Hegel in the 1820s and developed by Karl Marx in the 1840s. Its empirical discovery in terms of history was made by Sir Henry Sumner Maine in the Roman law categories of *status* and *contractus,* in the 1860s; finally, in the more comprehensive terms of economic anthropology, the position was restated by Bronislaw Malinowski in the 1920s.

Sir Henry Sumner Maine undertook to prove that modern society was built on *contractus,* while ancient society rested on *status. Status* is set by birth—a man's position in the family—and determines the rights and duties of a person. It derives from kinship and adoption; it persists under feudalism and, with some qualifications, right up to the age of equal citizenship as established in the nineteenth century. But already under Roman law *status* was gradually replaced by *contractus,* i.e., by rights and duties derived from bilateral arrangements. Later, Maine revealed the universality of *status* organization in the case of the village communities of India.

In Germany, Maine found a disciple in Ferdinand Tönnies. His conception was epitomized in the title of his work *Community and Society (Gemeinschaft und Gesellschaft),* 1888. "Community" corresponded to *"status,"* "society" to *"contractus."* Max Weber frequently employed *"Gesellschaft"* in the sense of contract-type group, and *"Gemeinschaft"* in that of status-type group. Thus his own analysis of the place of the economy in society, though at times influenced by Mises, was molded by the thought of Marx, Maine, and Tönnies.

The emotional connotation, however, given to *status* and *contractus,* as well as to the corresponding "community" and "society," was widely different with Maine and Tönnies. To Maine the pre-*contractus* condition of mankind stood merely for the dark ages of tribalism. The introduction of contract, so he felt, had emancipated the individual from the bondage of *status.* Tönnies' sympathies were for the intimacy of the community as against the impersonality of organized society. "Community" was idealized by him as a condition where the lives of men were embedded in a tissue of common experience, while "society" was never to him far removed from the *cash nexus,* as Thomas Carlyle called the relationship of persons connected by market ties alone. Tönnies' policy ideal was the restoration of community, not, however, by returning to the pre-society stage of authority and paternalism, but by advancing to a higher form of community of a post-society stage, which would follow upon our present civilization. He envisaged this community as a co-operative phase of human existence, which would retain the advantages of technological progress and individual freedom while restoring the wholeness of life.

Hegel's and Marx's, Maine's and Tönnies' treatment of the evolution of human civilization was accepted by many continental scholars as an epitome of the history of society. For a long time no advance was made on the trails they blazed. Maine had dealt with the subject chiefly as pertaining to the history of law, including its corporate forms as in rural India; Tönnies' sociology revived the outlines of medieval civilization. Not before Malinowski's fundamental stand on the nature of primitive society was that antithesis applied to the economy. It is now possible to say that *status* or *Gemeinschaft* dominate where the economy is embedded in non-economic institutions; *contractus* or *Gesellschaft* is characteristic of the existence of a motivationally distinct economy in society.

In terms of integration we can easily see the reason for this. *Contractus* is the legal aspect of exchange. It is not surprising, therefore, that a society based on *contractus* should possess an institutionally separate and motivationally distinct economic sphere of exchange, namely, that of the market. *Status,* on the other hand, corresponds to an earlier condition, which roughly goes with reciprocity and redistribution. As long as these latter forms of integration prevail, no concept of an economy need arise. The elements of the economy are here embedded in non-economic institutions, the economic process itself being instituted through kinship, marriage, age-groups, secret societies, totemic associations, and public solemnities. The term "economic life" would here have no obvious meaning.

This state of affairs, so puzzling to the modern mind, is often strikingly exhibited in primitive communities. It is often almost impossible for the observer to collect the fragments of the economic process and piece them together. To the individual his emotions fail to convey any experience that he could identify as "economic." He is simply not aware of any pervading interest in regard to his livelihood, which he could recognize as such. Yet the lack of such a concept does not appear to hamper him in the performance of his everyday tasks. Rather, it is doubtful whether awareness of an economic sphere would not tend to reduce his capacity of spontaneous response to the needs of livelihood, organized as they are mainly through other than economic channels.

All this is an outcome of the manner in which the economy is here instituted. The individual's *motives,* named and articulated, spring as a rule from situations set by facts of a non-economic—familial, political or religious—order; the site of the small family's economy is hardly more than a point of intersection between lines of activities carried on by larger kinship groups in various localities; land is either used in common as pasture or its various uses may be appropriated to members of different groups; labor is a mere abstraction from the "solicited" assistance offered by different teams of helpers, at definite occasions; as a result, the process itself runs in the grooves of different structures.

Accordingly, before modern times the forms of man's livelihood attracted much less of his conscious attention than did most other parts of his organized existence. In contrast to kinship, magic or etiquette with their powerful keywords, the economy as such remained nameless. There existed, as a rule, no term to designate the concept of economy. Accordingly, as far as one can judge, this concept was absent. Clan and totem, sex and age-group, the power of the mind and the ceremonial practices, custom and ritual were instituted through highly elaborate systems of symbols, while the economy was not designated by any one word conveying the significance of food supply for man's animal survival. It cannot be merely a matter of chance that until very recent times no name to sum up the organization of the material conditions of life existed in the languages even of civilized peoples. Only two hundred years ago did an esoteric sect of French thinkers coin the term and call themselves *économistes*. Their claim was to have discovered the economy.

The prime reason for the absence of any concept of the economy is the difficulty of identifying the economic process under conditions where it is embedded in non-economic institutions.

Only the concept of the economy, not the economy itself, is in abeyance, of course. Nature and society abound in locational and appropriational movements that form the body of man's livelihood. The seasons bring around harvest time with its strain and its relaxation; long-distance trade has its rhythm of preparation and foregathering with the concluding solemnity of the return of the venturers; and all kinds of artifacts, whether canoes or fine ornaments, are produced, and eventually used by various groups of persons; every day of the week food is prepared at the family hearth. Each single event contains necessarily a bundle of economic items. Yet for all that, the unity and coherence of those facts is not reflected in men's consciousness. For the series of interactions between men and their natural surroundings will, as a rule, carry various significances, of which economic dependence is only one. Other dependences, more vivid, more dramatic, or more emotionalized may be at work, which prevent the economic movements from forming a meaningful whole. Where these other forces are embodied in permanent institutions the concept of the economic would be more confusing than clarifying to the individual. Anthropology offers many examples:

1. Where the physical *site* of a man's life is not identifiable with any ostensible part of the economy, his habitat —the household with its tangible environment—has but little economic relevance. This will be so, as a rule, when movements belonging to different economic processes intersect in one site, while the movements forming part of

one and the same process are distributed over a number of disconnected sites.

Margaret Mead described how a Papuan-speaking Arapesh of New Guinea would envisage his physical surroundings:

A typical Arapesh man, therefore is living for at least part of the time (for each man lives in two or more hamlets, as well as in the garden huts, huts near the hunting bush, and huts near his sago palm) on land which does not belong to him. Around the house are pigs which his wife is feeding, but which belong either to one of her relatives or to one of his. Beside the house are coconut and betel palms which belong to still other people, and the fruit of which he will never touch without the permission of the owner, or someone who has been accorded the disposal of the fruit by the owner. He hunts on the bushland belonging to a brother-in-law or a cousin at least part of his hunting time, and the rest of the time he is joined by others on his bush, if he has some. He works his sago in others' sago clumps as well as in his own. Of the personal property in his house that which is of any permanent value, like large pots, well carved plates, good spears, has already been assigned to his sons, even though they are only toddling children. His own pig or pigs are far away in other hamlets: his palm trees are scattered three miles in one direction, two in another: his sago palms are still further scattered, and his garden patches lie here and there, mostly on the lands of others. If there is meat on his smoking rack over the fire, it is either meat which was killed by another, a brother, a brother-in-law, a sister's son, etc.—and has been given to him, in which case he and his family may eat it, or it is meat which he himself killed and which he is smoking to give away to someone else, for to eat one's own kill, even though it be only a small bird, is a crime to which only the morally, which usually means with the Arapesh mentally, deficient would stoop. If the house in which he is, is

87

nominally his, it will have been constructed in part at least from the posts and planks of other people's houses, which have been dismantled or temporarily deserted, and from which he has borrowed timber. He will not cut his rafters to fit his house, if they are too long, because they may be needed later for someone else's house which is of a different shape or size. . . . This then is the picture of a man's ordinary economic affiliations.[3]

The complexity of the social relations that account for these everyday items, is staggering. Yet it is only at the hand of such relations, familiar to him, articulated and meaningfully deployed in the course of his own personal experience, that the Arapesh is able to find his bearings in an economic situation, the elements of which are jigsawed into dozens of different social relationships of a non-economic character.

So much for the locational aspect of the economic process where reciprocity prevails.

2. Another broad reason for the absence in primitive society of an integrating effect of the economy is its *lack of quantitativity*. He who possesses ten dollars does not, as a rule, call each by a separate name, but conceives of them rather as interchangeable units that can be substituted one for another, added up or subtracted. Short of such an operational facility on which terms like fund or balance of profit and loss depend for a meaning, the notion of an economy would mostly be devoid of any practical purpose. It would fail to discipline behavior, to organize and sustain effort. Yet the economic process does not naturally offer such a facility; that matters of livelihood are subject to reckoning is merely a result of the manner in which they are instituted.

Trobriand economy, for instance, is organized as a continuous give-and-take, yet there is no possibility of setting

[3] *Cooperation and Competition among Primitive Peoples* (New York and London: 1937), p. 31.

up a balance, or of employing the concept of a fund. *Reciprocity demands adequacy of response, not mathematical equality.* Consequently, transactions and decisions cannot be grouped with any precision from the economic point of view, i.e., according to the manner in which they affect material want-satisfaction. Figures, if any, do not correspond to facts. Though the economic significance of an act may be great, there is no way of assessing its relative importance.

Malinowski listed the different kinds of give-and-take, from free gifts at the one extreme, to plain commercial barter at the other.[4] His grouping of "gifts, payments, and transactions" came under seven headings, which he correlated with the sociological relationships within which each occurred. These numbered eight. The results of his analysis were revealing:

(a) The category of "free gifts" was exceptional, since charity was neither needed nor encouraged, and the notion of gift was always associated with the idea of adequate counter-gift (but not, of course, of equivalency). Even actual "free gifts" were construed as counter-gifts, given in return for some fictitious service rendered to the giver. Malinowski found that "the natives would undoubtedly *not* think of free gifts as being all of the same nature." Where the notion of "dead loss" is lacking, the operation of balancing a fund is not feasible.

(b) In the group of transaction, where the gift is expected to be returned in an economically equivalent manner, we meet another confusing fact. This is the category which, according to our notions, ought to be practically indistinguishable from trade. Far from it. Occasionally the identically same object is exchanged back and forth between the partners, thus depriving the transaction of any conceivable economic purpose or meaning! By the simple device of handing back, though in a roundabout way, the

---

[4] [*Argonauts of the Western Pacific*, Chapter VI. Ed.]

pig to its donor, the exchange of equivalencies instead of being a step in the direction of economic rationality proves a safeguard against the intrusion of utilitarian considerations. The sole purpose of the exchange is to draw relationships closer by strengthening the ties of reciprocity.

(c) Utilitarian barter [*gimwali*] is distinct from any other type of mutual gift giving. While in ceremonial exchange of fish for yam [*wasi*] there is, in principle, adequacy between the two sides, a poor haul or a failure of crops, e.g., reducing the amount offered, in barter exchange of fish and yam there is at least a pretense of higgling and haggling. It is further characterized by an absence of special partnerships, and, if artifacts enter, by a restriction to newly manufactured goods—secondhand ones might have a personal value attached to them.

(d) Within the sociologically defined relationships—of which there are many—the exchange is usually unequal, as befits the relationship. Appropriational movements of goods and services are thus often instituted in a manner that renders some transactions irreversible and many goods noninterchangeable.

Thus quantitativity can hardly be expected to operate in that wide domain of livelihood, that comes under the heading of "gifts, payments, and transactions."

3. Another familiar concept that is inapplicable in primitive conditions is that of *property* as a right of disposing of definite objects. Consequently, no straight inventory of possessions is practicable. We have here a variety of rights of different persons in regard to the same object. By this fragmentation, the unity of the object under its property aspect is destroyed. The appropriational movement does not, as a rule, have the complete object, for instance a piece of land, as its referent, but only its discrete uses, thus depriving the concept of property of its effectiveness in regard to objects.

4. *Economic transactions* proper hardly crop up in kinship-organized communities. Transactions in early

times are public acts performed in regard to the status of persons and other self-propelling things: the bride, the wife, the son, the slave, the ox, the boat. With settled peoples changes in the status of a plot of land, too, were publicly attested.

Such status transactions would naturally carry important economic implications. Wooing, betrothal and marriage, adoption and emancipation, are accompanied by movements of goods, some of them immediate, some to follow in the long run. Great as the economic significance of such transactions was, it ranked second to their importance in establishing the position of the persons in the social context. How, then, did transactions in regard to goods eventually separate off from the typical kinship transactions in regard to persons?

As long as only a few status goods, such as land, cattle, slaves were alienable there was no need for separate economic transactions since the transfer of such goods accompanied the change in status, while a transfer of the goods without such a change would not have been approved of by the collectivity. Incidentally, no economic valuation could easily attach to goods the fate of which was inseparably linked with that of their owners.

Separate transactions in regard to goods were in early times restricted to the two most important ones, namely, land and labor. Thus precisely the "goods," which were the last to become freely alienable were the first to become objects of limited transactions. Limited, since land and labor for a long time to come remained part of the social tissue and could not be arbitrarily mobilized without destroying it. Neither land nor freemen could be sold outright. Their transfer was conditional and temporary. Alienation stopped short of an unrestricted transference of ownership. Amongst the economic transactions in fourteenth-century tribal-feudal Arrapha on the Tigris, those which refer to land and labor illustrate the point. Property, both in land and persons, belonged with the Nuzi to collectivities—clans, families, villages. Use alone was transferred. How exceptional in tribal times the transfer of property in land was, may be seen from the dramatic scenario of the episode of Abraham purchasing a family vault from the Hittite.

It is a peculiar fact that the transfer of "use alone" is rather more "economic" than would be the transfer of ownership. In the exchange of ownership, considerations of prestige and emotional factors may weigh heavily; in the alienation of use the utilitarian element prevails. In modern terms: interest, which is the price of use over time, may be said to have been one of the earliest economic quantities to be instituted.

Eventually, the thin economic layer may "peel off" from the status transaction, the referent of which is a person. The economic element may then change hands alone, the transaction being camouflaged as a status transaction which, however, is to be fictitious. Sale of land to non-clan members being prohibited, the residual rights of the clan to reclaim the land from the purchaser may be voided by legal devices. One of these was the fictitious adoption of the buyer or, alternatively, the fictitious consent of clan members to the sale.

Another line of development toward separate economic transactions led, as we saw, through the transference of "use only," thus expressly maintaining the residual property rights of the clan or family. The same purpose was served by a mutual exchange of "uses" of different objects, while pledging the return of the objects themselves.

The classical Athenian form of mortgage (*prasis epi lysei*) was probably such a transference of use alone, but (exceptionally) leaving the debtor *in situ* while pledging to the creditor by way of interest a part of the crop. The creditor was safeguarded by the setting up of a boundary stone inscribed with his name and the amount of the debt, neither the date of repayment nor interest being mentioned, however. If this interpretation of the Attican *horos* holds good, the plot of land was, in a friendly way, mortgaged for an indefinite period against some participation in the crop. Default with a subsequent distraint would occur only quite rarely, namely, on a confiscation of the debtor's lands or the ruin of his entire family.

Almost in every case the separate transference of "use" serves the purpose of strengthening the bonds of family and clan with its social, religious and political ties. Economic exploitation of the use is thus made compatible with the friendly mutuality of those ties. It maintains the control of the collectivity over the arrangements made by their individual members. As yet the economic factor hardly registers its claims in the transactions.

5. *Services, not goods, make up wealth in many archaic societies. They are performed by slaves, servants, and retainers.* But to make human beings disposed to serve as an outcome of their status is an aim of political (as against economic) power. With the increase of the material against the non-material ingredients of wealth, the political method of control recedes and gives way to so-called economic control. Hesiod, the peasant, was talking thrift and farming centuries before the gentlemen philosophers, Plato and Aristotle, knew of any other social discipline than politics. Two millennia later, in Western Europe, a new middle class produced a wealth of commodities and argued "economics" against their feudal masters, and another century later the working class of an industrial age inherited from them that category as an instrument of their own emancipation. The aristocracy continued to monopolize government and to look down on commodity production. Hence, as long as dependent labor predominates as an element in wealth, the economy has only a shadowy existence.

6. In the philosophy of Aristotle *the three prizes of fortune* were: honor and prestige; security of life and limb; wealth. The first stands for privilege and homage, rank and precedence; the second ensures safety from open and secret enemies, treason and rebellion, the revolt of the slave, the overbearing of the strong, and even protection from

the arm of the law; the third, wealth, is the bliss of proprietorship, mainly of heirloom or famed treasure. True, utilitarian goods, food and materials, accrue as a rule to the possessor of honor and security, but the glory outshines the goods. Poverty, on the other hand, goes with an inferior status; it involves working for one's living, often at the bidding of others. The less restricted the bidding, the more abject the condition. Not so much manual labor—as the farmer's ever-respected position shows—but dependence upon another man's personal whim and command causes the serving man to be despised. Again, the bare economic fact of a lower income is screened from view.

7. The *agatha* are the highest prizes of life, that which is most desirable and also rarest. This is indeed a surprising context in which to encounter that feature of goods, which modern theory has come to regard as the criterion of the "economic," namely, scarcity. For the discerning mind when considering those prizes of life must be struck by the utterly different source of their "scarcity" from that which the economist would make us expect. With him scarcity reflects either the niggardliness of nature or the burden of the labor that production entails. But the highest honors and the rarest distinctions are few for neither of these two reasons. They are scarce for the obvious reason that there is no standing room at the top of the pyramid. The fewness of the *agatha* is inherent in rank, immunity, and treasure: they would not be what they are if they were attainable to many. Hence the absence in early society of the "economic connotation" of scarcity, whether or not utilitarian goods sometimes also happen to be scarce. For the rarest prizes are not of this order. Scarcity derives here from the non-economic order of things.

8. The *self-sufficiency* of a body of humans, that postulate of bare life, is ensured when a supply of the "necessaries" is physically available. The things that are here meant are those that sustain life and are storable, that is, which keep. Corn, wine, and oil are *chrēmata*, but so are wool

and certain metals. The citizenry and the members of the family must be able to depend upon them in famine or war. The amount that the family or the city "needs" is an objective requirement. The household is the smallest, the polis is the largest unit of consumption: in either case that which is "necessary" is set by the standards of the community. Hence the notion of the intrinsically limited amount of the necessaries. This meaning is very near to that of "rations." Since equivalencies, whether by custom or law, were set only for such subsistence goods which actually served as units of pay, or of wages, the notion of the "necessary amount" was associated with the commonly stored staples. For operational reasons a boundlessness of human wants and needs—the logical correlate of scarcity—was a notion quite foreign to this approach.

These are some of the major reasons that so long stood in the way of the birth of a distinctively economic field of interest. Even to the professional thinker the fact that man must eat did not appear worthy of elaboration.

Aristotle's Probings

It may seem paradoxical to expect that the last word on the nature of economic life should have been spoken by a thinker who hardly saw its beginnings. Yet Aristotle, living, as he did, on the borderline of economic ages, was in a favored position to grasp the merits of the subject.

This may explain incidentally why in our own day, in the face of a change in the place of the economy in society comparable in scope only to that which in his time heralded the oncoming of market trade, Aristotle's insights into the connections of economy and society can be seen in their stark realism.

We have, therefore, every reason to seek in his works for far more massive and significant formulations on economic matters than Aristotle has been credited with in the past. In fact, the *disjecta membra* of the *Ethics* and *Politics* convey a monumental unity of thought.

Whenever Aristotle touched on a question of the economy he aimed at developing its relationship to society as a whole. The frame of reference was the community as such, which exists at different levels within all functioning human groups. In terms, then, of our modern speech Aristotle's approach to human affairs was sociological. In mapping out a field of study he would relate all questions of institutional origin and function to the totality of society. Community, self-sufficiency, and justice were the focal concepts. The group as a going concern forms a community (*koinonia*) the members of which are linked by the bond of good will (*philia*). Whether *oikos* or *polis*, there is a kind of *philia*, specific to that *koinonia*, apart from which the group could not remain. *Philia* expresses itself in a behavior of reciprocity (*anti-peponthos*),[5] that is, readiness to take on burdens in turn and share mutually. Anything that is needed to continue and maintain the community, including its self-sufficiency (*autarkeia*), is "natural" and intrinsically right. Autarchy may be said to be the capacity to subsist without dependence on resources from outside. Justice (contrary to our own view) implies that the members of the community possess unequal standing. That which ensures justice, whether in regard to the distribution of the prizes of life or the adjudication of conflicts, or the regulation of mutual services is good since it is required for the continuance of the group. Normativity, then, is inseparable from actuality.

These rough indications of his total system should permit us to outline Aristotle's views on trade and prices. External trade is natural when it serves the survival of the community by maintaining its self-sufficiency. The need for this arises as soon as the extended family grows overpopulous, and its members are forced to settle apart. Their au-

[5] Aristotle, *EN* 1132b 21, 35.

tarchy would now be impaired all round, but for the operation of giving a share (*metadosis*), from one's surplus. The rate at which the shared services (or, eventually, the goods) are exchanged follows from the requirement of *philia*, i.e., that the good will among the members persist. For without it, the community itself would cease. The just price, then, derives from the demands of *philia* as expressed in the reciprocity which is of the essence of all human community.

From these principles derive also his strictures on commercial trading and the maxims for the setting up of exchange equivalencies or the just price. Trade, we saw, is "natural" as long as it is a requirement of self-sufficiency. Prices are justly set if they conform to the standing of the participants in the community, thereby strengthening the good will on which community rests. Exchange of goods is exchange of services; this, again, is a postulate of self-sufficiency and is practiced by way of a mutual sharing at just prices. In such exchange no gain is involved; goods have their known prices, fixed beforehand. If exceptionally gainful retailing there must be for the sake of a convenient distribution of goods in the market-place, let it be done by non-citizens. Aristotle's theory of trade and price was nothing else than a simple elaboration of his general theorem of the human community.

Community, self-sufficiency, and justice: these pivots of his sociology were the frame of reference of his thought on all economic matters, whether the nature of the economy or policy issues were at stake.

The Sociological Bent

On the nature of the economy Aristotle's starting point is, as always, empirical. But the conceptualization even of the most obvious facts is deep and original.

The desire for wealth, Solon's verse had proclaimed, was unlimited with man. Not so, said Aristotle, in opening up the subject. Wealth is, in truth, the things necessary to sustain life when safely stored in the keeping of the community, whose sustenance they represent. Human needs, be they of the household or of the city, are not boundless; nor is there a scarcity of subsistence in nature. The argument, which sounds strange enough to modern ears, is powerfully pressed and carefully elaborated. At every point the institutional reference is explicit. Psychology is eschewed, sociology imposed.

The rejection of the scarcity postulate (as we would say) is based on the conditions of animal life, and is thence extended to those of human life. Do not animals from their birth find their sustenance waiting for them in their environment? And do not men, too, find sustenance in mother's milk and eventually in their environment, be they hunters, herdsmen, or tillers of the soil? Since slavery to Aristotle is "natural," he can without inconsistency describe slave raids as a hunt for peculiar game and consequently represent the leisure of the slave-owning citizenry as supplied by the environment. Otherwise, no need save that for sustenance is considered, much less approved of. Therefore, if scarcity springs "from the demand side," as we would say, Aristotle attributes it to a misconceived notion of the good life as a desire for a greater abundance of physical goods and enjoyments. The elixir of the good life—the elation of day-long theater, the mass jury service, the holding in turn of offices, canvassing, electioneering, great festivals, even the thrill of battle and naval combat—can be neither hoarded nor physically possessed. True, the good life requires, "this is generally admitted," that the citizen have leisure in order to devote himself to the service of the *polis*. Here again, slavery was part of the answer; another and much more incisive part lay in the payment of all citizens for the performance of public duties, or else, in not admitting artisans to citizenship, a measure Aristotle himself seemed to commend.

For yet another reason the problem of scarcity does not arise with Aristotle. The economy—as the root of the word shows, a matter of the domestic household or *oikos*—concerns directly the relationship of the persons who make up the natural institution of the household. Not possessions, but parents, offspring, and slaves constitute it. The techniques of gardening, breeding, or other modes of production Aristotle excluded from the purview of the economy. The emphasis is altogether institutional and only up to a point ecological, relegating technology to the subordinate sphere of useful knowledge. Aristotle's concept of the economy would almost permit us to refer to it as an instituted process through which sustenance is ensured. With a similar liberty of phrasing, Aristotle may be said to put down the erroneous conception of unlimited human wants and needs, or, of a general scarcity of goods, to two circumstances: first, the acquisition of foodstuffs through commercial traders, which introduces money-making into the quest for subsistence; second, a false notion of the good life as a utilitarian cumulation of physical pleasures. Given the right institutions in trade and the right understanding of the good life, Aristotle saw no room for the scarcity factor in the human economy. He did not fail to connect this with the existence of such institutions as slavery, infanticide, and a way of life that discounts comfort. Short of this empirical reference, his negation of scarcity might have been as dogmatic and as unfavorable to factual research as the scarcity postulate is in our days. But with him, once and for all, human needs presupposed institutions and customs.

Aristotle's adherence to the substantive meaning of economic was basic to his total argument. For why did he have to probe into the economy at all? And why did he need to set in motion an array of arguments against the popular belief that the significance of that dimly apprehended field lay in the lure of wealth, an insatiable urge common to the human frame? To what purpose did he develop a theorem comprising the origins of family and state, solely designed to demonstrate that human wants and needs are not boundless and that useful things are not, intrinsically, scarce? What was the motive behind this orchestration of an inherently paradoxical point which, moreover, must have appeared too speculative to be quite in keeping with his strongly empiricist bent?

The explanation is obvious. Two policy problems—trade and price—were pressing for an answer. Unless the question of commercial trade and the setting of prices could be linked to the requirements of communal existence and its self-sufficiency, there was no rational way of judging of either, be it in theory or in practice. If such a link did offer, then the answer was simple: first, trade that served to restore self-sufficiency was "in accordance with nature"; trade that did not, was "contrary to nature." Second, prices should be such as to strengthen the bond of community; otherwise exchange will not continue to take place and the community will cease to exist. The mediating concept was in either case the self-sufficiency of the community. The economy, then, consisted in the necessaries of life—grain, oil, wine, and the like—on which the community subsisted. The conclusion was stringent and no other was possible. So either the economy was about the material, substantive, things that sustained human beings, or else there was no empirically-given rational link between matters such as trade and prices on the one hand, and the postulate of a self-sufficient community, on the other. The logical necessity for Aristotle's insistence on the substantive meaning of economic is therefore evident.

Hence also that astonishing attack on the Solonic poem in an overture to a treatise on economics.

Natural Trade and Just Price

Commercial trade, or, in our terms, market trade, arose as a burning issue out of the circumstances of the time. It was a disturbing novelty, which could neither be placed nor explained nor judged adequately. Money was now being earned by respectable citizens through the simple device of buying and selling. Such a thing had been unknown, or rather, was restricted to low-class persons, known as hucksters, as a rule metics [resident aliens], who eked out a living by retailing food in the market place. Such individuals did make a profit by buying at one price and selling at another. Now this practice had apparently spread to the citizenry of good standing, and big sums of money were made by this method, formerly stamped as disreputable. How should the phenomenon itself be classified? How should profit, systematically made in this manner, be operationally explained? And what judgment should be passed on such an activity?

The origin of market institutions is in itself an intricate and obscure subject. It is hard to trace their historical beginnings with precision and even harder to follow the stages by which early forms of trade developed into market trade.

Aristotle's analysis struck to the root. By calling commercial trade *kapēlikē*—no name had yet been given to it—he intimated that it was nothing new, except for the proportions it assumed. It was hucksterism written large. The money was made "off" each other (*ap'allēlōn*), by the surcharging methods so often met with in the market place.

Aristotle's point, inadequate though such a notion of mutual surcharge was, reflected a crucial phase of transition in the history of the human economy: the juncture at which the institution of the market began to move into the orbit of trade.

One of the first city markets, if not the very first, was no other than the *agora* in Athens. Nothing indicates that it was contemporaneous with the founding of the city. The first authentic record of the *agora* is of the fifth century B.C. when it was already definitely established, though still contentious. Throughout the course of its early history the use of small coin and the retailing of food went together. Its beginnings in Athens should therefore coincide with the minting of obols sometime in the early sixth century B.C.

101

On Asian territory it may have had a precursor in Sardis, the Lydian capital, to all accounts a thoroughly Greek type of city. Here again pioneering in small change marks the trail, especially if we include as we should, the use of gold dust. On this point Herodotus leaves little doubt. The Midas legend dates the presence in Phrygia of large amounts of river gold about 715 B.C., while in Sardis the market place itself was crossed by a gold-bearing stream, the Pactolus. In Herodotus' birthplace, Halicarnassus, stood that huge monument to Alyattes to the cost of which the love trade of Lydian girls had so generously contributed, while Gyges, founder of the Mermnade dynasty, appears to have initiated the coinage of elektron. Alyattes' son, Croesus, adorned Delphi with the splendor of his massive gold gifts. No beads or shells that might be employed as money-stuffs are known from Asia Minor; the mention of gold dust is therefore crucial. The probability is strong that the twin Lydian innovations of coinage and the retailing of food were introduced together in Athens. They were not yet inseparable by any means. Aegina, which preceded Athens in matters of coinage, may have used coins only in foreign trade. The same might be true of the Lydian coins, while gold dust circulated in the food market and in love deals. Up to this day the market place in Bida, capital of Nupe, in Nigeria, is said to turn after midnight into a place of mercenary sociability, with gold dust presumably circulating as money. In Lydia, too, the presence of gold dust may have induced the retailing of food in the market. Attica followed in its wake, but replaced the specks of gold by fractions of obols of silver.

Broadly, coins spread much faster than markets. While trade was abounding and money as a standard was common, markets were few and far between.

By the end of the fourth century Athens was famous for her commercial *agora,* where anyone could buy a meal cheaply. Coinage had spread like wildfire, but outside of Athens the market habit was not particularly popular. During the Peloponnesian War fleets of sutlers accompanied the navy, for the troops could only exceptionally rely on subsisting from local markets. As late as the beginning of the fourth century, the Ionian countryside possessed no regular food markets. The chief promoters of markets were at that time the Greek armies, notably the mercenary troops now more and more frequently employed as a business venture. The traditional self-equipping hoplite army had been engaged only in brief campaigns on a sack of barley meal brought along from home. By the turn of the fifth century regular expeditionary forces were formed, only the cadres of which consisted of Spartan or Athenian citizens while the bulk was recruited from abroad. The employment of such a force, especially if it was supposed to cross friendly territory, raised logistic problems on which scholarly generals were fond to comment.

Xenophon's tracts offer many instances of the actual and the ideal role assigned to the market in the new strategy. The food market from which the troops could provision themselves from the hand money due to them from their Commanding Officer (unless local requisitioning was practicable) formed part of a broader issue—the sale of booty, especially slaves and cattle, as well as provisioning from sutlers who followed the army in the hope of profit. It all boiled down to so many market problems. Concerning each we have evidence of organizational and financial activities initiated by kings, generals, or governments responsible for the military undertaking. The campaign itself was quite often no more than a rationalized booty raid, if not of the renting out of an army to serve some foreign government for the benefit of the home country that financed the venture on business grounds. Military efficiency, of course, was the paramount requirement. An expedition's sale of booty, if only for reasons of military tactics, formed as much part of efficiency as did the regular provisioning of the troops, while it avoided, as far as could be, the antagonizing of friendly neutrals. Go-ahead generals devised up-to-date methods of stimulating local market activities, financing sutlers to wait upon the troops, and engaging local craftsmen in improvised markets for the supply of armaments. They boosted market supply and market services by all means at their disposal, however tentative and hesitant local initiative sometimes may have been. There was, in effect, but little reliance on the spontaneous business spirit of the residents. The Spartan government sent a civilian commission of "booty sellers" along with the king who commanded the army in the field. Their task was to have the captured slaves and cattle auctioned on the spot. King Agesilaos busied himself to have markets "prepared," "set up," and "offered" to his troops by the friendly cities along his prospective itinerary. In the Cyropaedian utopia, Xenophon described how any trader who wished to accompany the army and needed money for supplies, would go to the commander and, after giving references as to his reliability, would be advanced money out of a fund kept for that purpose. (*Cyr.* VI ii 38 f.) Around that time Timotheus, the Athenian general, heedful of the sutlers' financial needs, acted on lines similar to Xenophon's educational novel. In the Olynthian war (364 B.C.), having substituted copper for silver in paying his soldiers, he persuaded the traders to accept it from the soldiers at that value, firmly promising them that it will be accepted from them at that rate for the purchase of booty, and that anything left over after purchasing booty would be redeemed in silver. (Ps. Arist. *Oecon.* II 23 a.) It all goes to show how small the reliance on local markets still was, both as a means of provisioning and as a vent for booty unless fostered by the military.

Local markets, then, in Aristotle's time were a delicate growth. They were put up on occasion, in an emergency or for some definite purpose and not unless political expediency so advised. Nor does the local food market present itself in any way as an organ of long-distance trade. Separation of [external] trade and market is the rule.

The institution which eventually was to link the two, the

supply-demand-price mechanism, was unknown to Aristotle. It was, of course, the true originator of these commercial practices, which were now becoming noticeable in trade. Traditionally, [external] trade carried no taint of commerce. In its origins a semi-warlike occupation, it never cut loose from governmental associations, apart from which but little trading could take place under archaic conditions. Gain sprang from booty and gifts (whether voluntary or blackmailed), public honors and prizes, the golden crown and the land grant bestowed by prince or city, the arms and luxuries acquired—the *kerdos* of the Odyssey. Between all this and the local food market of the *polis* there was no physical connection. The Phoenician *emporos* would display his treasures and trinkets at the prince's palace or the manorial hall, while the crew would settle down to grow their own food on foreign soil—a yearly turnover. Later forms of trade ran in administrative grooves, smoothed by the urbanity of port of trade officialdom. Customary and treaty prices loomed large. The trader, unless compensated from commission fees, would make his "gain" from the proceeds of the imports that were the trophy of the venture.

Treaty prices were matters of negotiation, with much diplomatic higgling-haggling to precede them. Once a treaty was established, bargaining was at an end. For treaty meant a set price at which trading took its course. As there was no trade without treaty, so the existence of a treaty precluded the practices of the market. Trade and markets had not only different locations, status, and personnel, they differed also in purpose, ethos, and organization.

We cannot yet tell for certain, when and in what form higgling-haggling and gain made on prices entered the realm of trade, as implied in Aristotle. Even in the absence of international markets gain made in overseas trade had been normal. There can be no doubt, however, that the sharp eye of the theoretician had discerned the links between the petty tricks of the huckster in the *agora* and novel kinds of trading profits that were the talk of the day. But the gadget that established their kinship—the supply-demand-price mechanism—escaped Aristotle. The distribution of food in the market allowed as yet but scant room to the play of that mechanism; and long-distance trade was directed not by individual competition, but by institutional factors. Nor were either local markets or long-distance trade conspicuous for the fluctuation of prices. Not before the third century B.C., was the working of a supply-demand-price mechanism in international trade noticeable. This happened in regard to grain, and later, to slaves, in the open port of Delos. The Athenian *agora* preceded, therefore, by some two centuries the setting up of a market in the Aegean which could be said to embody a market mechanism. Aristotle, writing in the second half of this period, recognized the early instances of gain made on price differentials for the symptomatic development in the organization of trade which they actually were. Yet in the absence of price-making markets he would have seen nothing but perversity in the expectation that the new urge for money-making might conceivably serve a useful purpose. As to Hesiod, his famous commendation of peaceful strife had never transcended the prizes of pre-market competition on the manorial level—praise for the potter, a joint for the lumberman, a gift to the singer who won.

Exchange of Equivalencies

This should dispose of the notion that Aristotle was offering in his *Ethics* a theory of prices. Such a theory is indeed central to the understanding of the market, the main function of which is to produce a price that balances supply and demand. None of these concepts, however, was familiar to him.

The postulate of self-sufficiency implied that such trade as was required to restore autarchy was natural and, therefore, right. Trade went with acts of exchange, which again implied a definite rate at which the exchange was to take

106

place. But how to fit acts of barter into a framework of community? And, if barter there was, at what rate was it to be performed?

As to the origin of barter, nothing could appeal less to the philosopher of *Gemeinschaft* than the Smithian propensity allegedly inherent in the individual. Exchange, Aristotle said, sprang from the needs of the extended family the members of which originally used things in common which they owned in common. When their numbers increased and they were compelled to settle apart, they found themselves short of some of the things they formerly used in common and had therefore to acquire the needed things from amongst each other.[6] This amounted to a mutual sharing. Briefly,[7] reciprocity in sharing was accomplished through acts of barter.[8] Hence exchange.

The rate of exchange must be such as to maintain the community.[9] Again, not the interests of the individuals, but those of the community were the governing principle. The skills of persons of different status had to be exchanged at a rate proportionate to the status of each: the builder's performance exchanged against many times the cobbler's performance; unless this was so, reciprocity was infringed and the community would not hold.[10]

Aristotle offered a formula by which the rate (or price) is to be set:[11] it is given by the point at which two diagonals cross, each of them representing the status of one of the two parties.[12] This point is formally determined by four quantities—two on each diagonal. The method is obscure, the result incorrect. Economic analysis represented the four determinative quantities with correctness and precision by

[6] Aristotle, *Pol.* 1257a 24.
[7] Ibid., 1257a 19.
[8] Ibid., 1257a 25.
[9] Aristotle, *EN* 1133b 16, 1133b 8.
[10] Ibid., 1133b 29.
[11] Ibid., 1133a 8.
[12] Ibid., 1133a 10.

pointing out the pair of indices on the demand curve, and the pair of indices on the supply curve, which are determinative of the price that clears the market. The crucial difference was that the modern economist was aiming at a description of the *formation of prices* in the market, while such a thought was far from Aristotle's mind. He was busied with the quite different and essentially practical problem of providing a formula by which the *price was to be set*.

Surprisingly enough, Aristotle seemed to see no other difference between set price and bargained price than a point of time, the former being there before the transaction took place, while the latter emerged only afterward.[13] The bargained price, he insisted, would tend to be excessive because it was agreed to when the demand was not yet satisfied. This in itself should be sufficient proof of Aristotle's naïveté concerning the working of the market. He apparently believed that the justly set price must be different from the bargained one.

The set price, besides its justness, also offered the advantage of setting natural trade apart from unnatural trade. Since the aim of natural trade is exclusively to restore self-sufficiency, the set price ensures this through its exclusion of gain. Equivalencies—as we will henceforth call the set rate—serve therefore to safeguard "natural" trade. The bargained price might yield a profit to one of the parties at the expense of the other, and thus undermine the coherence of the community instead of underpinning it.

To the modern market-adjusted mind the chain of thought here presented and ascribed to Aristotle must appear as a series of paradoxes:

It implies the ignoring of the market as a vehicle of trade; of price formation as a function of the market; of any other function of trade than that of contributing to self-sufficiency; of the reasons why set price might differ from market-formed price, and why market prices should

13 Ibid., 1133b 15.

be expected to fluctuate; finally, of competition as the device that produced a price unique in that it clears the market and can therefore be regarded as *the* natural rate of exchange.

Instead, market and trade are here thought of as separate and distinct institutions; prices, as produced by custom, law, or proclamation; gainful trade, as "unnatural"; the set price, as "natural"; fluctuation of prices, as undesirable; and the natural price, far from being an impersonal appraisal of the goods exchanged, as expressing the mutual estimation of the statuses of the producers.

For the resolution of these apparent contradictions the concept of equivalencies enters as crucial.

In the key passage on the origin of exchange (*allagē*) Aristotle gave perfect precision to that basic institution of archaic society—exchange of equivalencies. The increase in the size of the family spelled the end of their self-sufficiency. Lacking one thing or another, they had to rely on one another for supply. Some barbarian peoples, Aristotle said, still practice such exchange in kind "for such people are expected to give in exchange necessaries of life for other necessaries of life, for example, wine for corn, as much as required in the circumstances and no more, handing over the one and taking the other in return, and so with each of the staples of the sort. The practice of barter of this manner and type was not, therefore, contrary to nature, nor was it a branch of the art of wealth-getting, for it was instituted for the restoring of man's natural self-sufficiency."[14]

The institution of equivalency exchange was designed to ensure that all householders had a claim to share in the necessary staples at given rates, in exchange for such staples as they themselves happened to possess. For no one was expected to give away his goods for the asking, receiving nothing in return; indeed, the indigent who possessed no

[14] Aristotle, *Pol.*, 1257a 24–31.

equivalent to offer in exchange had to work off his debt (hence the great social importance of the institution of debt bondage). Thus barter derived from the institution of sharing of the necessities of life; the purpose of barter was to supply all householders with those necessities up to the level of sufficiency; it was institutionalized as an obligation of householders to give of their surplus to any other householder who happened to be short of that definite kind of necessity, at his request, and to the extent of his shortage, but only to that extent; the exchange was made at the established rate (equivalency) against other staples of which the householder happened to have a supply. Insofar as legal terms are applicable to so primitive conditions, the obligation of the householder was directed toward a transaction in kind, limited in extent to the claimant's actual need, performed at equivalency rates by exclusion of credit, and comprising all staples.

In the *Ethics*, Aristotle stressed that in spite of the equivalency of goods exchanged, one of the parties benefited, namely, the one who felt compelled to suggest the transaction. Nevertheless, in the long run, the procedure amounted to a mutual sharing, since at another time it was the other's turn to benefit by the chance. "The very existence of the state depends on such acts of proportionate reciprocity . . . failing which no sharing happens, and it is the sharing which binds us together. This is why we set up a shrine of the Graces in a public place to remind men to return a kindness; for that is a special characteristic of Grace, since it is a duty not only to repay a service done one, but another time to take the initiative in doing a service oneself."[15] Nothing, I feel, could show better the meaning of reciprocity than this elaboration. It might be called reciprocity on the square. Exchange is here viewed as part of reciprocity behavior in contrast to the marketing view that invested barter with the qualities which are the very reverse of

[15] Aristotle, *EN* 1133a 3–6.

the generosity and grace that accompanied the idea of reciprocity.

But for these strategic passages, we might still be unable to identify this vital institution of archaic society, in spite of the sheaves of documentary evidence unearthed by archeologists within the last two or three generations. Figures representing mathematical rates between units of goods of different kinds were throughout translated by Orientalists as "price." For markets were assumed as a matter of course. Actually those figures connoted equivalencies quite unconnected with markets and market prices, their quality of fixedness being an inborn one, not implying any antecedent fluctuations brought to an end by some process of "setting" or "fixing" as the phrase seems to imply. Language itself betrays us here.

The Texts

This is not the place to elaborate on the numerous points at which our presentation differs from previous ones. However, in brief we must refer back to the texts themselves. Almost inevitably an erroneous view had been formed of the subject matter of Aristotle's discourse. Commercial trading, which was taken to be that subject, was, as it now appears, just only beginning to be practiced in his time. Not Hammurabi's Babylonia, but the Greek-speaking fringe of Western Asia together with Greece herself were responsible for that development—well over a thousand years afterward. Aristotle could not, therefore, have been describing the working of a developed market mechanism and discussing its effects on the ethics of trade. Again, it follows that some of his key terms, notably *kapēlikē, metadosis* and *chrēmatistikē*, were misinterpreted in translation. Sometimes the error becomes subtle. *Kapēlikē* was rendered as the art of retail trade instead of the art of "commercial trade," *chrēmatistikē* as the art of money-making instead of that of supply, i.e., the procuring of the necessaries of

111

life in kind. In another instance, the distortion is manifest: *metadosis* was taken to be exchange or barter, while patently meaning its opposite, namely, "giving one's share."

Briefly, in sequence:

Kapēlikē, grammatically denotes the art of the *kapēlos*. The meaning of *kapēlos* as used by Herodotus in the middle of the fifth century, is broadly established as some kind of retailer, especially of food, a keeper of a cookshop, a seller of foodstuffs and cooked food. The invention of coined money was linked by Herodotus with the fact that the Lydians had turned *kapēloi*. Herodotus also recounts that Darius was nicknamed *kapēlos*. Indeed, under him military stores may have begun the practice of retailing food. Eventually *kapēlos* became synonymous with "trickster, fraud, cheat." Its pejorative meaning was congenital.

Unfortunately, this still leaves the Aristotelian meaning of the word *kapēlikē* wide open. The suffix *-ikē* indicates "art of," and so makes *kapēlikē* signify the art of the *kapēlos*. Actually, such a word was not in use; the dictionary mentions only one instance (apart from Aristotle) and in this instance it designates, as one would expect, the "art of retailing." How, then, did Aristotle come to introduce it as the heading for a subject of the first magnitude noways restricted to retail trading, namely, commercial trade? For that and no other is without any possible doubt the subject of his discourse.

The answer is not hard to find. In his passionate diatribe against gainful trading Aristotle was using *kapēlikē* with an ironical overtone. Commercial trade was, of course, not huckstering; nor was it retail trading; and whatever it was, it deserved to be called some form or variant of *emporia*, which was the regular name for seafaring trade, together with any other form of large-scale or wholesale trade. When Aristotle referred specifically to the various kinds of maritime trade, he fell back on *emporia*, in the usual sense. Why, then, did he not do so in the main theoretical analysis

112

of the subject but use instead a new-fangled word of pejorative connotation?

Aristotle enjoyed inventing words, and his humor, if any, was Shavian. The figure of the *kapēlos* was an unfailing hit of the comic stage. Aristophanes in his *Acharnians* had made his hero turn *kapēlos* and in that guise earn the solemn praises of the chorus, which lauded him as the philosopher of the day. Aristotle wished drastically to convey his unimpressedness with the *nouveaux riches* and the allegedly esoteric sources of their wealth. Commercial trade was no mystery. When all is said, it was but huckstering written large.

Chrēmatistikē was deliberately employed by Aristotle in the literal sense of providing for the necessities of life, instead of its usual meaning of "money-making." Laistner rendered it correctly as "the art of supply," and Ernest Barker in his commentary recalled the original sense of *chrēmata*, which, he warned, was not money, but the necessities themselves, an interpretation also upheld by Defourny and by M. I. Finley in an unpublished lecture. Indeed, with Aristotle the stress on the non-monetary meaning of *chrēmata* was logically unavoidable, since he held on to the autarchy postulate which was pointless outside of a naturalistic interpretation of wealth.

The signal error in rendering *metadosis* as "exchange" in the three crucial passages of the *Politics* and the *Ethics* cut deeper still.[16] In the case of *metadosis* Aristotle kept to the common meaning of the word. It was the translators who brought in an arbitrary interpretation. In an archaic society of common feasts, raiding parties, and other acts of mutual help and practical reciprocity the term *metadosis* possessed a specific operational connotation—it signified "giving a share," especially to the common pool of food, whether a religious festivity, a ceremonial meal, or other public venture was in question.[17] That is the dictionary mean-

[16] Ps.-Arist., *Oec.* II, 1353a 24–28.
[17] Ibid., 1133a 2; *Pol.* 1257a 24; 1280b 20.

ing of *metadosis*. Its etymology underlines the unilateral character of the giving, contributing, or sharing operation. Yet we are faced with the astonishing fact that in the translation of these passages in which Aristotle insisted on the derivation of exchange from *metadosis*, this term was rendered as "exchange" or "barter," which turned it into its opposite. This practice was sanctioned by the leading dictionary, which recorded *s. v. metadosis* those crucial three passages as exceptions! Such a deviation from the plain text is understandable only as an expression of the marketing bias of latter-day translators, who at this point were unable to follow the meaning of the text. Exchange to them was a natural propensity of men and stood in no need of explanation. But even assuming it did, it certainly could not have sprung from *metadosis* in its accepted meaning of "giving a share." Accordingly, they rendered *metadosis* by "exchange," and thus turned Aristotle's statement into an empty truism. This mistake endangered the whole edifice of Aristotle's economic thought at the pivotal point. By his derivation of exchange from "giving one's share" Aristotle provided a logical link between his theory of the economy in general and the practical questions at issue. Commercial trade, we recall, he regarded as an unnatural form of trade; natural trade was gainless since it merely maintained self-sufficiency. In support of this he could effectively appeal to the circumstance that, to the limited amount needed to maintain self-sufficiency, and only to that amount, exchange in kind was still widely practiced by some barbarian peoples in regard to the necessities of life, at set equivalences, benefiting at one time the one, at another time the other, as chance would have it. Thus the *derivation of exchange from contributing one's share to the common pool of food* was the linchpin that held together a theory of the economy based on the postulate of self-sufficiency of the community and the distinction between natural and unnatural trade. But all this appeared so foreign to the marketing mind that translators took refuge in turning the text upside down, eventually losing their hold of the argument. Perhaps the most daring thesis of Aristotle, which up to this day must stagger the thinking mind by sheer force of originality, was in this manner reduced to a platitude that, had it carried any definite meaning at all, would have been rejected by him as a shallow view of the ultimate forces on which the human economy rested.

6

The Place of Economies in Societies

Few social scientists today accept in the whole the Enlightenment's ingenuous view of pristine man contracting for his freedoms and bartering his goods in bush and jungle to form his society and economy. The discoveries of Comte, Quetelet, Marx, Maine, Weber, Malinowski, Durkheim, and Freud figure predominantly in the accretion of our current knowledge that the social process is a tissue of relationships between man as biological entity and the unique structure of symbols and techniques that results in maintaining his existence. But while in this sense we have discovered the reality of society, the new knowledge has not produced a vision of society comparable in popularity to the traditional picture of an atomistic individualism. At important junctures we fall back on the earlier rationalizations of man as a utilitarian atom. And nowhere is this lapse more apparent than in our ideas concerning the economy. Approaching the economy in any of its widely varied aspects, the social scientist is still hampered by an intellectual heritage of man as an entity with an innate propensity to truck, barter, and exchange one thing for another. This remains so in spite of all the protestations against "economic man" and the intermittent attempts to provide a social framework for the economy.

FROM Chapter 12, "The Place of Economies in Societies," pp. 239–242, of Karl Polanyi, Conrad M. Arensberg, and Harry W. Pearson (eds.), *Trade and Market in the Early Empires.* Glencoe: The Free Press, 1957. Reprinted by permission of the publisher.

The economic rationalism to which we are heir posits a type of action as *sui generis* economic. In this perspective an actor—a single man, a family, a whole society—is seen facing a natural environment that is slow to yield its life-giving elements. Economic action—or, more precisely, economizing action, the essence of rationality—is, then, regarded as a manner of disposing of time and energy so that a maximum of goals are achieved out of this man-nature relationship. And the economy becomes the locus of such action. It is, of course, admitted that, in reality, the operation of this economy may be influenced in any number of ways by other factors of a non-economic character, be they political, military, artistic, or religious. But the essential core of utilitarian rationality remains as the model of the economy.

This view of the economy as the locus of units allocating, saving up, marketing surpluses, forming prices, grew out of the Western milieu of the eighteenth century and it is admittedly relevant under the institutional arrangements of a market system, since actual conditions here roughly satisfy the requirements set by the economistic postulate. But does this postulate allow us to infer the generality of a market system in the realm of empirical fact? The claim of formal economics to an historically universal applicability answers in the affirmative. In effect this argues the virtual presence of a market system in every society, whether such a system is empirically present or not. All human economy might then be regarded as a potential supply-demand-price mechanism, and the actual processes, whatever they are, explained in terms of this hypostatization.

If empirical research is ever to enhance our understanding of the basic operation and the position of various forms of the economy in different societies, we must put the test of relevance to this economistic postulate. Approaching the economic process from the vantage point of the new knowledge we have gained of the reality of society, we must say that there is no necessary relationship between economizing action and the empirical economy. The institutional structure of the economy need not compel, as with the market system, economizing actions. The implications of such an insight for all the social sciences which must deal with the economy could hardly be more far-reaching. Nothing less than a fundamentally different starting point for the analysis of the human economy as a social process is required.

In search for a new beginning, we turn from the economizing to the substantive meaning of the term "economic," unfashionable though it is. This is not to ignore the popular use of "economic," which compounds economizing with materiality: it is merely to urge the limited applicability of that common-sense compound. Unless a man has food to eat, he must starve, be he rational or not: but his safety, indeed his education, art, and religion also require material means, weapons, schools, temples of wood, stone, or steel. This fact was, of course, never overlooked. Time and again it was urged that economics should be based upon the whole range of man's material want-satisfaction—his material wants, on the one hand, the means of satisfying his wants, be these material or not, on the other.

As experts are unanimous to recognize, all strivings for such a naturalistic economics remained unsuccessful. The reason is simple. No merely naturalistic concept of the economy can even approximately compete with economic analysis in explaining the mechanics of livelihood under a market system. And since the economy in general was equated with the market system those naïve attempts to replace economic analysis by a naturalistic scheme stood justly discredited.

But was this a conclusive argument against the use of the substantive concept of the economy in the social sciences? By no means. It was overlooked that economic theory, economic analysis, or plain economics is only *one* of several disciplines that busy themselves with the livelihood of man from the material angle, that is, the economy.

118

Practically, it is no more than a study of market phenomena; apart from mere generalities its relevance to other than market systems, e.g., a planned economy, is negligible. What can it do, for instance, for the anthropologist to disentangle the economy from the general tissues of society under a kinship system? In the absence of markets and market prices, the economist cannot be of help to the student of primitive economies; indeed, he may hinder him. Or take the sociologist faced with the question of the changing place occupied by economies in societies as a whole. Unless we keep to times and regions where price-making markets are extant, economics cannot supply him with orientation of any value. This is even more true of the economic historian outside of that slim strip of a few centuries in which the price-making markets and consequently money as a means of exchange have become general. Prehistory, early history, and indeed, as Karl Bücher was the first to proclaim, the whole of history apart from those last centuries, had economies the organization of which differed from anything assumed by the economist. And the difference, we now begin to infer, can be reduced to one single point—they possessed no system of price-making markets. In the whole range of economic disciplines, the point of common interest is set by the process through which material want-satisfaction is provided. Locating this process and examining its operation can only be achieved by shifting the emphasis from a type of rational action to the configuration of goods and person movements, which actually make up the economy.

To shift in natural science from one conceptual framework to another is one thing; to do so in the social sciences is quite another. It is like rebuilding a house, foundation, walls, fittings and all, while continuing to live in it. We must rid ourselves of the ingrained notion that the economy is a field of experience of which human beings have necessarily always been conscious. To employ a metaphor, the facts of the economy were originally embedded in situations that were not in themselves of an economic nature, neither the ends nor the means being primarily material. The crystallization of the concept of the economy was a matter of time and history. But neither time nor history has provided us with those conceptual tools required to penetrate the maze of social relationships in which the economy was embedded. This is the task of what we will here call institutional analysis.

Karl Polanyi, Conrad M. Arensberg, and Harry W. Pearson

APPENDIX[1]

Here are some indications why it is essential to restrict the use of the term "economic" to reference to "provision for material want-satisfaction," and to employ the formal meaning of economic only if expressly required.

Our main interest connected with the study of general economic history is the question of the place of the economic system in society. Several issues of importance arise in this connection, and unless the meaning of the term economic employed is neutral in respect to these issues, we are in danger of prejudging them.

To the query as to the place of economic institutions in society the answer may be that such institutions have a separate and distinct existence, as under a market system, or, alternatively, that they are, as a rule, embedded in other, non-economic institutions, or something in between the two.

Now if we use the term economic to denote the gainful manner in which men behave in the market, then their behavior in regard to economic matters in primitive and ar-

[1] This appendix is compiled from unpublished memoranda Polanyi wrote in 1947 and distributed as mimeographed notes to his students in courses in economic history at Columbia University. The unpublished material is printed by permission of Ilona Polanyi and Kari Polanyi Levitt. Ed.

chaic economies must inevitably appear as some kind of marketing behavior. For example, Mueller-Lyer, the sociologist and author of *The History of Social Development* (1920), wrote on the subject of primitive economics: Commerce in many savage societies takes on the form of reciprocal exchange of guest-gifts. Business-like exchange is unknown. To this he added that "the guest-gift was a remnant of barter after the true meaning of it had been lost" (p. 161). This is a classical instance of forcing our preconceptions on the facts. The fact is the institution of guest-gifts: the market pattern is superimposed on the fact, by the simple device of assuming that the savages originally started with bartering, then continued to do so as a matter of habit, until they lost all recollection of their original practice. As a result, reciprocal gifts are made to appear as their opposite, namely, as barter [i.e., moneyless market exchanges].

Another example is from the field of economic analysis. The marketing definition of economic may lead to the result that *all* economic activity is regarded as barter and exchange. Archbishop Whately (1787–1863), a Victorian economist, suggested that economics should be called the science of exchange, or catallactics. This suggestion was taken up in our time by Joseph Schumpeter and Ludwig von Mises. Production may then usefully be construed as exchange of less preferable for more preferable uses of scarce means. Obviously for the economic historian such a translation of production into terms of exchange would be worse than useless, since it would make it impossible to discover to what extent the institution of the market was or was not in existence in any given society. We would see markets and exchange everywhere. This is precisely what happened to some of our most eminent economic historians.

Another aspect of this issue is that of the actual psychological motives on which the individual participates in economic institutions at various times and places. Again, the question is meaningless, unless the term economic is employed in a neutral fashion. If economic is made to mean "gainful," then, by definition, economic institutions are run on gainful motives. The question concerning the actual motives is answered beforehand, or, rather, does not arise.

Still another question refers to possible laws of development in regard to economic institutions. Is there anything in the nature of a law of economic progress? If so, how far does it consist in an increasing economic rationality, in the sense of efficiency? How far in an improved adjustment of economic institutions to non-economic institutions in society, under given technological conditions? A difficult question to which no simple approach is possible.

To sum up: The problem of the place of the economic system in society involves several important questions such as the separateness or the embeddedness of these institutions; the actual psychological motives on which individuals participate in running those institutions; or possible laws of progress in the evolution of economic institutions. Significant issues such as these are in danger of being prejudged, unless "economic" is taken simply to mean "referring to the provision of material means of want-satisfaction."

Views on the Place of the Economic System in Society from Montesquieu to Max Weber

To establish the study of general economic history on the foundations of adequate method, it is necessary to safeguard against the unconscious influence of definitions developed in the field of economic analysis.

It will be found useful, therefore, to give a bird's-eye view of the history of economics from Montesquieu and the Physiocrats to Marx, Menger, and Max Weber. We are taking here the term "economics" in the broadest sense, in which the study of economic institutions as well as that of the laws governing the price system are comprised, so that the distinction of economic history and economic theory is merged in the term.

This brief survey offers to assess how far the questions which we described above as important in the study of general economic history have been dealt with in the past.

We should fix our attention on two points: (1) How far does the assumption of a separate economic system in society underlie, and how far, on the contrary, is the view indicative of an approach to society as a whole of which the economic forms merely one aspect? (2) What assumptions in regard to actual psychological motives underlie the views of the authors? How far do they assume the existence of specifically economic motives?

We will list the chief thinkers according to our main viewpoint in roughly five chronologically overlapping groups:

(1) Original societal approach:
 Montesquieu (1748)
 François Quesnay (1758)
 Adam Smith (1776)
(2) Original economistic approach:
 Townsend (1786)
 Malthus (1798)
 Ricardo (1817)
(3) Return to societal approach:
 Carey (1837)
 List (1841)
 Marx (1859)
(4) Return to economistic approach:
 Menger (1871)
(5) Synthesis of (3) and (4):
 Max Weber (1905)

On the whole, the movement was swinging back and forth, from societal to economistic approach; from the meaning of economic as "provision for material goods" to that of "gainful pursuit" or "business-like attitude"; from the broad view which fixes on society as a whole to the narrower view which centers on the economic system as an institutionally separate and distinct sphere in society.

(1) The original starting point was societal: Montesquieu, Quesnay, and Adam Smith shared it. (2) With Malthus and Ricardo, political economy cuts loose from all dependence upon society as a whole. It is autonomous; it stands under laws of its own. (3) A world-wide reaction against the classics set it, the manifold directions of which were typified by Henry Carey, List, and Marx. This swing back to the societal approach was institutionalist and historicist. (Schmoller and his school in Germany, as well as Veblen and his even more important school in the United States, belong, of course, in this context.) (4) Early, however, in the Germany of Marx and Schmoller, the attack on the neo-societal school set in. The neo-classics represented a return to the economistic approach, in a logically extreme form. This movement, too, was world-wide. (5) About the turn of the century, Max Weber initiated a synthetic move of great importance to the economic historian by returning to the societal approach, this time with emphasis on the rationalistic aspect of economics proper. This represented a compromise between the societal and the economistic view, which proved fruitful. Max Weber, however, had formulated his views before the significant discoveries in the field of primitive economics were made and before the implications of his own inquiries into the origin of capitalism could be clearly discerned. Moreover, the course of history after his death tended to refute his dogmatic belief in the necessarily increasing dominance of "purposeful rationality" in the economic field.

Montesquieu (1748)

In modern language, Montesquieu's thesis was that the institutions of a society reflect the needs of that society in the given environment. Economic institutions also were formed according to their function in the framework of society as a whole. Montesquieu defined commerce "as the exportation and importation of merchandise with a view to the advantage of the State" (p. 348). "The constraint of the merchant," he wrote, "is not the constraint of commerce. It is in the freest countries that the merchant finds innumerable obstacles. The English constrain the merchant, but it is in favor of commerce." Montesquieu declared he would give up the use of money for the benefits of a planned economy as realized by the Jesuits in Paraguay. Many of his views reflected mercantilist theories and practices. It might, however, be inferred from this that some of these practices could not have been quite as "absurd" as W. Lippmann asserts in his *Good Society* (p. 10). If the Physiocrats are regarded as the founders of social science, Montesquieu was the precursor of the institutionalist school of that science. His approach was sociological, historical, anthropological, and institutional—in effect, it comprised the traits of the modern approach.

François Quesnay (1758)

The Physiocrats widened Montesquieu's societal approach in regard to economic life. But while his inspiration had been the unity of society as expressed in the organic concept of the Middle Ages, Quesnay's organic conception was essentially biological. He started life as a "vet" and his *Essai physique sur l'économie animale* (1736) was a physiology reflecting mainly two ideas: Harvey's discovery of the circulation of the blood (1628) and his Hippocratic attitude to illness relying on the healing powers of nature. (In his physiology Quesnay had used the word economy in the sense of husbandry or householding of the animal body.) The twin ideas of natural circulation and of reliance on the healing powers of Nature were expressed in Quesnay's most original contribution to the social sciences, namely his *Tableau économique* (1758). Here for the first time human economy (or at least an approximation to it) was presented as a cyclical process. (K. Marx was greatly impressed by this achievement and followed in Quesnay's footsteps in his *Capital,* in attempting to outline a similar cycle in regard to capitalist economy.) Quesnay's *Tableau* showed the circulation of the *produit net* in the body social. The *produit net* was the alleged surplus that remained over from the year's crops after all advances and investments (including the profits of the tenant) had been subtracted. That Nature alone produced such a surplus was a basic tenet of the Physiocrats. Of course, this was false in whatever way we interpret it.

The science founded by the Physiocrats was the science of society, not that of economics. They were a sect based on social philosophical tenets, believers in the laws of Nature and the rule of Nature (or Physiocracy). They called themselves *économistes* because in their opinion the health of the community and the State rested on natural laws similar to those that regulate the household of the animal body. In spite of the *Tableau* their philosophy referred not so much to economic life as to the State and society as a whole.

The school of Gournay, the "intendant" to whom the slogan laissez faire has been traced, was distinct from that of the Physiocrats. The latter stood not only for "legal absolutism" and the maintenance of the feudal regime, but also for systematic and scientific "interventionalism." As a doctor who believes in the healing forces of Nature applies treatment in such a manner as to assist the work of Nature, the Physiocrats thought they had discovered the laws according to which Nature does her work in society, and believed that it was the task of the authorities to intervene in such a way as to remove the obstacles to, and support the working of, the forces of Nature.

This is the explanation of the three most important documents of Physiocracy. They represent a thoroughly modern idea. The documents were: (1) The *Tableau économique,*

(2) the *Maximes,* some twenty-five in number, published in the *Encyclopédie,* (3) the *Détails,* or periodical surveys, of a descriptive and statistical kind. The *Tableau* indicated the circulation of wealth in the body social, according to the *ordre naturel,* the *Maximes* laid down the principles of treatment or policy. The *Détails,* or surveys, should supply the factual or quantitative data, so that the policy could be applied scientifically. Manifestly, the method contained very valuable elements, but, unfortunately, the alleged science on which the policy was to be based, did not exist.

From the policy point of view the Physiocrats were one-sidedly agrarian. They objected to embargoes on the export of grain, which were maintained in order to keep wages low in the interest of the export trade. The Physiocrats insisted that the aim should be the *bon prix* for grain, which would keep the landlords in affluence (and, incidentally, provide the State with a single tax). The concept of the *bon prix* (a close relative of the just price) indicated how much removed they were from the view that the free market was the best judge of the right price. It is true that the Physiocrats also argued, in a vague way, that the interest of the individual and the interest of the community harmonized in the *ordre naturel.* This was the principle later taken up by Adam Smith. But the unit to which the self-regulation under the *ordre naturel* referred, was not the economic system, but human society as a whole.

Adam Smith (1776)

Adam Smith, not Quesnay, became the founder of political economy. This was due to important advances beyond his predecessor's position, especially to the more realistic methods of the Scotsman. But Adam Smith still ranges with the societal group of writers. His subject was the *wealth* of a society, its *material welfare.* To him, wealth is an aspect of national life, no more. Its special reference is to production, and accordingly his interest

127

centered on the increase of productive efficiency, depending on the skill of the laborer and the organization of labor. The division of labor in the workshop appeared to him as the paradigm of the division of labor in society. Thus he made his great discovery that division of labor can be applied to the extent to which markets are developed. It should be noted that both division of labor and market are dealt with here in institutional terms.

Adam Smith defined the problem of wealth sharply, both in regard to Nature and to society. In regard to Nature, he refused to follow in the footsteps of the Physiocrats who had put natural resources in the foreground. Adam Smith's first remarks exclude the consideration of natural resources, since these should be regarded as given. In respect to the condition of society, his attitude is the opposite. Whether the society is improving, declining, or stagnant is regarded by him as a distinction governing his treatment of the subject. Economic life is only an aspect of national life, and must therefore reflect the state of health or ill-health of national life. Even the question whether the government's policy is favorable to agriculture or to manufactures should be considered as vital, since such a policy depends upon general considerations of statecraft (not as we tend to think today, on economic considerations). Finally, the political exigencies of national safety and security are taken for granted, and upheld as, e.g., in regard to the Navigation Laws of 1649 and 1651.

Reference to the "hidden hand," which made the self-interest of the butcher and baker "serve me with a meal," have been exaggerated out of all proportion. Adam Smith wished to discourage the idea that the self-interest of the merchant naturally benefited the community. He demanded, e.g., that the British government should rule India, not the merchants of the East India Company, whose interests, he asserted, were contrary to those of the population, while the government's interests ran parallel to that interest (for instance, in terms of taxation). Self-interest is not yet differentiated into economic motives of employers and employed. All through, the approach is still institutional, historical, and societal.

Joseph Townsend (1786)

Classical economists, after Adam Smith, based their approach on the assumption of an institutionally separate economic sphere in society. To employ a physiological analogy: With the societal writers, economy was in the nature of assimilation and dissimilation, i.e., a function of the social organism as a whole. Now economy became something more definite, rather like the digestive organs of the body. The transition was to some extent gradual: Townsend merely grasped the autonomy of the labor market; Malthus was still held back by his conservative outlook and attachment to the traditional system of landholding from relinquishing the societal approach altogether. This was fully accomplished only by Ricardo.

Townsend was the immediate precursor of Malthus. His *Observations on the Poor Laws* were written only ten years after the publication of the *Wealth of Nations.* (Like Mandeville and Quesnay, he had a medical training.) He was much concerned about the effects of the Poor Laws, a survival from Elizabethan times. Parishes had been recently enjoined to provide employment for the able-bodied poor in the neighborhood, failing which outdoor relief could be administered according to Gilbert's Act, 1782. Townsend, like many others of his contemporaries, proposed that the Poor Laws should be abolished, and the poor compelled to search for work at whatever wages they could get. Poor Law relief, he argued, artificially raised the birth rate at the expense of others whose lives were shortened accordingly. There was, he insisted, a natural equilibrium between food supplies and population, if there was no "intervention" such as the Poor Laws.

129

His paradigm was taken from Robinson Crusoe's island, Juan Fernandez, off the coast of Chile. It was recorded that pirates, who infested the Spanish main, used the island as a station whence to provision themselves. Juan Fernandez, the discoverer of the island, had landed a pair of goats, which multiplied prodigiously. The Spanish government determined to destroy this pirates' nest, and landed a dog and a bitch on the same island. These also started to multiply lustily, since the dogs found ample food in the form of goats. After a time the goats had to take refuge in the rocky parts of the island until only the swiftest and sturdiest dogs were able to catch and kill them. Eventually, the increase of the dogs was checked, and a balance between the numbers of the goats and the dogs was reached. This condition of peace and order had been attained, without any intervention of a magistrate, Townsend proclaimed. The most powerful force of all, the dependence of all animals on food supplies for their survival, had achieved it. In the same fashion, he argued, the simple abolition of poor relief would automatically solve the problem of pauperism. Hunger could force the poor to work at any wages they could get, and their numbers would be regulated by the amount of food available. Townsend here pointedly referred to the economic motive, i.e., the motive which would, in the absence of Poor Laws, force everyone to participate in production, without any administrative compulsion.

Malthus (1798)

Malthus made Townsend's thoughts world-famous. He reacted sharply against his father's optimistic humanitarianism, and admiration for Godwin's *Political Justice* (1793). The humanitarians seemed to deny that poverty was unavoidable and that more than a good wish was needed to abolish pauperism. Townsend's theorem of the goats and the dogs reached Malthus by way of Condorcet. But why should food be always scarce in human society? Malthus made the answer explicit, which was implied in Townsend's story. There was a force in Nature, which had the effect of perpetuating *hunger,* namely *sex.* It would see to it that the number of human beings should always be such as to force upon the limits of food supplies. If more children were born than the supply of food could carry, the supernumerary had to be killed off by war and pestilence, vice and famine.

Now, the autonomy of the economic sphere was safeguarded by the sanction of Nature herself. Nothing that government can do, could alter these laws. The place of the economic system in society was worked out by the force, not of society and government, but of Nature herself.

Ricardo (1817)

Ricardo's main interest was in determining the laws according to which the various classes of the population shared in the national dividend. He combined the hunger and gain motives with the *profit motive* as a general incentive determining human behavior. The self-interest vaguely apostrophized by Adam Smith now differentiated into fear of starvation with the worker and hope of profit with the owner of capital. The market, which Adam Smith had brought in as the determinant of the extent to which division of labor was possible, was now developed into a supply-demand-price system, including labor and land. Society was now imbedded in the economic system, rather than vice versa. Social classes were defined by their market role, since they personified the supply-and-demand factor, respectively, in various markets, such as the market for labor, land, capital, professional services, and so on.

The place of the economic system in society was now defined by the "economic motives" of hunger and gain.

They accounted for the economic laws, like the iron law of wages, as well as the law of rent (in combination with the Malthusian law and the law of diminishing returns, another law of Nature). Both ideological and political endeavors to change the course of economic processes were futile. Society was ruled by the laws governing the market, and these, in their turn, were determined by Nature herself.

This theoretical shift in the place of the economic system in society was, of course, accompanied by a great development of actual markets, which did not yet exist to a similar extent in Adam Smith's time. Competitive markets, money economics, and profit motive together resulted in compulsion to reduce costs. This implied the application of the economic principle, as it began to be called. Townsend, Malthus, and Ricardo between them established the modern concept of a separate autonomous economic system, governed by economic motives, and subject to the economic principle of formal rationality [i.e., economizing].

Carey (1837)

Ricardian economics were attacked from all sides as abstract, dogmatic, deductive, removed from life and institutions, cosmopolitan and inhuman. The reaction was world-wide. Actually Ricardian economics fitted English conditions, and expressed English interests. The Industrial Revolution was an English event. Free trade advocates of the Ricardian school knew the advantages to England's superior manufacturing power.

Henry Carey formulated American protectionist needs. In doing so he appealed (a) to history, and (b) to the institutionalist argument. (a) His attempt to refute the Ricardian rent theory was based on factual historical sequence of land settlement. He argued that not the best soil was selected first since it was marshy and inaccessible. This has proved true not only of the United States—see Turner's work on the "Frontier"—but also in regard to ancient history. In England the Pilgrim's Way, which connects neolithic Stonehenge with Canterbury, runs along the slopes of the hills.

(b) Carey's arguments in regard to neighborhood development were sociological in character and anticipated Thunen's Law. It amounted to the argument that division of labor has to be qualified in respect to agricultural regions by the needs of urban centers, and that intensive agriculture depends upon the presence of farms.

Frederick List (1840)

Frederick List was much influenced by Henry Carey and applied Carey's method to his own country, Germany. In List's hands it produced the theorem of stages of development: the so-called relativity principle. The stages were (a) pastoral life, (b) agriculture, (c) agriculture united with manufactures, (d) final stage: agriculture, manufacture, plus commerce. "The economic task of the state is to bring into existence through legislative and administrative action the conditions required for the progress of the nation through these stages." Young countries needed protection, he argued, until they reached the stage of industrialization similar to that of the more advanced countries. List's arguments were based on social anthropology, economic history and the institutional aspects of societal affairs. He is looked on today as the specific precursor, if not the founder, of the German Historical School in economics.

Marx (1859)

The third writer of this group stands apart. Karl Marx's opposition to Ricardian economics was not societal in the name of a country, but of that of a class. Malthus and Ricardo had doomed the workers to perpetual destitution. Marx accepted the Ricardian analysis as valid. Consequently, his only alternative was to reject the whole institutional system of market economy. He asserted that industrial capitalism was a historical phenomenon which would disappear again as it had come. The argument was anthropological, institutional, and historical. It centered on a view of society as a whole. It was supplemented by a whole philosophy, which distinguished Marx sharply from writers like Carey or List who accepted the bourgeois order.

Marx emphatically ranks as a representative of the return to the societal approach. Yet at the same time he also involuntarily strengthened the economistic position. Having accepted Ricardian economics, he turned it into an argument against capitalist society. This was the meaning of *Das Kapital*. Capitalist society, Marx argued, was economic society, and therefore it was ruled by the laws governing the economic system, i.e., the laws of the market. Marx, however, failed to emphasize (to put it at the least) that such a state of affairs existed only in capitalist society. The discovery of the importance of the "economic" under a market economy induced him to overstress the influence of the economic factor generally, at all times and places. This proved a grave mistake. Although Marx himself insisted on the influence of non-economic factors in history, especially in early history, nevertheless Marxists made a veritable creed of the economic interpretation of history. This amounted to an assertion not only of the predominance of economic factors, but also of economic motives. This enormously strengthened the classics. The societal approach personified in Marx was sapped by the economistic element inherited from the classics.

Menger (1871)

Menger was the first economist to make a deliberate distinction between concern with material want-satisfaction, and a concern with allocation of scarce means. By relating the theory of choice or "formal economics" to allocation of material goods, the neo-classical school defined the sphere of *economic theory*. It was hence no more open to the criticism of relying on laws of Nature such as the Malthusian Law or the law of diminishing returns. A general theory of price was produced, and economic analysis gained a precision which was formerly lacking. Equilibrium formulae permitted the introduction of optimum theorems which made the "economic principle" supreme.

Gustav Schmoller published an unfavorable review of Menger's work. The Battle of Methods was joined, in which the societal approach of the German Historical School was subjected to attack by Menger.

Menger was essentially right against the Historical School, but he overstated his case. Consequently, the Battle of Methods tended to discredit neo-classical theories in Germany. However, a quarter of a century later, when neo-classical theory had been greatly advanced by English, French, Italian, and American contributions, it gained acceptance in Germany. The *Handwoerterbuch der Staatswissenschaften* as well as the *Grundriss der Sozialoekonomik* invited adherents of the "Austrian School" to contribute articles dealing with basic theoretical subjects. This was largely the result of Max Weber's intervention.

Max Weber (1905)

For him the societal approach was represented chiefly by Marxism, the economic one by Menger, Mises, and the other members of the neo-classical school. Marxist influence was not restricted to orthodox Marxism. It was reflected in the work of such non-Marxist scholars as Ferdinand Tönnies, Franz Oppenheimer, Werner Sombart, Carl Lamprecht, and Robert Michlses.

Max Weber was an economic liberal and a strong believer in the vitality of capitalist economy. Though no adherent of laissez faire, he was even further removed from any form of planned economy. So, the Marxian influence produced with him a paradoxical result; he accepted the primacy of the economic factor (at least, heuristically), but being convinced of the superiority of the market system, he became not so much a Marxist as a "marketist."

Weber consciously included *both* the substantive and the formal meaning in the definition of "economic" (in conformity with common usage). He asserted that "economic" meant provision for the means of material want-satisfaction, but also insisted that the intrinsically *"economic" behavior* was of "pure rationality" (*zweckrational*), the most typical form of which we encounter on the stock exchange. Owing to this ambiguity, Weber's terms proved a very useful instrument of inquiry into capitalist economy, in which the same conjunction of meanings prevails. However, outside of capitalism, the inclusion of pure rationality into the definition of "economic behavior" made that term unsuitable for general economic history.

Note Weber's definition of "economic goods": Bundle of utilities! The utilities themselves are defined as a bundle of strains and stresses, as, i.e., an aggregate of separate single physical effects. (Weber's example) "Not the *horse as such* is the point of reference in economic life but merely as separate and distinct services."

Yet, during the greater part of human history, the possession of a *horse* was coveted, *not* so much on account of the separate and distinct effects of pull and push, stress and strain, [i.e., services provided by the horse] but rather on account of the horse as such, conveying social distinctions, etc.

While economic theory must be able to determine the factors influencing the price of mechanical power, whether there is a horse attached to the power or not, economic history deals *inter alia* with the actual motives leading to the domestication of the horse, its role in prestige-economy, and so on. From this angle, measurement in "horse-power" would be of little use.

Weber also distinguishes between goods and services. "Useful services, when provided for us by *things,* will be briefly called "goods"; when provided by human beings "services." The human being is thus brought into formal analogy with things. Man is being treated as a service-rendering thing. Thus only can the term "useful services" be effectively detached from things and persons alike. Such a separation is necessary for the purposes of economic theory which employs the "useful services" as a unit; for only so can economic analysis be made to apply to *all* types of goods and their various relationships such as sub-stitutibility, complementarity, etc. Yet, from the viewpoint of economic *history,* this definition is useless. In the realm of economic institutions, the useful services of things and those rendered by human beings must be sharply distinguished. The first are attached to a dead object, the other to a live person, from the point of view of economic *institutions* they are therefore in an entirely different category. The question of actual motives, e.g., arises in a different way in regard to the production or the transfer of objects than in regard to the rendering of personal services. To equate the two under the heading of useful push and pull would be nonsensical. Motives for service are in a different category from motives for the transfer of goods. The one is essentially personal, the other essentially impersonal. To mix up these two groups of motives must confuse the institutional aspect of economic history.

Eventually, Max Weber, who fused the two meanings of "economic" for the sake of the common usage, found himself contradicting common usage on a vital point. The criterion of rationality assumes a person striking a choice between uses of scarce means, of which he disposes. Weber proceeds: "Disposal comprises disposal of one's labor power." This is inevitable, for how could otherwise a theory of the labor market be developed? Yet, it follows that the only economic activity of the worker is that of selling

137

his labor power, and, maybe, activities in his own domestic sphere.

Weber says: As a slave working under the lash of his master is no more than a tool and is not himself carrying on an "economic activity," neither is the factory worker in the factory engaged in "economic activity" (though he may be "economically active" in his own household!).

This is entirely logical. Since the worker has sold his labor power, which is now not his anymore, he is in the factory not choosing or disposing of any kinds of scarce means of his own. Consequently, it would be senseless to argue that he is "economically active" there. However, common usage is very different. To argue that the worker in the factory is *not* engaged in any kind of economic activity, is not only contrary to common usage, but sounds like a paradox of questionable taste. The exclusion of everyday activities of producers from the scope of economic activities, is utterly unacceptable to the student of economic institutions. That the only economic activity carried on in a mine or a factory should be that of the shareholder who sells his shares, is a useless proposition to the student of the institution of the mine or factory. Yet Weber's definition denies that even the manager carries on "economic activity" in the giant establishment, the operation of which he is directing, since he does not dispose of his own means.

From the point of view of economic history, Weber's attempt at a synthesis of societal and economistic approach is open to criticism. His inability to decide in favor of the substantive meaning of "economic" vitiated his endeavors to clarify the problems of general economic history.

7

The Economy as Instituted Process

Our main purpose in this chapter is to determine the meaning that can be attached with consistency to the term "economic" in all the social sciences.

The simple recognition from which all such attempts must start is the fact that in referring to human activities the term economic is a compound of two meanings that have independent roots. We will call them the substantive and the formal meaning.

The substantive meaning of economic derives from man's dependence for his living upon nature and his fellows. It refers to the interchange with his natural and social environment, insofar as this results in supplying him with the means of material want-satisfaction.

FROM Chapter 13, "The Economy as Instituted Process," pp. 243–270, of Karl Polanyi, Conrad M. Arensberg, and Harry W. Pearson (eds.), *Trade and Market in the Early Empires,* Glencoe: The Free Press, 1957. Reprinted by permission of the publisher. [Polanyi packed into this single chapter all the important conceptual categories he devised for analyzing non-market economies: the two meanings of "economic"; reciprocity, redistribution, and (market) exchange; forms of (external) trade, money uses, and markets; operational devices; etc. It is therefore a dense and difficult essay, and I have made editorial insertions more frequently than elsewhere. The Introduction to this volume was written at such length in order to clarify some of the important analytical concepts mentioned here. See, also, George Dalton, "Economic Theory and Primitive Society," *American Anthropologist,* February 1961; "Traditional Production in Primitive African Economies," *The Quarterly Journal of Economics,* August 1962; "Primitive Money," *American Anthropologist,* February 1965. Ed.]

139

The formal meaning of economic derives from the logical character of the means-ends relationship, as apparent in such words as "economical" or "economizing." It refers to a definite situation of choice, namely, that between the different uses of means induced by an insufficiency of those means. If we call the rules governing choice of means the logic of rational action, then we may denote this variant of logic, with an improvised term, as formal economics.

The two root meanings of economic, the substantive and the formal, have nothing in common. The latter derives from logic, the former from fact. The formal meaning implies a set of rules referring to choice between the alternative uses of insufficient means. The substantive meaning implies neither choice nor insufficiency of means; man's livelihood may or may not involve the necessity of choice and, if choice there be, it need not be induced by the limiting effect of a "scarcity" of the means; indeed, some of the most important physical and social conditions of livelihood such as the availability of air and water or a loving mother's devotion to her infant are not, as a rule, so limiting. The cogency that is in play in the one case and in the other differs as the power of syllogism differs from the force of gravitation. The laws of the one are those of the mind; the laws of the other are those of nature. The two meanings could not be further apart; semantically they lie in opposite directions of the compass.

It is our proposition that only the substantive meaning of economic is capable of yielding the concepts that are required by the social sciences for an investigation of all the empirical economies of the past and present. The general frame of reference that we endeavor to construct requires, therefore, treatment of the subject matter in substantive terms. The immediate obstacle in our path lies, as indicated, in that concept of economic in which the two meanings, the substantive and the formal, are naïvely compounded. Such a merger of meanings is, of course, unexceptionable as long as we remain conscious of its restrictive effects. But the current concept of economic fuses the "subsistence" and the "scarcity" meanings of economic without a sufficient awareness of the dangers to clear thinking inherent in that merger.

This combination of terms sprang from logically adventitious circumstances. The last two centuries produced in Western Europe and North America an organization of man's livelihood to which the rules of choice happened to be singularly applicable. This form of the economy consisted in a system of price-making markets. Since acts of exchange, as practiced under such a system, involve the participants in choices induced by an insufficiency of means, the system could be reduced to a pattern that lent itself to the application of methods based on the formal meaning of economic. As long as the economy was controlled by such a system, the formal and the substantive meanings would in practice coincide. Laymen accepted this compound concept as a matter of course; a Marshall, Pareto, or Durkheim equally adhered to it. Menger alone in his posthumous work criticized the term, but neither he nor Max Weber, nor Talcott Parsons after him, apprehended the significance of the distinction for sociological analysis. Indeed, there seemed to be no valid reason for distinguishing between two root meanings of a term which, as we said, were bound to coincide in practice [when applied to our own economy].

While it would have been, therefore, sheer pedantry to differentiate in common parlance between the two meanings of economic, their merging in one concept nevertheless proved a bane to a precise methodology in the social sciences. Economics naturally formed an exception, since under the market system its terms were bound to be fairly realistic. But the anthropologist, the sociologist, or the historian, each in his study of the place occupied by the economy in human society, was faced with a great variety of institutions other than markets, in which man's livelihood was embedded. Its problems could not be attacked with the

141

help of an analytical method devised for a special form of the economy, which was dependent upon the presence of specific market elements.[1]

This lays down the rough sequence of the argument.

We will begin with a closer examination of the concepts derived from the two meanings of economic, starting with the formal and thence proceeding to the substantive meaning. It should then prove possible to describe the empirical economies—whether primitive or archaic—according to the manner in which the economic process is instituted. The three institutions of trade, money, and market will provide a test case. They have previously been defined in formal terms only; thus any other than a marketing approach was barred. Their treatment in substantive terms should then bring us nearer to the desired universal frame of reference.

The Formal and the Substantive Meanings of "Economic"

Let us examine the formal concepts starting from the manner in which the logic of rational action produces formal economics, and the latter, in turn, gives rise to economic analysis.

Rational action is here defined as choice of means in relation to ends. Means are anything appropriate to serve the end, whether by virtue of the laws of nature or by virtue of the laws of the game. *Thus "rational" does not refer either to ends or to means, but rather to the relating of means to*

[1] The uncritical employment of the compound concept fostered what may well be called the "economistic fallacy." It consisted in an artificial identification of the economy with its market form. From Hume and Spencer to Frank H. Knight and Northrop, social thought suffered from this limitation wherever it touched on the economy. Lionel Robbins' essay, *The Nature and Significance of Economic Science* (1932), though useful to economists, fatefully distorted the problem. In the field of anthropology Melville Herskovits' recent work, *Economic Anthropology* (1952), represents a relapse after his pioneering effort of 1940, *The Economic Life of Primitive Peoples.*

ends. It is not assumed, for instance, that it is more rational to wish to live than to wish to die, or that, in the first case, it is more rational to seek a long life through the means of science than through those of superstition. For whatever the end, it is rational to choose one's means accordingly; and as to the means, it would not be rational to act upon any other test than that which one happens to believe in. Thus it is rational for the suicide to select means that will accomplish his death; and if he be an adept of black magic, to pay a witch doctor to contrive that end.

The logic of rational action applies, then, to all conceivable means and ends covering an almost infinite variety of human interests. In chess or technology, in religious life or philosophy ends may range from commonplace issues to the most recondite and complex ones. Similarly, in the field of the economy, where ends may range from the momentary assuaging of thirst to the attaining of a sturdy old age, while the corresponding means comprise a glass of water and a combined reliance on filial solicitude and open-air life, respectively.

Assuming that the choice is induced by an insufficiency of the means, the logic of rational action turns into that variant of the theory of choice which we have called formal economics. It is still logically unrelated to the concept of the human economy, but it is closer to it by one step. Formal economics refers, as we said, to a situation of choice that arises out of an insufficiency of means. This is the so-called scarcity postulate. It requires, first, insufficiency of means; second, that choice be induced by that insufficiency. Insufficiency of means in relation to ends is determined with the help of the simple operation of "earmarking," which demonstrates whether there is or is not enough to go round. For the insufficiency to induce choice there must be given more than one use to the means, as well as graded ends, i.e., at least two ends ordered in sequence of preference. Both conditions are factual. It is irrelevant whether the reason for which means can be used in one way only happens to be conventional or technological; the same is true of the grading of ends.

Having thus defined choice, insufficiency and scarcity in operational terms, it is easy to see that as there is choice of means without insufficiency, so there is insufficiency of means without choice. Choice may be induced by a preference for right against wrong (moral choice) or, at a crossroads, where two or more paths happen to lead to our destination, possessing identical advantages and disadvantages (operationally induced choice). In either case an abundance of means, far from diminishing the difficulties of choice, would rather increase them. Of course, scarcity may or may not be present in almost all fields of rational action. Not all philosophy is sheer imaginative creativity, it may also be a matter of economizing with assumptions. Or, to get back to the sphere of man's livelihood, in some civilizations scarcity situations seem to be almost exceptional, in others they appear to be painfully general. In either case the presence or absence of scarcity is a question of fact, whether the insufficiency is due to Nature or to Law.

Last but not least, economic analysis. This discipline results from the application of formal economics to an economy of a definite type, namely, a market system. The economy is here embodied in institutions that cause individual choices to give rise to interdependent movements that constitute the economic process. This is achieved by generalizing the use of price-making markets. All goods and services, including the use of labor, land, and capital are available for purchase in markets and have, therefore, a price; all forms of income derive from the sale of goods and services—wages, rent, and interest, respectively, appearing only as different instances of price according to the items sold. The general introduction of purchasing power as the means of acquisition converts the process of meeting requirements into an allocation of insufficient means with alternative uses, namely, money. It follows that both the conditions of choice and its consequences are quantifiable in the form of prices. It can be asserted that by concentrating on price as the economic fact par excellence, the formal method of approach offers a total description of the economy as determined by choices induced by an insufficiency of means. The conceptual tools by which this is performed make up the discipline of economic analysis.

From this follow the limits within which economic analysis can prove effective as a method. The use of the formal meaning denotes the economy as a sequence of acts of economizing, i.e., of choices induced by scarcity situations. While the rules governing such acts are universal, the extent to which the rules are *applicable* to a definite economy depends upon whether or not that economy is, in actual fact, a sequence of such acts. To produce quantitative results, the locational and appropriational movements, of which the economic process consists, must here present themselves as functions of social actions in regard to insufficient means and oriented on resulting prices. Such a situation obtains only under a market system.

The relation between formal economics and the human economy is, in effect, contingent. Outside of a system of price-making markets economic analysis loses most of its relevance as a method of inquiry into the working of the economy. A centrally planned economy, relying on nonmarket prices is a well-known instance.

The fount of the substantive concept is the empirical economy. It can be briefly (if not engagingly) defined as an instituted process of interaction between man and his environment, which results in a continuous supply of want-satisfying material means. Want-satisfaction is "material," if it involves the use of material means to satisfy ends; in the case of a definite type of physiological wants, such as food or shelter, this includes the use of so-called services only.

145

The economy, then, is an instituted process. Two concepts stand out, that of "process" and its "institutedness." Let us see what they contribute to our frame of reference.

Process suggests analysis in terms of motion. The movements refer either to changes in location or in appropriation or both. In other words, the material elements may alter their position either by changing place or by changing "hands"; again, these otherwise very different shifts of position may go together or not. Between them, these two kinds of movements may be said to exhaust the possibilities comprised in the economic process as a natural and social phenomenon.

Locational movements include production, alongside of transportation, to which the spatial shifting of objects is equally essential. Goods are of a lower order or of a higher order, according to the manner of their usefulness from the consumer's point of view. This famous "order of goods" sets consumers' goods against producers' goods, according to whether they satisfy wants directly, or only indirectly, through a combination with other goods. This type of movement of the elements represents an essential of the economy in the substantive sense of the term, namely, production.

The appropriative movement governs both what is usually referred to as the circulation of goods and their administration. In the first case, the appropriative movement results from transactions, in the second case, from dispositions. Accordingly, a transaction is an appropriative movement as between hands; a disposition is a one-sided act of the hand, to which by force of custom or of law definite appropriative effects are attached. The term "hand" here serves to denote public bodies and offices as well as private persons or firms, the difference between them being mainly a matter of internal organization. It should be noted, however, that in the nineteenth century private hands were commonly associated with transactions, while public hands were usually credited with dispositions.

146

In this choice of terms a number of further definitions are implied. Social activities, insofar as they form part of the process, may be called economic; institutions are so called to the extent to which they contain a concentration of such activities; any components of the process may be regarded as economic elements. These elements can be conveniently grouped as ecological, technological, or societal according to whether they belong primarily to the natural environment, the mechanical equipment, or the human setting. Thus a series of concepts, old and new, accrue to our frame of reference by virtue of the process aspect of the economy.

Nevertheless, reduced to a mechanical, biological, and psychological interaction of elements, that economic process would possess no all-round reality. It contains no more than the bare bones of the processes of production and transportation, as well as of the appropriative changes. In the absence of any indication of societal conditions from which the motives of the individuals spring, there would be little, if anything, to sustain the interdependence of the movements and their recurrence on which the unity and the stability of the process depends. The interacting elements of nature and humanity would form no coherent unit, in effect, no structural entity that could be said to have a function in society or to possess a history. The process would lack the very qualities that cause everyday thought as well as scholarship to turn toward matters of human livelihood as a field of eminent practical interest as well as theoretical and moral dignity.

Hence the transcending importance of the institutional aspect of the economy. What occurs on the process level between man and soil in hoeing a plot or what on the conveyor belt in the constructing of an automobile is, prima facie a mere jigsawing of human and non-human movements. From the institutional point of view it is a mere referent of terms like labor and capital, craft and union, slacking and speeding, the spreading of risks and the other

147

semantic units of the social context. The choice between capitalism and socialism, for instance, refers to two different ways of instituting modern technology in the process of production. On the policy level, again, the industrialization of underdeveloped countries involves, on the one hand, alternative techniques; on the other, alternative methods of instituting them. Our conceptual distinction is vital for any understanding of the interdependence of technology and institutions as well as their relative independence.

The instituting of the economic process vests that process with unity and stability; it produces a structure with a definite function in society; it shifts the place of the process in society, thus adding significance to its history; it centers interest on values, motives and policy. Unity and stability, structure and function, history and policy spell out operationally the content of our assertion that the human economy is an instituted process.

The human economy, then, is embedded and enmeshed in institutions, economic and non-economic. The inclusion of the non-economic is vital. For religion or government may be as important for the structure and functioning of the economy as monetary institutions or the availability of tools and machines themselves that lighten the toil of labor.

The study of the shifting place occupied by the economy in society is therefore no other than the study of the manner in which the economic process is instituted at different times and places.

This requires a special tool box.

Reciprocity, Redistribution, and [Market] Exchange[2]

A study of how empirical economies are instituted should start from the way in which the economy acquires unity and stability, that is the interdependence and recurrence of

[2] [Throughout, Polanyi means by "exchange," market exchange. Ed.]

148

its parts. This is achieved through a combination of a very few patterns, which may be called forms of integration. Since they occur side by side on different levels and in different sectors of the economy it may often be impossible to select one of them as dominant so that they could be employed for a classification of empirical economies as a whole. Yet by differentiating between sectors and levels of the economy those forms offer a means of describing the economic process in comparatively simple terms, thereby introducing a measure of order into its endless variations.

Empirically, we find the main patterns to be reciprocity, redistribution, and exchange. Reciprocity denotes movements between correlative points of symmetrical groupings; redistribution designates appropriational movements toward a center and out of it again; exchange refers here to vice versa movements taking place as between "hands" under a market system. Reciprocity, then, assumes for a background symmetrically arranged groupings; redistribution is dependent upon the presence of some measure of centricity in the group; exchange in order to produce integration requires a system of price-making markets. It is apparent that the different patterns of integration assume definite institutional supports.

At this point some clarification may be welcome. The terms reciprocity, redistribution, and exchange, by which we refer to our forms of integration, are often employed to denote personal interrelations. Superficially, then, it might seem as if the forms of integration merely reflected aggregates of the respective forms of individual behavior: If mutuality between individuals were frequent, a reciprocative integration would emerge; where sharing among individuals was common, redistributive integration would be present; similarly, frequent acts of barter between individuals would result in exchange as a form of integration. If this were so, our patterns of integration would be indeed no more than simple aggregates of corresponding forms of behavior on the personal level. To be sure, we insisted that the integrative effect was conditioned by the presence of definite institutional arrangements, such as symmetrical organizations, central points, and market systems, respectively. But such arrangements seem to represent a mere aggregate of the same personal patterns the eventual effects of which they are supposed to condition.

The significant fact is that mere aggregates of the personal behaviors in question do not by themselves produce such structures. Reciprocity behavior between individuals integrates the economy only if symmetrically organized structures, such as a symmetrical system of kinship groups, are given. *But a kinship system never arises as the result of mere reciprocating behavior on the personal level.* Similarly, in regard to redistribution. It presupposes the presence of an allocative center in the community, yet the organization and validation of such a center does not come about merely as a consequence of frequent acts of sharing as between individuals. Finally, the same is true of the market system. Acts of exchange on the personal level produce prices only if they occur under a system of price-making markets, an institutional setup which is nowhere created by mere random acts of exchange.

We do not wish to imply, of course, that those supporting patterns are the outcome of some mysterious forces acting outside the range of personal or individual behavior. We merely insist that if, in any given case, the societal effects of individual behavior depend on the presence of definite institutional conditions, these conditions do not for that reason result from the personal behavior in question. Superficially, the supporting pattern may *seem* to result from a cumulation of a corresponding kind of personal behavior, but the vital elements of organization and validation are necessarily contributed by an altogether different type of behavior.

The first writer to our knowledge to have hit upon the factual connection between reciprocative behavior on the interpersonal level, on the one hand, and given symmetrical groupings, on the other, was the anthropologist Richard Thurnwald, in 1915, in an empirical study on the marriage system of the Bánaro of New Guinea. Bronislaw Malinowski, some ten years later, referring to Thurnwald, predicted that socially relevant reciprocation would regularly be found to rest on symmetrical forms of basic social organization. His own description of the Trobriand kinship system as well as of the Kula trade bore out the point. This lead was followed up by this writer, in regarding symmetry as merely *one* of several supporting patterns. He then added redistribution and exchange to reciprocity, as further forms of integration; similarly, he added centricity and market to symmetry, as other instances of institutional support. Hence our forms of integration and supporting structure patterns.

This should help to explain why in the economic sphere interpersonal behavior so often fails to have the expected societal effects in the absence of definite institutional preconditions. Only in a symmetrically organized environment will reciprocative behavior result in economic institutions of any importance; only where allocative centers have been set up can individual acts of sharing produce a redistributive economy; and only in the presence of a system of price-making markets will exchange acts of individuals result in fluctuating prices that integrate the economy. Otherwise such acts of barter will remain ineffective and therefore tend not to occur. Should they nevertheless happen, in a random fashion, a violent emotional reaction would set in, as against acts of indecency or acts of treason, since trading behavior is never emotionally indifferent behavior and is not, therefore, tolerated by opinion outside of the approved channels.

Let us now return to our forms of integration.

A group that deliberately undertook to organize its economic relationships on a reciprocative footing would, to effect its purpose, have to split up into sub-groups the corresponding members of which could identify one another as such. Members of Group A would then be able to establish relationships of reciprocity with their counterparts in Group B and vice versa. But symmetry is not restricted to duality. Three, four, or more groups may be symmetrical in regard to two or more axes; also members of the groups need not reciprocate with one another but may do so with the corresponding members of a third group toward which they stand in analogous relations. A Trobriand man's responsibility is toward his sister's family. But he himself is not on that account assisted by his sister's husband, but, if he is married, by his own wife's brother—a member of a third, correspondingly placed family.

Aristotle taught that to every kind of community (*koinōnia*) there corresponded a kind of good will (*philia*) amongst its members, which expressed itself in reciprocity (*antipeponthos*). This was true both of the more permanent communities such as families, tribes, or city states as of those less permanent ones that may be comprised in, and subordinate to, the former. In our terms this implies a tendency in the larger communities to develop a multiple symmetry in regard to which reciprocative behavior may develop in the subordinate communities. The closer the members of the encompassing community feel drawn to one another, the more general will be the tendency among them to develop reciprocative attitudes in regard to specific relationships limited in space, time, or otherwise. Kinship, neighborhood, or totem belong to the more permanent and comprehensive groupings; within their compass voluntary and semi-voluntary associations of a military, vocational, religious, or social character create situations in which, at least transitorily or in regard to a given locality or a typical situation, there would form symmetrical groupings the members of which practice some sort of mutuality.

Reciprocity as a form of integration gains greatly in power through its capacity of employing both redistribution and exchange as subordinate methods.[3] Reciprocity may be attained through a sharing of the burden of labor according to definite rules of redistribution as when taking things "in turn." Similarly, reciprocity is sometimes attained through exchange at set equivalencies for the benefit of the partner who happens to be short of some kind of necessities—a fundamental institution in ancient Oriental societies. In non-market economies these two forms of integration —reciprocity and redistribution—occur in effect usually together.

Redistribution obtains within a group to the extent to which the allocation of goods is collected in one hand and takes place by virtue of custom, law, or *ad hoc* central decision. Sometimes it amounts to a physical collecting accompanied by storage-cum-redistribution, at other times the "collecting" is not physical, but merely appropriational, i.e., rights of disposal in the physical location of the goods. Redistribution occurs for many reasons, on all civilizational levels, from the primitive hunting tribe to the vast storage systems of ancient Egypt, Sumeria, Babylonia, or Peru. In large countries differences of soil and climate may make redistribution necessary; in other cases it is caused by discrepancy in point of time, as between harvest and consumption. With a hunt, any other method of distribution would lead to disintegration of the horde, or band, since only "division of labor" can here ensure results; a redistribution of purchasing power may be valued for its own sake, i.e., for the purposes demanded by social ideals as in the modern welfare state. The principle remains the same—collecting into, and distributing from, a center. Re-

---

[3] [I add italics to emphasize that Polanyi was quite clear in regarding reciprocity, redistribution, and (market) exchange as modes of transaction, not as designations for entire economies or economic systems. Ed.]

distribution may also apply to a group smaller than society, such as the household or manor irrespective of the way in which the economy as a whole is integrated. The best-known instances are the Central African *kraal,* the Hebrew patriarchal household, the Greek estate of Aristotle's time, the Roman *familia,* the medieval manor, or the typical large peasant household before the general marketing of grain. Only under a comparatively advanced form of agricultural society, however, is householding practicable, and then, fairly general. Before that, the widely spread "small family" is not economically instituted, except for some cooking of food; the use of pasture, land, or cattle is still dominated by redistributive or reciprocative methods on a wider than family scale.

Redistribution, too, is apt to integrate groups at all levels and all degrees of permanence from the state itself to units of a transitory character. Here, again, as with reciprocity, the more closely knit the encompassing unit, the more varied will the subdivisions be in which redistribution can effectively operate. Plato taught that the number of citizens in the state should be 5040. This figure was divisible in 59 different ways, including division by the first ten numerals. For the assessment of taxes, the forming of groups for business transactions, the carrying of military and other burdens "in turn," etc., it would allow the widest scope, he explained.

Exchange in order to serve as a form of integration requires the support of a system of price-making markets. Three kinds of exchange should therefore be distinguished: The merely locational movement of a "changing of places" between the hands (operational exchange); the appropriational movements of exchange, either at a set rate (decisional exchange) or at a bargained rate (integrative exchange). Insofar as exchange at a set rate is in question, the economy is integrated by the factors, which fix that rate, not by the market mechanism. Even price-making markets are integrative only if they are linked up in a system that tends to spread the effect of prices to markets other than those directly affected.

Higgling-haggling has been rightly recognized as being of the essence of bargaining behavior. In order for exchange to be integrative the behavior of the partners must be oriented on producing a price that is as favorable to each partner as he can make it. Such a behavior contrasts sharply with that of exchange at a set price. The ambiguity of the term "gain" tends to cover up the difference. Exchange at set prices involves no more than the gain to either party implied in the decision of exchanging; exchange at fluctuating prices aims at a gain that can be attained only by an attitude involving a distinctive antagonistic relationship between the partners. The element of antagonism, however diluted, that accompanies this variant of exchange is ineradicable. No community intent on protecting the fount of solidarity between its members can allow latent hostility to develop around a matter as vital to physical existence and, therefore, capable of arousing as tense anxieties as food. Hence the universal banning of transactions of a gainful nature in regard to food and foodstuffs in primitive and archaic society. The very widely spread ban on higgling-haggling over victuals automatically removes price-making markets from the realm of early institutions.

Traditional groupings of economies, which roughly approximate a classification according to the dominant forms of integration, are illuminating. What historians are wont to call "economic systems" seem to fall fairly into this pattern. *Dominance of a form of integration is here identified with the degree to which it comprises land and labor in society*. So-called savage society, is characterized by the integration of land and labor into the economy by way of the ties of kinship. In feudal society the ties of fealty determine the fate of land and the labor that goes with it. In the floodwater empires land was largely distributed and sometimes redistributed by temple or palace, and so was labor, at least in its dependent form. *The rise of the market to a ruling force in the economy can be traced by noting the extent to which land and food were mobilized through [market] exchange, and labor was turned into a commodity free to be purchased in the market.* This may help to explain the relevance of the historically untenable stages theory of slavery, serfdom, and wage labor that is traditional with Marxism—a grouping, which flowed from the conviction that the character of the economy was set by the status of labor. The integration of the soil into the economy, however, should be regarded as hardly less vital.

In any case, forms of integration do not represent "stages" of development. No sequence in time is implied. Several subordinate forms may be present alongside of the dominant one, which may itself recur after a temporary eclipse. Tribal societies practice reciprocity and redistribution, while archaic societies are predominantly redistributive, though to some extent they may allow room for exchange. Reciprocity, which plays a dominant part in some Melanesian communities, occurs as a not-unimportant although subordinate trait in the redistributive archaic empires, where foreign trade (carried on by gift and countergift) is still largely organized on the principle of reciprocity. Indeed, during a war emergency it was reintroduced on a large-scale in the twentieth century, under the name of lend-lease, with societies where otherwise marketing and exchange were dominant. Redistribution, the ruling method in tribal and archaic society beside which exchange plays only a minor part, grew to great importance in the later Roman Empire and is actually gaining ground today in some modern industrial states. The Soviet Union is an extreme instance. Conversely, more than once before in the course of human history markets have played a part in the economy, although never on a territorial scale, or with an institutional comprehensiveness comparable to that of the nineteenth century. However, here again a change is noticeable. In our century, with the lapse of the gold standard, a recession of the world role of markets from their nineteenth-century peak set in—a turn of the trend which, incidentally, takes us back to our starting point, namely, the increasing inadequacy of our limited marketing definitions for the purposes of the social scientist's study of the economic field.

Forms of [External] Trade,[4] Money Uses, and Market Elements

The restrictive influence of the marketing approach on the interpretation of trade and money institutions is incisive: inevitably, the market appears as the locus of exchange, trade is the actual exchange, and money as the means of exchange. Since trade is directed by prices and prices are a function of the market, all trade is market trade, just as all money is exchange money. The market is the generating institution of which trade and money are the functions.

Such notions are not true to the facts of anthropology and history. Trade, as well as some money uses, are as old as mankind; although meetings of an economic character may have existed as early as the neolithic, markets did not gain importance until comparatively late in history. Price-making markets, which alone are constitutive of a market system, were to all accounts non-existent before the first millennium of antiquity, and then only to be eclipsed by other forms of integration. Not even these main facts, however, could be uncovered as long as trade and money were thought to be limited to the exchange form of integration, as its specifically economic form. The long periods of history when reciprocity and redistribution integrated the economy, and the considerable ranges within which, even in modern times, they continued to do so, were put out of bounds by a restrictive terminology.

[4] [Almost invariably, Polanyi means by "trade," foreign or external trade. Ed.]

Viewed as an exchange system, or, in brief, catallactically,[5] trade, money and market form an indivisible whole. Their common conceptual framework is the market. Trade appears as a two-way movement of goods through the market, and money as quantifiable goods used for indirect exchange in order to facilitate that movement. Such an approach must induce a more or less tacit acceptance of the heuristic principle according to which, where trade is in evidence, markets should be assumed, and where money is in evidence trade, and therefore markets, should be assumed. Naturally, this leads to seeing markets where there are none and ignoring trade and money where they are present, because markets happen to be absent. The cumulative effect must be to create a stereotype of the economies of less familiar times and places, something in the way of an artificial landscape with only little or no resemblance to the original.

A separate analysis of trade, money, and markets is therefore in order.

1. Forms of Trade

From the substantive point of view, trade is a relatively peaceful method of acquiring goods which are not available on the spot. It is external to the group, similar to activities that we are used to associating with hunts, slaving expeditions, or piratic raids. In either case the point is acquisition and carrying of goods from a distance. What distinguishes trade from the questing for game, booty, plunder, rare woods, or exotic animals, is the two-sidedness of the movement, which also ensures its broadly peaceful and fairly regular character.

[5] [Polanyi means by "catallactic," pertaining to market exchange. Throughout this essay I have substituted the words "market" or "formal economics," or "market economics," for "catallactic." Ed.]

From the market viewpoint, [all] trade is the movement of goods on their way through the market. All commodities—goods produced for sale—are potential objects of trade; one commodity is moving in one direction, the other in the opposite direction; the movement is controlled by prices: trade and market are co-terminous. All trade is market trade.

Again, like hunt, raid, or expedition under native conditions, [external] trade is not so much an individual as a group activity, in this respect closely akin to the organization of wooing and mating, which is often concerned with the acquisition of wives from a distance by more or less peaceful means. Trade thus centers in the meeting of different communities, one of its purposes being the exchange of goods. Such meetings do not, like price-making markets, produce rates of exchange, but on the contrary they rather presuppose such rates. Neither the persons of individual traders nor motives of individual gain are involved. Whether a chief or king is acting for the community after having collected the "export" goods from its members, or whether the group meets bodily their counterparts on the beach for the purpose of exchange—in either case the proceedings are essentially collective. Exchange between "partners in trade" is frequent, but so is, of course, partnership in wooing and mating. Individual and collective activities are intertwined.

Emphasis on "acquisition of goods from a distance" as a constitutive element in trade should bring out the dominant role played by the import interest in the early history of trade. In the nineteenth century export interests loomed large—a typical market phenomenon.

Since something must be carried over a distance and that in two opposite directions, trade, in the nature of things, has a number of constituents such as personnel, goods, carrying, and two-sidedness, each of which can be broken down according to sociologically or technologically significant criteria. In following up those four factors we may

159

hope to learn something about the changing place of trade in society.

First, the persons engaged in trade.

"Acquisition of goods from a distance" may be practiced either from motives attaching to the trader's standing in society and, as a rule, comprising elements of duty or public service (status motive); or it may be done for the sake of the material gain accruing to him personally from the buying and selling transaction in hand (profit motive).

In spite of many possible combinations of those incentives, honor and duty on the one hand, profit on the other, stand out as sharply distinct primary motivations. If the "status motive," as is quite often the case, is reinforced by material benefits, the latter do not as a rule take the form of gain made on exchange, but rather of treasure or endowment with landed revenue bestowed on the trader by king or temple or lord, by way of recompense. Things being what they are, gains made on exchange do not usually add up to more than paltry sums that bear no comparison with the wealth bestowed by his lord upon the resourceful and successfully venturing trader. Thus he who trades for the sake of duty and honor grows rich, while he who trades for filthy lucre remains poor—an added reason why gainful motives are under a shadow in archaic society.

Another way of approaching the question of personnel is from the angle of the standard of life deemed appropriate to their status by the community to which they belong.

Archaic society in general knows, as a rule, no other figure of a trader than that which belongs either to the top or to the bottom rung of the social ladder. The first is connected with rulership and government, as required by the political and military conditions of trading, the other depends for his livelihood on the coarse labor of carrying. This fact is of great importance for the understanding of the organization of trade in ancient times. There can be no middle-class trader, at least among the citizenry. Apart from the Far East, which we must disregard here, only three significant instances of a broad commercial middle class in premodern times are on record: the Hellenistic merchant of largely metic [resident alien] ancestry in the eastern Mediterranean city-states; the ubiquitous Islamitic merchant who grafted Hellenistic maritime traditions on to the ways of the bazaar; lastly, the descendants of Pirenne's "floating scum" in Western Europe, a sort of continental metic of the second third of the Middle Ages. The classical Greek middle class preconized by Aristotle was a landed class, not a commercial class at all.

A third manner of approach is more closely historical. The trader types of antiquity were the *tamkarum*, the metic, or resident alien, and the "foreigner."

The *tamkarum* dominated the Mesopotamian scene from the Sumerian beginnings to the rise of Islam, i.e., over some 3000 years. Egypt, China, India, Palestine, pre-conquest Mesoamerica, or native West Africa knew no other type of trader. The *metic* became first historically conspicuous in Athens and some other Greek cities as a lower-class merchant, and rose with Hellenism to become the prototype of a Greek-speaking or Levantine commercial middle class from the Indus Valley to the Pillars of Hercules. The *foreigner* is, of course, ubiquitous. He carries on trade with foreign crews and in foreign ships; he neither "belongs" to the community, nor enjoys the semi-status of resident alien, but is a member of an altogether different community.

A fourth distinction is anthropological. It provides the key to that peculiar figure, the trading foreigner. Although the number of "trading peoples" to which these "foreigners" belonged was comparatively small, they accounted for the widely spread institution of "passive trade." Amongst themselves, trading peoples differed again in an important respect: trading peoples proper, as we may call them, were exclusively dependent for their subsistence on trade in which, directly or indirectly, the whole population was engaged, as with the Phoenicians, the Rhodians, the inhabitants of Gades (the modern Cadix), or at some periods Armenians and Jews; in the case of others—a more numerous group—trade was only *one* of the occupations in which from time to time a considerable part of the population engaged, traveling abroad, sometimes with their families, over shorter or longer periods. The Hausa and the Mandingo in the Western Sudan are instances. The latter are also known as Duala, but, as recently turned out, only when trading abroad. Formerly they were taken to be a separate people by those whom they visited when trading.

Second, the organization of trade in early times must differ according to the goods carried, the distance to be traveled, the obstacles to be overcome by the carriers, the political and the ecological conditions of the venture. For this, if for no other reason, all trade is originally specific [i.e., expeditions to acquire specific items]. The goods and their carriage make it so. There can be, under these conditions, no such thing as trading "in general."

Unless full weight is given to this fact, no understanding of the early development of trading institutions is possible. The decision to acquire some kinds of goods from a definite distance and place of origin will be taken under circumstances different from those under which other kinds of goods would have to be acquired from somewhere else. Trading ventures are, for this reason, a discontinuous affair. They are restricted to concrete undertakings, which are liquidated one by one and do not tend to develop into a continuous enterprise. The Roman *societas,* like the later *commenda,* was a trade partnership limited to one undertaking. Only the *societas publicanorum,* for tax farming and contracting, was incorporated—it was the one great exception. Not before modern times were permanent trade associations known.

The specificity of trade is enhanced in the natural course of things by the necessity of acquiring the imported goods with exported ones. For under non-market conditions imports and exports tend to fall under different regimes. The process through which goods are collected for export is mostly separate from, and relatively independent of, that by which the imported goods are repartitioned. The first may be a matter of tribute or taxation or feudal gifts or under whatever other designation the goods flow to the center, while the repartitioned imports may cascade along different lines. Hammurabi's "Seisachtheia" appears to make an exception of *simu* goods, which may have sometimes been imports passed on by the king via the *tamkarum* to such tenants who wished to exchange them for their own produce. Some of the pre-conquest long-distance trading of the *pochteca* of the Aztec of Mesoamerica appears to carry similar features.

What nature made distinct, the market makes homogeneous. Even the difference between goods and their transportation may be obliterated, since in the market both can be bought and sold—the one in the commodity market, the other in the freight and insurance market. In either case there is supply and demand, and prices are formed in the same fashion. Carrying and goods, these constituents of trade, acquire a common denominator in terms of cost. Preoccupation with the market and its artificial homogeneity thus makes for good economic theory rather than for good economic history. Eventually, we will find that trade routes, too, as well as means of transportation may be of no less incisive importance for the institutional forms of trade than the types of goods carried. For in all these cases the geographical and technological conditions interpenetrate with the social structure.

According to the rationale of two-sidedness we meet with three main types of trade: gift trade, administered trade, and market trade.

Gift trade links the partners in relationships of reciprocity, as with guest-friends, Kula partners, and other visiting parties. Over millennia trade between empires was carried on as gift trade—no other rationale of two-sidedness would

163

have met quite as well the needs of the situation. The organization of trading is here usually ceremonial, involving mutual presentation, embassies, or political dealings between chiefs or kings. The goods are treasure, objects of elite circulation; in the border case of visiting parties they may be of a more "democratic" character. But contacts are tenuous and exchanges few and far between.

Administered trade has its firm foundation in treaty relationships that are more or less formal. Since on both sides the import interest is as a rule determinative, trading runs through government-controlled channels. The export trade is usually organized in a similar way. Consequently, the whole of trade is carried on by administrative methods. This extends to the manner in which business is transacted, including arrangements concerning "rates" or proportions of the units exchanged; port facilities; weighing; checking of quality; the physical exchange of the goods; storage; safekeeping; the control of the trading personnel; regulation of "payments"; credits; price differentials. Some of these matters would naturally be linked with the collection of the export goods and the repartition of the imported ones, both belonging to the redistributive sphere of the domestic economy. The goods that are mutually imported are standardized in regard to quality and package, weight, and other easily ascertainable criteria. Only such "trade goods" can be traded. Equivalencies are set out in simple unit relations; in principle, trade is one-to-one.

Higgling and haggling is not part of the proceedings; equivalencies are set once and for all. But since to meet changing circumstances adjustments cannot be avoided, higgling-haggling is practiced only on *other items than price,* such as measures, quality, or means of payment. Endless arguments are possible about the quality of the foodstuffs, the capacity and weight of the units employed, the proportions of the currencies if different ones are jointly used. Even "profits" are often "bargained." The rationale of the procedure is, of course, to keep prices unchanged; if they must adjust to actual supply situations, as in an emergency, this is phrased as trading two-to-one or two-and-a-half-to-one, or, as we would say, at 100% or 150% profit. This method of haggling on profits at stable prices, which may have been fairly general in archaic society, is well authenticated from the Central Sudan as late as the nineteenth century.

Administered trade presupposes relatively permanent trading bodies such as governments or at least companies chartered by them. The understanding with the natives may be tacit, as in the case of traditional or customary relationships. Between sovereign bodies, however, trade assumes formal treaties even in the relatively early times of the second millennium B.C.

Once established in a region, under solemn protection of the gods, administrative forms of trade may be practiced without any previous treaty. The main institution, as we now begin to realize, is the port of trade, as we here call this site of all administered foreign trade. The port of trade offers military security to the inland power; civil protection to the foreign trader; facilities of anchorage, debarkation and storage; the benefit of judicial authorities; agreement on the goods to be traded; agreement concerning the "proportions" of the different trade goods in the mixed packages or "sortings."[6]

Market trade is the third typical form of trading. Here exchange is the form of integration that relates the partners to each other. This comparatively modern variant of trade released a torrent of material wealth over Western Europe and North America. Though presently in recession, it is still by far the most important of all. The range of tradable goods—the commodities—is practically unlimited and the organization of market trade follows the lines traced out by

[6] [On "ports of trade," "sortings," and other features of administered trade, see Essays 9, 10, and 11 in this volume; also Rosemary Arnold, "A Port of Trade: Whydah on the Guinea Coast," in *Trade and Market in the Early Empires*. Ed.]

the supply-demand-price mechanism. The market mechanism shows its immense range of application by being adaptable to the handling not only of goods, but of every element of trade itself—storage, transportation, risk, credit, payments, etc.—through the forming of special markets for freight, insurance, short-term credit, capital, warehouse space, banking facilities, and so on.

The main interest of the economic historian today turns toward the questions: When and how did [foreign] trade become linked with markets? At what time and place do we meet the general result known as market trade?

Strictly speaking, such questions are precluded under the sway of the logic of market economics, which tends to fuse trade and market inseparably.

2. Money Uses

The definition of money in market economics is that of means of indirect exchange. Modern money is used for payment and as a "standard" precisely because it is a means of [commercial] exchange. Thus our money is "all-purpose" money. Other uses of money are merely unimportant variants of its exchange use, and all money uses are dependent upon the existence of markets.

The substantive definition of money, like that of trade, is independent of markets. It is derived from definite uses to which quantifiable objects are put. These uses are payment, standard and exchange. Money, therefore, is defined here as quantifiable objects employed in any one or several of these uses. The question is whether independent definitions of those uses are possible.

The definitions of the various money uses contain two criteria: the sociologically defined situation in which the use arises, and the operation performed with the money objects in that situation.

Payment is the discharge of obligations in which quantifiable objects change hands. The situation refers here not to one kind of obligation only, but to several of them, since only if an object is used to discharge more than one obligation can we speak of it as "means of payment" in the distinctive sense of the term (otherwise merely an obligation to be discharged in kind is so discharged).

The payment use of money belongs to its most common uses in early times. The obligations do not here commonly spring from [economic] transactions. In unstratified primitive society payments are regularly made in connection with the institutions of bride-price, blood-money, and fines.[7] In archaic society such payments continue, but they are overshadowed by customary dues, taxes, rent, and tribute that give rise to payments on the largest scale.

The standard, or accounting use of money is the equating of amounts of different kinds of goods for definite purposes. The "situation" is either barter or the storage and management of staples; the "operation" consists in the attaching of numerical tags to the various objects to facilitate the manipulation of those objects. Thus in the case of barter, the summation of objects on either side can eventually be equated; in the case of the management of staples the possibility of planning, balancing, budgeting, as well as general accounting is attained.

The standard use of money is essential to the flexibility of a redistributive system. The equating of such staples as barley, oil, and wool, in which taxes or rent have to be paid, or, alternatively, rations or wages may be claimed, is vital, since it ensures the possibility of choice between the different staples for payer and claimant alike. At the same time the precondition of large scale finance "in kind" is created, which presupposes the notion of funds and balances, in other words, the interchangeability of staples.

The exchange use of money arises out of a need for quantifiable objects for indirect exchange. The "operation" con-

[7] [See Essay 8 of this volume, "The Semantics of Money-Uses"; also George Dalton, "Primitive Money," *American Anthropologist*, February 1965. Ed.]

sists in acquiring units of such objects through direct exchange, in order to acquire the desired objects through a further act of exchange. Sometimes the money objects are available from the start, and the twofold exchange is merely designed to net an increased amount of the same objects. Such a use of quantifiable objects develops not from random acts of barter—a favored fancy of eighteenth-century rationalism—but rather in connection with organized trade, especially in markets. In the absence of markets the exchange use of money is no more than a subordinate culture trait. The surprising reluctance of the great trading peoples of antiquity such as Tyre and Carthage to adopt coins, that new form of money eminently suited for exchange, may have been due to the fact that the trading ports of the commercial empires were not organized as markets, but as "ports of trade."

Two extensions of the meaning of money should be noted. The one extends the definition of money other than physical objects, namely, ideal [or accounting] units; the other comprises alongside of the three conventional money uses, also the use of money objects as operational devices.

Ideal units are mere verbalizations or written symbols employed as if they were quantifiable units, mainly for payment or as a standard. The "operation" consists in the manipulation of debt accounts according to the rules of the game. Such accounts are common facts of primitive life and not, as was often believed, peculiar to monetized economies. The earliest temple economies of Mesopotamia as well as the early Assyrian traders practiced the clearing of accounts without the intervention of money objects.

At the other end it seemed advisable not to omit the mention of operational devices among money uses, exceptional though they be. Occasionally quantifiable objects are used in archaic society for arithmetical, statistical, taxation, administrative, or other non-monetary purposes connected with economic life. In eighteenth-century Whydah cowrie money was used for statistical purposes, and *damba* beans (never employed as money) served as a gold weight and, in that capacity, were cleverly used as a device for accountancy.[8]

Early money is, as we saw, special-purpose money. Different kinds of objects are employed in the different money uses; moreover, the uses are instituted independently of one another. The implications are of the most far-reaching nature. There is, for instance, no contradiction involved in "paying" with a means with which one cannot buy, nor in employing objects as a "standard," which are not used as a means of exchange. In Hammurabi's Babylonia barley was the means of payment; silver was the universal standard; in exchange, of which there was very little, both were used alongside of oil, wool, and some other staples. It becomes apparent why money uses—like trade activities—can reach an almost unlimited level of development, not only outside of market-dominated economies, but in the very absence of markets.

3. Market Elements[9]

Now, the market itself. From the viewpoint of formal economics, the market is the *locus* of exchange; market and exchange are co-extensive and economic life is reducible to acts of exchange all embodied in markets. Exchange is thus described as *the* economic relationship, with the market as *the* economic institution. The definition of the market derives logically from the underlying premise that all "exchange" may be regarded as market exchange.

Under the substantive range of terms, market and exchange have independent empirical characteristics. What,

[8] [Other examples of "operational devices" used in census counting, measurement, and accounting, are *quipu* strings used by the Inca, and the use of pebble counts for statistical enumeration in eighteenth-century Dahomey. Ed.]

[9] [The first paragraph of this section has been rewritten by the editor.]

then, is here the meaning of exchange and market? And to what extent are they necessarily connected?

Exchange, substantively defined, is the mutual appropriative movement of goods between hands. Such a movement as we saw may occur either at set rates or at bargained rates. The latter only is the result of higgling-haggling between the partners.

Whenever, then, there is exchange, there is a rate. This remains true whether the rate be bargained or set. It will be noted that exchange at bargained prices is identical with catallactic exchange or "exchange as a form of integration." This kind of exchange alone is typically limited to a definite type of market institution, namely price-making markets.

Market institutions shall be defined as institutions comprising a supply crowd or a demand crowd or both. Supply crowds and demand crowds, again, shall be defined as a multiplicity of hands desirous to acquire, or alternatively, to dispose of, goods in exchange. Although market institutions, therefore, are exchange institutions, market and exchange are *not* co-terminous. Exchange at set rates occurs under reciprocative or redistributive forms of integration; exchange at bargained rates, as we said, is limited to price-making markets. It may seem paradoxical that exchange at set rates should be compatible with any form of integration except that of [market] exchange: yet this follows logically since only bargained exchange represents exchange in the catallactic sense of the term, in which it is a form of integration.[10]

The best way of approaching the world of market institutions appears to be in terms of "market elements." Eventually, this will not only serve as a guide through the va-

[10] [On the distinction between petty market place exchange and the integrative role of market transactions and prices in national economies such as the United States, see Paul Bohannan and George Dalton, "Introduction," in *Markets in Africa*, New York: Natural History Press, 1965. Ed.]

riety of configurations subsumed under the name of markets and market type institutions, but also as a tool with which to dissect some of the conventional concepts that obstruct our understanding of those institutions.

Two market elements should be regarded as specific, namely, supply crowds and demand crowds; if either is present, we shall speak of a market institution (if both are present, we call it a market, if one of them only, a market-type institution). Next in importance is the element of equivalency, i.e., the rate of the exchange; according to the character of the equivalency, markets are set-price markets or price-making markets.

Competition is another characteristic of some market institutions, such as price-making markets and auctions, but in contrast to equivalencies, economic competition is restricted to markets. Finally, there are elements that can be designated as functional. Regularly, they occur apart from market institutions, but if they make their appearance alongside of supply crowds or demand crowds, they pattern out those institutions in a manner that may be of great practical relevance. Amongst these functional elements are physical site, goods present, custom, and law.

This diversity of market institutions was in recent times obscured in the name of the formal concept of a supply-demand-price mechanism. No wonder that it is in regard to the pivotal terms of supply, demand, and price that the substantive approach leads to a significant widening of our outlook.

Supply crowds and demand crowds were referred to above as separate and distinct market elements. In regard to the modern market this would be, of course, inadmissible; here there is a price level at which bears turn bulls, and another price level at which the miracle is reversed. This has induced many to overlook the fact that buyers and sellers are separate in any other than the modern type of market. This again gave support to a twofold misconception. Firstly, "supply and demand" appeared as combined elemental forces while actually each consisted of two very different components, namely, an amount of *goods,* on the one hand, and a number of *persons,* related as buyers and sellers to those goods, on the other. Secondly, "supply and demand" seemed inseparable like Siamese twins, while actually forming distinct groups of persons, according to whether they disposed of the goods as of resources, or sought them as requirements. Supply crowds and demand crowds need not therefore be present together. When, for instance, booty is auctioned by the victorious general to the highest bidder only a demand crowd is in evidence; similarly, only a supply crowd is met with when contracts are assigned to the lowest submission. Yet auctions and submissions were widespread in archaic society, and in ancient Greece auctions ranked amongst the precursors of markets proper. This distinctness of supply and demand crowds shaped the organization of all premodern market institutions.

As to the market element commonly called "price," it was here subsumed under the category of equivalencies. The use of this general term should help avoid misunderstandings. Price suggests fluctuation, while equivalency lacks this association. The very phrase "set" or "fixed" price suggests that the price, before being fixed or set was apt to change. Thus language itself makes it difficult to convey the true state of affairs, namely, that price is originally a rigidly fixed quantity, in the absence of which trading cannot start. Changing or fluctuating prices of a competitive character are a comparatively recent development and their emergence forms one of the main interests of the economic history of antiquity. Traditionally, the sequence was supposed to be the reverse: price was conceived of as the result of trade and exchange, not as their precondition.

Price is the designation of quantitative ratios between goods of different kinds, effected through barter or higgling-haggling. It is that form of equivalency that is characteristic of economies that are integrated through exchange.

But equivalencies are by no means restricted to exchange relations. Under a redistributive form of integration equivalencies are also common. They designate the quantitative relationship between goods of different kinds that are acceptable in payment of taxes, rents, dues, fines, or that denote qualifications for a civic status dependent on a property census. Also the equivalency may set the ratio at which wages or rations in kind can be claimed, at the beneficiary's choosing. The elasticity of a system of staple finance—the planning, balancing, and accounting—hinges on this device. The equivalency here denotes not what should be given *for* another good, but what can be claimed *instead* of it. Under reciprocative forms of integration, again, equivalencies determine the amount that is "adequate" in relation to the symmetrically placed party. Clearly, this behavioral context is different from either exchange or redistribution.

Price systems, as they develop over time, may contain layers of equivalencies that historically originated under different forms of integration. Hellenistic market prices show ample evidence of having derived from redistributive equivalencies of the cuneiform civilizations that preceded them. The thirty pieces of silver received by Judas as the price of a man for betraying Jesus was a close variant of the equivalency of a slave as set out in Hammurabi's Code some 1700 years earlier. Soviet redistributive equivalencies, on the other hand, for a long time echoed nineteenth-century world market prices. These, too, in their turn, had their predecessors. Max Weber remarked that for lack of a costing basis Western capitalism would not have been possible but for the medieval network of statuated and regulated prices, customary rents, etc., a legacy of guild and manor. Thus price systems may have an institutional history of their own in terms of the types of equivalencies that entered into their making.

It is with the help of non-catallactic concepts of trade, money, and markets of this kind that such fundamental problems of economic and social history as the origin of fluctuating prices and the development of market trading can best be tackled and, as we hope, eventually resolved.

To conclude: A critical survey of the definitions of trade, money, and market should make available a number of concepts which form the raw material of the social sciences in their economic aspect. The bearing of this recognition on questions of theory, policy, and outlook should be viewed in the light of the gradual institutional transformation that has been in progress since the first World War. Even in regard to the market system itself, the market as the sole frame of reference is somewhat out of date. Yet, as should be more clearly realized than it sometimes has been in the past, the market cannot be superseded as a general frame of reference unless the social sciences succeed in developing a wider frame of reference to which the market itself is referable. This indeed is our main intellectual task today in the field of economic studies. As we have attempted to show, such a conceptual structure will have to be grounded on the substantive meaning of economic.

8

The Semantics of Money-Uses

Because of the exchange-use of money under our market organization of economic life we are apt to think of money in too narrow terms. No object is money per se, and any object in an appropriate field can function as money. In truth, money is a system of symbols similar to language, writing, or weights and measures. These differ from one another mainly in the purpose served, the actual symbols employed, and the degree to which they display a single unified purpose.

Pseudo-Philosophies of Money

Money is an incompletely unified system, a search for its single purpose a blind alley. This accounts for the many, unavailing attempts at determining the "nature and essence" of money. We must be content with listing the purposes to which the quantifiable objects actually called money are put. This is achieved by pointing to the *situation* in which we operate those objects and with what effect. We will find them called money, when used in any one of the following ways: for payment; as a standard; as a means of indirect exchange. The human situation is, of course, given independently of the notion of money, just as the handling of the objects is described in operational terms independently of that notion. Payment occurs in a situa-

FROM *Explorations,* the University of Toronto, October 1957. Reprinted by permission of the publisher.

tion of obligation, and a handing over of the objects has the effect of wiping out the obligation. Money used as a standard is a quantitative tag attached to units of goods of different kinds, either for the purpose of barter with the effect that, by adding up the numerals, we can readily equalize the two sides in the exchange, or for budgeting and balancing stores of different staples, thus producing staple finance. Finally, there is the exchange use of such objects, that is, acquiring them in order to acquire other objects through a further act of exchange. The objects employed in direct exchange thereby gain the character of money. They become symbols through their participation in a definite human situation.

A few sidelines are here avoided. First: The distinction between tokens and what they "represent" is ignored. Either function as money objects and form part of the symbolic system. No difference is therefore made between barley money, gold money or paper money. To confuse the basic problem of money with that of token money is a source of frequent misunderstandings. Tokens as such are no novelty—fiction and abstraction belong to the original endowment of man. In Herodotus' well-known story of compulsory temple prostitution in Babylonia, he records this operational detail: "The silver coin may be of any size; it cannot be refused for that is forbidden by the law, since, once thrown, it is sacred." Nor are mere tokens unknown in the primitive societies of our ethnographers. Some peoples of the Congo employ "simply as a token" straw mats or grass cloth originally of square shape, but eventually reduced to a tangle of hay, "practically of no value at all." Strips of blue cloth of standard width that had become in time useless rags were current as token money in parts of the Western Sudan. Since paper money came to the fore, however, scholars felt induced to focus on the tokens instead of on the massive physical objects themselves. This modernizing fashion carried the day. The latest outstanding

THE SEMANTICS OF MONEY-USES

work of an ethnographer, Mrs. Quiggin,[1] takes the token to be the true money and accordingly dubs the actual money objects that it describes exhaustively, "money substitutes."

Historians of antiquity have proved hardly less susceptible to modernizing on the matter of money. Since third millennium Babylonia possessed no paper money, the metals were regarded by historians as the orthodox money material. Actually, all payments were made in barley. Bruno Meissner, the Assyriologist, put this in the terms "Money was primarily replaced by grain." His colleague Lutz thought that the scarcity of silver "necessitated the use of a substitute. Thus grain often took the place of metals." Throughout, token money ranks as true money, since it is the most abstract and the least useful; next comes gold and silver, as substitutes; in their absence, even grain will do. This is a consistent reversal of the sequence in which the physical money objects are primary empirical evidence. Yet the existence of tokens should cause no complications; it is a matter of course in a monetary system. If paper money viewed as a token, "symbolizes" coins, then in our terms it symbolizes that which is already a symbol, namely, money. Symbols do not merely "represent" something. They are material, oral, visual, or purely imaginary signs that form part of the definite situation in which they participate; thus they acquire meaning.

Second, a similar disregard of the semantics of economic theory is forced upon us in the choice of terms when referring to the various money-uses. Payment, standard, and means of exchange are distinctions originally developed by classical economists. Hence the understandable belief of some anthropologists that their application to primitive money implies an economistic bias. The reverse would be truer. Actually, modern economics does not rely for its monetary theories on such distinctions at all. Archaic

[1] [A. H. Quiggin, *A Survey of Primitive Money*, London: Methuen and Co., 1949. Ed.]

society, on the other hand, shows an institutional setting where the use of quantifiable objects typically occurs in precisely those three ways.

All-Purpose and Special-Purpose Money

From a formal angle, modern money, in contrast to primitive money, offers a striking resemblance to both language and writing. They all possess a uniform grammar. All three are organized in an elaborate code of rules concerning the correct way of employing the symbols—and general rules applicable to all the symbols. Archaic society did not know "all-purpose" money. Various money-uses may be supplied here by different money objects. Consequently, there is no grammar with which all money-uses must comply. No one kind of object deserves the distinctive name of money; rather the term applies to a small group of objects, each of which may serve as money in a different way. While in modern society the money employed as a means of exchange is endowed with the capacity of performing all the other functions as well, in early society the position is rather the reverse. One encounters slaves or horses or cattle used as a standard when judging of prestige conveying wealth, or anyway of large amounts, while cowrie shells are solely employed for small amounts. (Eventually, the unit slave or horse may stand for a conventional value representing a mere unit of account, real slaves and horses being actually sold at varying prices.) We might also find that while real slaves are a means of payment of tribute to a foreign overlord, cowrie shells function as a domestic means of payment or even as a medium of exchange. This may not exclude the use of precious metals for hoarding wealth, while such metals may not otherwise serve as money except perhaps as a standard, and in exchange for imports. Where the market habit is fairly widespread money might, moreover, serve as a means of exchange to which

178

end several trade goods might be in use, which otherwise are not employed as money at all. Numerous combinations of these variants occur. No *one* rule is universally valid, except for the very general, but no less significant, rule that money-uses are distributed between a multiplicity of different objects.

No such fragmentation in the use of sounds is known in any language. In speech all articulate oral sounds, in script all letters of the alphabet are eligible for use in all types of words, while archaic money in extreme cases employs one kind of object as means of payment, another as a standard of value, a third for storing wealth, and a fourth for exchange purposes—like a language where verbs consisted of one group of letters, nouns of another, adjectives of a third, and adverbs of yet a fourth.

Moreover, in primitive society [commercial] exchange is not the fundamental money-use. If any one be more "basic" than another it is rather the use for [non-commercial] payment or standard. These are common even where the exchange-use of money is not practiced. Accordingly, while in modern society the unification of the various uses of money happened on the basis of its exchange-use, in early communities we find the different money-uses institutionalized separately from one another. Insofar as there is interdependence between them, we find use for payment or as a standard or for storing of wealth, having precedence over use for exchange. Thus nineteenth-century money, employing exchange symbols for various other uses, appears as an almost complete parallel to language and writing with its all-purpose sounds and signs. But to some extent the analogy holds also for primitive and archaic money, which differs from its modern counterpart only in the lesser degree to which the systems are unified. Since the second quarter of the twentieth century, however, starting with Nazi Germany, "modern" money begins to show a definite tendency toward a reverting to disunification. Half a dozen "marks" were current under Hitler and each of them restricted to some special purpose or other.[2]

Exchange-Money

"Money is a means of exchange." This presumption belongs among the most powerful in the field of modern thought. Its authority may be gauged by the axiomatic manner in which it was formulated to cover the whole course of human history and even extended by anthropologists to primitive society. It is forcefully expressed in the following quotation: "In any economic system, however primitive, an article can only be regarded as true money," Professor Raymond Firth declares, "when it acts as a definite and common medium of exchange, as a convenient stepping stone in obtaining one type of goods for another. However, in so doing, it serves as a measure of value, allowing the worth of all other articles to be expressed in terms of itself. Again, it is a standard of value, with reference to past or future payments, while as a store of value it allows wealth to be condensed and held in reserve." (Art. 'Currency, Primitive' in *Encyclopedia Britannica*, 14th ed.)

According to this still current view, the exchange-use to which money can be put is its essential criterion, not only in modern, but also in primitive society. Even under primitive conditions the various money-uses are asserted to be inseparable. Only quantifiable objects serving as means of exchange can, therefore, be regarded as money. Their functioning as means of payment, as standard of value, or as means of hoarding wealth, is not decisive for their character as money, unless it implies their use as media of exchange. For it is this use that logically unifies the system,

[2] [On the roles of money in the Soviet economy see Gregory Grossman, "Gold and the Sword: Money in the Soviet Command Economy," in H. Rosovsky (ed.), *Industrialization in Two Systems: Essays in Honor of Alexander Gershenkron*, New York: John Wiley & Sons, Inc., 1966. Ed.]

since it allows a consistent linking up of the various functions of money. Without it there cannot be true money. Such a modernizing approach to the problem, we submit, is largely responsible for the obscurity in which the characteristics of primitive money still abide.

The Payment-Use of Money

Payment is the discharge of an obligation through the handing-over of quantifiable objects, which then function as money. The connectedness of payment with money and of obligations with economic transactions appears to the modern mind self-evident. Yet the quantification, which we associate with payment, operated already at a time when the obligations discharged were quite unconnected with economic transactions. The story starts with the propinquity of payment and punishment on the one hand, obligation and guilt on the other. No unilineal development should be inferred, however. Rather, obligations may have origins different from guilt and crime, such as wooing and marriage; punishment may spring from other than sacral sources, such as prestige and precedence; eventual payment, then, with its quantitative connotation, may include operational elements not entailed in punishment as such.

It is only broadly true that civil law followed on penal law, penal law on sacral law. Payment was due alike from the guilty, the defiled, the impure, the weak and the lowly; it was owed to the gods and their priests, the honored, the pure, and the strong. Punishment, accordingly, aimed at diminution in power, sanctity, prestige, status, or wealth of the payer, not stopping at his physical destruction.

Pre-legal obligations mostly spring from custom and give rise to an offense only in case of default. Even so the restoring of the balance need not involve payment. Obligations are, as a rule, specific, and their fulfilment is a qualitative affair, thus lacking an essential of payment—its quantitative character. Infringement of sacral and social obligations, whether toward god, tribe, kin, totem, village, age-group, caste, or guild, is repaired not through payment but by action of the right *quality*. Wooing, marrying, avoiding, dancing, singing, dressing, feasting, lamenting, lacerating, or even killing oneself may occur in discharge of an obligation, but they are not for that reason payments.

The specific characteristic in the payment-use of money is quantification. Punishment approximates payment when the process of riddance of guilt is numerable, as when lashes of the whip, turns of the praying mill, or days of fasting dispose of the offense. But though it has now become an "obligation to pay," the offense is atoned for not by depriving one's self of quantifiable objects, but primarily by a loss of personal qualitative values or sacral and social status.

The payment-use of money links up with the economy when the units discharged by the person under obligation happen to be physical objects such as sacrificial animals, slaves, ornamental shells, or measures of food stuffs. The obligations may still be predominantly non-transactional, such as paying a fine, composition,[3] tax, tribute, making gifts and counter-gifts, honoring the gods, ancestors, or the dead. There is now, however, a significant difference. For the payee does gain what the payer loses—the effect of the operation fits the legal concept of payment.

The ultimate intent of the obligation to pay may still be the diminution in power and status of the payer. In archaic society an exorbitant fine did not only bankrupt but politically degraded the victim. For a long time power and status in this way retained their precedence over economic possessions as such. The political and social importance of accumulated wealth under these conditions lay in the rich man's capacity of making a big payment without undermining his status. (This is the condition of affairs in archaic

[3] [In this context, composition means payment as part of an "agreement for cessation of hostilities." Oxford Concise Dictionary. Ed.]

democracies where political confiscation takes the form of exorbitant fines.) Treasure gains great political importance, as witness Thucydides' memorable passages in the Archeology. Wealth is here directly transmuted into power. It is a self-maintaining institution. Because the rich man is powerful and honored he receives payments: gifts and dues are showered upon him without his having to use power to torture and kill. Yet his wealth, used as a fund for gifts, would procure him a sufficiency of power to do so.

Once money as a means of exchange is established in society, the practice of payment spreads far and wide. For with the introduction of markets as the physical locus of exchange a new type of obligation comes into prominence as the legal residue of transactions. Payment appears as the counterpart of some material advantage gained in the transaction. Formerly a man was made to pay taxes, rent, fines, or blood-money. Now he pays for the goods he bought. Money is now means of payment *because* it is means of exchange. The notion of an independent origin of payment fades, and the millennia in which it sprang not from economic transactions, but directly from religious, social, or political obligations, are forgotten.

Hoarding or Storage-Use of Money

A subordinate money-use—storing of wealth—has its origin largely in the need for payments. Payment is not primarily an economic phenomenon. Neither is wealth. In early society it consisted largely of treasure, which is again rather a social than a subsistence category. The subsistence connotation of wealth (as of payment) derives from the frequency with which wealth is accumulated in the form of cattle, slaves, and non-perishable goods of common consumption. Both that which feeds the store of wealth and that which is disbursed from it gains then a subsistence significance. Only within limits, however, since payments are still made, as a rule, for non-transactional reasons. This is true both of the rich who own the store of wealth, and the subjects who fill the store by their payments. He who owns wealth is thereby enabled to pay fines, composition, taxes, etc., for sacral, political, and social ends. The payments, which he receives from his subjects, high or low, are paid to him as taxes, rents, gifts, etc., not for transactional but for social and political reasons ranging from pure gratitude for protection or admiration of superior endowment, to stark fear of enslavement and death. This again, is not to deny that once exchange-money is present money will readily lend itself as a store of wealth. But, as in the case of payment, the condition is the previous establishment of quantifiable objects as media of exchange.

Use of Money as a Standard

Money as a standard of value seems more closely linked with the exchange use of money than is either payment or hoarding. For barter and storage of staples are the two very different sources from which the need for a standard springs. At first sight the two have little in common. The first is akin to transaction, the other to administration and disposal. Yet neither can be effectively carried out in the absence of some standard. For how otherwise than with the help of computation could, for instance, a piece of land be bartered against an assortment consisting of a chariot, horse-harness, asses, ass-harness, oxen, oil, clothes and other minor items? In the absence of a means of exchange the account in a well-known case of barter in ancient Babylonia shaped up like this. The land was valued at 816 shekels of silver, while the articles given in exchange were valued in shekels of silver as follows: chariot 100, 6 horse-harnesses 300, an ass 130, ass-harness 50, and ox 30, the rest were distributed over the smaller items.

The same principle applied, in the absence of exchange, to the administration of vast palace and temple stores (staple finance). Their keeper handled subsistence goods under conditions which, from more than one angle, required a gauging of the relative importance of these goods. Hence the famed rule of accountancy of "one unit of silver = one unit of barley" on the stele of Manistusu as well as at the head of the Laws of Eshnunna.

Research data reveal that the exchange-use of money cannot have given rise to the other money-uses. On the contrary, the payment, storage, and accountancy uses of money had their separate origins and were institutionalized independently of one another.

Élite Circulation and Staple Finance

It seems almost self-contradictory to expect that one could pay with money with which one cannot buy. Yet that precisely is implied in the assertion that money was not used as a medium of exchange and still was used as a means of payment. Two institutions of early society offer a partial explanation: treasure and staple finance.

Treasure, as we saw, should be distinguished from other forms of stored wealth. The difference lies mainly in its relation to subsistence. In the proper sense of the term, treasure is formed of prestige goods, including "valuables" and ceremonial objects, the mere possession of which endows the holder with social weight, power, and influence. It is, then, a peculiarity of treasure that both the giving and the receiving enhances prestige; it largely circulates for the sake of the turnover, which is its proper use. Even when food is "treasured" it is liable to pass backward and forward between the parties, however absurd this might appear from the subsistence point of view. But food rarely functions as treasure, for interesting food, like slaughtered pigs, does not keep, and that which keeps, such as barley or oil, is not exciting. The precious metals, on the other hand, which are almost universally valued as treasure, cannot readily be exchanged for subsistence, since apart from exceptionally auriferous regions such as the Gold Coast

185

or Lydia, display of gold by the common people is opprobrious.

Nevertheless, treasure, like other sources of power, may be of great economic importance, since gods, kings, and chiefs can be made to put the services of their dependents at the disposal of the giver, thus indirectly securing for him food, raw materials, and labor services, on a large scale. Ultimately, this power of indirect disposal, which may comprise the important power of taxation, arises, of course, from the enhanced influence exerted by the recipient of treasure over his tribe or people.

All this holds good, whether the treasure consists of quantifiable units or not. If it does, the handling of treasure may give rise to something in the nature of finance. In archaic Greece, for instance, he who owned treasure employed it to gain the favor of gods and chiefs or other politically influential agents, by forming the gold and silver into conventionally acceptable gifts, such as tripods or bowls. But this did not make tripods into money, for only by an artificial construction could such an honorific gift-use be subsumed under either payment or exchange. Transactions of treasure finance were restricted to the narrow circle of the gods and chiefs. While some things could be paid for with treasure, very many more could not be bought with it.

Storage of wealth as an institution of the subsistence economy starts from the collecting and stacking of *staples*. While treasure and treasure finance does not, as a rule, belong to the subsistence economy, the storing of staples represents an accumulation of subsistence goods involving, as a rule, their use as a means of payment. For once staples are stored on a large scale by temple, palace, or manor, this must be accompanied by such a use. Thus treasure-finance is replaced by staple-finance.

Most archaic societies possess an organization of staple-finance of some kind or other. It was in the framework of the planned transfer and investment of staples stored on a

186

gigantic scale that the accounting devices were first developed, which characterized the redistributive economies of the ancient empires over long periods of time. For only well after the introduction of coined money in Greece some six centuries before our era, did money-finance begin to supersede staple-finance in these empires, especially in the Roman Republic. Nevertheless, even later, Ptolemaic Egypt continued in the traditions of staple-finance, which it raised to unparalleled levels of efficiency.

Redistribution as a form of integration often involves under primitive conditions the storage of goods at a center, whence they are distributed and fall out of circulation. Goods passed on as payment to the center are passed out from there and are consumed. They provide subsistence for army, bureaucracy and labor force, whether paid out in wages, in soldiers' pay or in other forms. The personnel of the temples consumes a large part of the payments made to the temple in kind. The raw materials are required for the equipment of the army, for public works and government exports; wool and cloth are exported too; barley, oil, wine, dates, garlic, and so on, are distributed and consumed. Thus the means of payment are destroyed. Maybe some of them are eventually bartered privately by their recipients. To that extent a "secondary circulation" is started, which might even become the mainspring of local markets, without disrupting the redistributive economy. Actually, no evidence of the existence of such markets has yet turned up. The relevance of treasure and staple to the question of money-uses is therefore that they explain the functioning of the various money-uses in the absence of the market system.

Treasure goods, which happen to be quantifiable, may be used for payment. Yet such elite goods are not normally exchanged and cannot be used for purchase except in the sacral and foreign policy spheres. The much larger sector of payments concerns, of course, subsistence goods. Such objects, when used for the discharge of obligations, i.e., for payment, are stored at the center whence they revert through redistributive payment and are consumed.

Treasure and staples, between them, offer therefore broadly the answer to the institutional problem set by the conditions of early society, where means of payment may be independent of the exchange use of money. The absence of money as a means of exchange in the irrigational empires helped to develop a kind of banking enterprise —actually large estate managements practicing staple finance—in order to facilitate transfer and clearing in kind. It might be added that similar methods were employed by the administrations of the larger temples. Thus clearing, book-transfer and non-transferable checks were first developed, not as expedients in a money economy, but on the contrary, as administrative devices designed to make barter more effective and therefore the developing of market methods unnecessary.

Babylonia and Dahomey

In regard to its monetary organization, Hammurabi's Babylonia, in spite of its complex economic administration and elaborate operational practices, was typically "primitive," for the principle of differentiation of money-objects was firmly established. With many important reservations as to detail, the following broad generalization can be made: rents, wages, and taxes were paid in barley, while the standard of value was universally silver. The total system was governed by the rule of accountancy, unshakably grounded on the equation "1 *shekel* of silver $=$ 1 *gur* of barley." In case of a permanent improvement in the average yield of the land (as would be caused by large-scale irrigational works), the barley content of the *gur* was raised by solemn proclamation. The general use of silver as money of account facilitated barter enormously; the equally general employment of barley as a means of domestic payment made the storage system possible on which the re-distributive economy of the country rested.

It appears that all the important staples functioned to some extent as means of exchange, none of them being permitted to attain the status of "money" (as opposed to goods). This may also be put in the following terms: an elaborate system of barter was practiced, which was based on the function of silver as money of account; the use of barley as a means of payment; and the simultaneous employment of a number of staples such as oil, wool, dates, bricks, etc. as means of exchange. Amongst the latter should be counted barley and silver, care being taken to prevent these or any other staple developing into a "preferred means of exchange," or, as we should say, money. These safeguards included the avoidance of coined money, the hoarding of precious metals in palace and temple treasury, and, more effective than all, strict legal provisions as to the documentation of transactions. The outstanding provision appears to have been the restriction of formal "sale-purchase" transactions to *specific* goods such as a plot of land, a house, heads of cattle, individual slaves, a boat—all of them specimens which might be designated by a name. In regard to staples or fungible goods, such as barley, oil, wool, or dates, no documentation of exchange against each other is in evidence during the millennia of cuneiform civilization.

On a very much smaller scale the eighteenth-century Negro kingdom of Dahomey shows monetary conditions not so dissimilar to those of Babylonia. Cowries were used as domestic currency in all four uses, but as a standard of value they were supplemented by slaves, which served as money of account for larger amounts. Accordingly, the wealth of rich persons, the customs payments of foreign ships to the king, tribute to foreign sovereigns, were reckoned (but only in this last instance, paid) in slaves. These did not, however, here serve as a means of exchange, as in some Hausa regions. In this latter use cowrie was supplemented by gold dust, which was especially employed in ports of trade and other foreign contacts. As to storage of wealth, not only cowrie but also slaves were used. It is reminiscent of Babylonia that the rule of accountancy governing the system involved equation between slaves and cowrie, which it seems, was a matter of public proclamation; so was the export price of slaves, which was reckoned in ounces of gold dust.

APPENDIX: NOTES ON PRIMITIVE MONEY[4]

I. GENERAL PROPOSITIONS ON TRADE, MONEY, AND MARKETS

(1) Trade and money originate separately and independently of markets. They do not arise, as has been thought, from individual barter and exchange. Trade and money are much more widely spread institutions than markets. The various forms of trade and the different money-uses should be regarded, therefore, independently of markets and market elements. Much of economic history consists precisely in the linking up of trade and money-uses with market elements, thus leading to market-trade and exchange-money. All this may be subsumed under the thesis of the *independent origins of trade and money from markets.*

(2) The development of trade, money, and markets follows different lines according to whether these institutions are primarily external or internal to the community. One of the characteristics of the nineteenth-century type of economy [laissez-faire capitalism] was the almost complete

[4] This appendix is compiled from unpublished memoranda Polanyi wrote between 1947 and 1950 and distributed as mimeographed notes to his students in courses in economic history at Columbia University. The unpublished material is printed by permission of Ilona Polanyi and Kari Polanyi Levitt. Ed.

obliteration of this distinction. We may call this the thesis of the *separate origins of external and internal trade, money, and markets.*

(3) We are familiar with the manner in which trade, money uses and market elements are integrated under a market system. Their manner of integration, however, in the absence of a dominant market system is obscure. It is submitted that it is explained through the part played in the process by non-economic institutions, more especially by the reciprocating and redistributive elements comprised in (a) basic social organization and (b) political administration. The latter has a predominant role in archaic society. This may be referred to as the thesis of the *integrative role of reciprocity and redistribution in non-market societies.*

II. PROPOSITIONS IN REGARD TO PRIMITIVE MONEY

Money Uses

(1) In modern society the distinction between the various money uses is of hardly more than a historical or theoretical, but rarely of practical interest. The reason is that modern money, at least up to recently, was all-purpose money—i.e., the medium of exchange was also employed for the other money uses. Primitive money, on the contrary, is special-purpose money—i.e., different objects are, as a rule, employed in different money uses. The various money uses are, therefore, institutionalized separately and, mostly, independently from one another. Consequently, the distinction between the various money uses is here of utmost practical importance for the understanding of the money use of quantifiable objects.

(2) The definition of primitive money is derived from its uses. The money uses are payment, standard, hoarding, and exchange. Money is defined as quantifiable objects employed for any of the above uses.

191

(3) Thus the emphasis shifts to the definition of the various money uses. They should contain (a) the sociological situation in which the use arises and (b) the operation performed with the objects in that situation.

(a) Payment is the discharging of obligations through the handing over of quantifiable objects or, in the case of "ideal units," of some definite manipulation of debt accounts. The "sociological situation" refers here not to one single use but to a number of them, for only in regard to different obligations can we speak of "payment" in the distinctive sense of the term, i.e., as involving a money use. If only one type of obligation is involved, its discharge through the handing over of quantifiable objects may well be a non-monetary operation, as when an obligation is discharged "in kind."

(b) Standard, or Accounting, use of money is the equating of amounts of different goods either for the purposes of barter or in any other situation involving the need for accountancy. The sociological situation is that of bartering, or of administrative management of quantifiable objects, e.g., staples. The "operation" consists in attaching numerical values to the various objects so that their summations may be eventually equated.

(c) Hoarding is the accumulation of quantifiable objects for future disposal or simply to hold as treasure. The sociological situation is one of the numerous ones in which persons prefer not to consume or otherwise dispose of quantifiable objects, but to defer their use for the future, unless they altogether prefer the advantages of sheer possession, especially the power, prestige, and influence accruing from it. The operation involved consists in keeping, storing, and conserving the objects so that their possession and, preferably, ostentatious display should redound to the credit of the owner and all those whom he may represent.

(d) Exchange use of money is the use of quantifiable objects for indirect exchange. The sociological situation is that of the possession of some objects together with the desire for other objects. The operation consists of acquiring units of quantifiable objects through direct exchange in order to acquire other objects through another act of exchange. It may be, however, that the money objects are possessed, and the indirect exchange is designed to net an increased amount of such objects.

The Definitions of Money in Primitive Economics, Cultural Anthropology, and Economic Analysis

(1) This definition of money is most suited to the purpose of primitive economics. It refers to quantifiable (physical) objects used for definite purposes, these latter being, again, defined with the help of sociological situations and operations performed in them. This definition should, however, be supplemented (a) in regard to money objects, by ideal units, and (b) in regard to money uses, by operational devices. Ideal units are non-physical objects employed in money uses, as for payment or standard, in which case the operation does not primarily involve physical objects, but is rather the manipulation of debt accounts. Operational devices, i.e., solutions primarily achieved through manipulation of objects, are not limited to money uses. Objects employed in some money use, however, may be also employed for some device, as for arithmetical, statistical, taxation, administrative, or other purposes connected with economic life. Examples: (i) Double cowrie numeration, employed for automatic regulation of retail span. Cf. Mage, Baillaud, Binger, Bovill, etc. (ii) The relating of gold dust, cowrie, and trade-good prices. Gold dust is measured by weight with the help of seeds of grain; cowrie is counted by tale, the current unit containing a definite round number of cowrie (2000); the trade goods are priced variously: in gold, in European silver currencies, in cowrie, in iron bars, or copper wire. The native may be selling gold dust and may be paid in trade goods. The European trader (i) translates the value of the gold into £ s.d. or Spanish silver dollars, and (ii) then the value of the trade goods into

cowrie. The native simply counts the value of the gold dust by the number of beans to which that weight amounts, and then equates the number of beans with the cowrie units owed to him by the trader. By removing a bean from a sack for each cowrie unit paid to him, he keeps track of how much is still owed to him by the number of beans remaining in the sack.

(2) Cultural anthropology deals with money as a semantic system similar to writing, language, or weights and measures. Money as a semantic system links symbols to quantifiable objects, but the purpose served by the system as a whole must be inferred from the actual uses, and can hardly be said to be as clear as that of writing or language.

(3) The classical and neo-classical economists' definition of money was, up till recently, that of means of indirect exchange. The other money uses are here merely unimportant variants of that use.

Independent Institutional Origins of Money Uses

1. Payment
   (a) In unstratified primitive society, as a rule, payments are made in connection with the institutions of bridewealth, bloodwealth and fines.
   (b) In stratified, and especially in archaic society, institutions such as customary dues, taxes, rent, and tribute similarly give rise to payments.
2. Standard or Accountancy use of money is found in connection with
   (a) complex barter, i.e., different articles being summed up on both sides;
   (b) the administration of staples (staple-finance).
3. Hoarding of wealth may serve the purpose of
   (a) accumulating treasure,
   (b) providing against future dearth,
   (c) disposal over military and labor forces by providing subsistence in kind.

4. Exchange develops as a rule not from random barter acts of individuals, but in connection with organized external trade and internal markets.

III. MONEY: THEORETICAL AND INSTITUTIONAL CONCEPTS

Classical Economics

Money is defined as a commodity primarily used in exchange. Money is therefore a function of barter and exchange. Monetary problems should be resolved by reducing them to commodity problems. Token money (such as paper currency) is not money proper.

The logical derivation of money is identified with its historical evolution: The propensity to barter, truck, and exchange leads to individual acts of barter. Such acts are limited by the specific quality of the commodities being offered more often than others. This again leads to the establishment of one of them as preferred to all others for purposes of exchange. This commodity is adopted as "money," on account of its suitability for indirect exchange. To increase its fungibility the commodity may be quantified, and divided into parts which are stamped by public authority. For the sake of convenience, which governs the whole process, these coins may be replaced by tokens, such as bank notes, which, however, are money only insofar as they insure the possession of the actual commodity, which in modern times consists in coins made from precious metals.

The semblance of a "parallel" between logic and history: The use of coin is thus logically preceded by the use of metal money measured by weight; the monopoly of metal money is logically preceded by competing commodities used in indirect exchange; this again must have derived from the preferred non-monetary use of a number of commodities—all this originating in individual acts of exchange, explained by man's propensity to barter. According to this

195

type of rationalistic argument, in following back the thread of logical deduction to its sources, we are allegedly also retracing the developmental stages embodied in history.

The various uses of money appear in this system as logically interdependent. The commodity character of money, i.e., its being an object possessing utility in itself, is presupposed. (1) "Means of exchange" is defined as the original use; (2) "Means of payment" follows later, for how could one pay with a thing that cannot be used in exchange? (3) "Standard of value" comes next, comprising (1) and (2); (4) "Means of hoarding wealth or treasure" presupposes the other three. The commodity and exchange concepts are cornerstones of the system.

Neo-classical economics

(1) Pre-Keynesian system. Mostly some kind of "exchange" derivation was a legacy from the classics. Schumpeter, e.g., retained the definition of "indirect exchange" for money. Böhm-Bawerk had previously introduced exchange as a special type of use for commodities, and Wieser proceeded to elaborate the marginal utility of money. In this early phase, neo-classical theory was as yet unconscious of the conceptual difficulty of putting money into the scheme.

(2) Keynesian system. In the Keynesian system the role of money is purely pragmatic. No attempt is made to deduce its presence from the allocation of scarce means. Money itself is here one of the scarce means, but a means, which is contrasted with commodities. The classical system denied this contrast (and, consequently, was unable to explain specifically monetary phenomena). The presence of money is here rightly taken for granted—since it can only be institutionally explained, not conceptually deduced. The phrase about the "veil of money" as used by the classics was a remnant of Humean solecism in regard to the allegedly conventional value of money, and the (opposite)

Ricardian fallacy of the commodity character of money. Actually, the value of money does not derive from convention and is not therefore illusory, but neither does it derive from "value in use," as the commodity theory would have it. Its utility derives from the fact that one can buy things with it, and its value, from its scarcity. This, however, does not account for its origin, which lies with the institutions of government and banking.

Institutional terms

The various uses of money were originally institutionalized separately. Connections between these four uses were more or less accidental. We will deal with these uses in the following sequence: (1) Means of payment; (2) Means of hoarding wealth or treasure; (3) Means of exchange; (4) Standard of value.

Means of Payment

For money to be in use as a means of payment, it is necessary that there be (a) some kind of debt or obligation to pay *for;* (b) something to pay *with.* From the traditional point of view, the need, therefore, is to explain (a) how do debts or obligations arise in primitive society outside of economic transactions? (b) how can there be means of payment where money is not also used as a means of exchange?

Something to pay for (How do debts arise?)

(1) That early society is built on *status* means that rights and obligations are mostly derived from birth, whether the kinship is real or fictitious. This is largely true of stratified societies. Negative privilege is also acquired through birth. Men are born to debts, and the discharge of obligation.

(2) The dominant institution is *kinship* and its extensions; this entails obligations of various kinds, the outstanding ones being those of the blood feud group. On the one

197

hand, obligation to take revenge, on the other, to pay fines or composition.[5]

(3) In many primitive societies (e.g., the Manus) customary obligations are under the severe sanction of magic.

(4) Sacral character of early law (formal and ritualistic). Transactions under the sanction of religion. Obligations incurred in this way are of the utmost stringency.

(5) The great importance of prestige, rank, prerogative attaching to honorific actions, names, titles, counts (coups), ceremonial transactions, explains that (even intentional) debts are incurred by infringement of recognized prerogatives as among the Tolowa and the Kwakiutl.

(6) Another rich source lies in the growth of authority, which creates political obligation.

All these factors contribute to the capacity of primitive society to produce *indebtedness of a non-economic nature.* The obligation is based on status, blood, feud, prestige, kinship, and betrothal or marriage, and involves paying off, making good, or resolving the debt; the whole procedure under the sanction of magic, ritualistic law, sacral ceremony. The debt is incurred not as a result of economic transaction, but of events like marriage, killing, coming of age, being challenged to potlatch, joining a secret society etc. While in primitive society, economic interests and corresponding obligations lack stringency and tend toward leniency, elasticity, and equity treatment, economic self interests are usually in the category of non-approved motives. The opposite is the case in regard to debts and obligations having non-economic sources, such as magic, sacral command, *stricti juris negotis,* ritual performances honorific or prestige matters, formal law, including *ju talionis,* the *nexum,* or the formalities connected with the buying and selling of *res mancipi.* (Cf. also Roman

[5] [In this context composition means payment as part of a "agreement for cessation of hostilities." Oxford Concise Dictionary. Ed.]

"Twelve Tables" codifying "customary law" [about middle fifth century B.C.]. The Hebrew Laws of Deuteronomy credited to late seventh century B.C., but using much earlier material.) On Suque (Bank Islands) entrance fees, grades, "freemasonry," Daryll Forde writes: "This system gives a far more mercenary cast to society in such areas and money acquires a greater importance than in the rest of Melanesia."[6] Payments are made in conventional media of payment, e.g., feathers for dances are paid in dentalia, or shell necklaces; songs for suque admission are paid in strings of shell money. Whole strings of shell, etc., are used, *not* single units. Such payments are restricted to different communities.

How are debts paid in the absence of exchange?

Wealth primarily consists of valuables, which are objects capable of arousing emotion and prized for their own sake. The "use" of these valuables may consist merely in possessing them—as in the case of crown jewels.

Pelew money. The Pelew Island (North Pacific), also called Palau, belong to the Carolines. Porcelain and glass mixture of relatively prehistoric origin is a fact. Some of the glass beads are found on Yap, but *not* used there as money (instead huge aragonite stones are used). Yellow and red Pelew money. These are shell-like and glassy, but opaque. Different white sorts of Pelew money exchanged specifically, e.g., sails are bought for high-valued type. The most highly valued are loaned at interest! Bridewealth according to rank; the higher pays more!

The most valuable type of money is secreted by the chieftains. Few people know of even one-sixth of the kinds of money. Fines are paid in Pelew money. Some kinds used in exchange at fixed prices. Glass beads similar to

[6] [Daryll Forde, *Habitat, Economy, and Society,* London: Methuen, 8th ed., 1950, p. 203. Ed.]

199

those of West Africans found in Anglo-Saxon burrows. The Ashanti pay "weight in gold" for such "Aggry pearls." The development of Pelew money is highly specific. Each type of money has its own use, a circle within which it moves. This harmonizes with the idea of wealth and treasure, but not with that of a means of exchange. Although there is also exchange-use, the main uses are in the nature of payment, as in bridewealth—an outstanding instance of money as a means of payment being based on its use as a means of hoarding treasure.

Otherwise, the disposing of the "valuable" is its main "use," as with the Kula, where the relatives and dependents of the proprietor are permitted to wear the objects. Retainers, vassals, and allies in war are secured with the help of such valuables. The point is that the recipient values them as valuables, *not* for their use in [commercial] exchange, the chances of which are usually nil; value is bound inextricably with rank. (Some Kula objects are big, greasy white arm shells, without any value except for the associations that go with earlier possessors.)

Yet money as a means of payment could never have developed to any great extent if its utility had been restricted to being hoarded as treasure. Another use accrued through the development of redistribution as a form of integrating economic activity. The beginnings are, of course, with hunters. In the stratified societies like those of Micronesia and Polynesia, the high chief as representative of the first clan, receives the revenue, redistributing it later in the form of largesse among the population. The principle of redistribution is practiced on a gigantic scale in the despotically governed aristocracies of shepherds and hoe-cultivators, as in Mexico and Peru. The tax payments of subjects and subject peoples are stored in enormous storehouses and redistributed to the in-groups and in-peoples. The same principles reigned in Sumer, Babylonia, Assyria, as well as in ancient China and the New Kingdom of Egypt. All

THE SEMANTICS OF MONEY-USES

this goes to explain the relative independence of "payment" from "exchange."

Money as a means of exchange

External use of money. The origins of money as a means of exchange are linked to external trade. This is in accordance with the equally established fact of trade and markets as "external" institutions.

Some articles are in prominence in foreign trade, as food versus manufactures. Specific products are traded. Geographical factors assert themselves, as in East- and West-Central Africa. With some simpler communities, this tendency toward specialization produces this phenomenon, even in the absence of geographical determination, as in Melanesia. But the broad fact is the tendency of external trade to specialize in a few main articles. Some of these, like salt or iron, are favored for indirect exchange. This is one origin of exchange-money.

Only rarely do we see money emerging primarily out of the need for a means of indirect exchange. This type of external money is deliberate, like the use of cowrie shells. They are little used otherwise, yet extremely popular with all peoples as money in external trade.

Internal use of money. Since money as a means of exchange originated in external trade, when and how, if at all, did it become a means of exchange internally? Though, in general, money as a means of exchange may have originated in external trade, it might be the case that the internal or domestic use of money in exchange may have originated independently. This might have happened as a result of individual acts of barter and exchange, and eventually from local markets. This, however, appears not to have been the case.

In simple, i.e., unstratified, primitive society, money originates as a means of payment, and although used in prestige economy, to a limited extent as a means of exchange, it is only exceptionally used in subsistence economy. Food always remains an article of external trade, and is not domestically exchanged for money.

In stratified primitive society, money is, of course, widely used in redistribution, i.e., as a means of payment. This may be in the form of "valuables," such as Pelew money, or as cattle as in East Africa. Yet we see no money arising as a means of exchange, for acts of exchange on local markets (as in Africa) are limited to the exchange of specific types of goods, and trade is, in principle, exclusively external trade.

Let us mention here Heinrich Schurtz's "internal" and "external" money (*Grundriss einer Entstehungsgeschichte des Geldes,* 1898). Two different types of money originating from different sources. This appeared to suit some important facts stressed by Schurtz. But Schurtz mistook some uses of money for internal, which by origin are external. (1) Bridewealth, payment is originally an exogamy institution and the payment is, in principle, "external"; (2) the composition of blood feud is "external," since there is no blood feud and originally no composition inside the group.

The internal use of money in exchange in the ancient oriental empires of Egypt, Sumer, Babylonia, and China was, on the whole, very restricted. In Egypt, no coins have been assigned of a date anterior to Alexander the Great. The elaborate Ptolemaian money system is, of course, of late origin. Silver and gold were in the keeping of the temples. The highly developed goldsmith's art did not induce them to coin metal, which was used in rings of silver and gold by weight. On the whole, the economy was one of redistribution on a vast scale. Foreign trade was mostly in the hands of foreigners. Internal business was transacted in kind, sometimes in gold and silver, according to weight. The immensely developed redistributive economy kept the system on the money as use of payment basis, and discouraged the formation of internal markets of any importance. In this respect Egypt was typical of ancient oriental empires.

Money as a standard of value

Money as a standard of value reaches its greatest development in modern society on the basis of a market-integrated exchange economy in which money takes the form of general purchasing power.

Money, however, is used as a standard of value in ancient empires as a result of widespread redistributive institutions. This use is restricted to the most important economic goods, such as land, corn, and metals, and it is not a result of market functions, but of price fixing on the part of authorities. In this connection it is of interest to note that insofar as metals (by weight) were used as a means of payment, there is in ancient history no evidence of attempts at a "debasement of currency." The "money" character of commodities was more often due to the extension of government to larger areas than to barter in commodities. By these means external trade became "interiorized."

PART II
PRIMITIVE AND ARCHAIC ECONOMIES

9

Redistribution: The State Sphere in Eighteenth-Century Dahomey

The monarchy was the central institution of the state sphere. It was accepted as of divine origin. The king was the link between the people and the deified ancestors, as well as the guardian of the people's livelihood. As such the king played a central role in the Dahomean economy. It was he who annually reviewed economic conditions, formulated plans for the future, distributed a minimum of cowrie to the population to buy food, set certain equivalents, received and dispensed gifts and levied tolls, taxes, and tribute.

Annual Customs

The place of the monarch in Dahomean life comes into focus at the great redistributive ceremony of the Annual Customs. On this occasion the king appeared before an assembly of all Dahomey to discharge his various duties as sovereign.

The Annual Customs was the major event of the economic cycle. In terms of gross national product and foreign import, as well as popular participation, it was an economic institution of unique proportions. The king himself was the central actor in an assembly of all the personages, administrators, and office holders of the land, in which literally

FROM Chapter III, "Redistribution: The State Sphere," of Karl Polanyi, *Dahomey and the Slave Trade,* Seattle: The University of Washington Press for the American Ethnological Society, 1966. Reprinted by permission of the publisher.

every family was represented at least by one member for part of the time. In a day-long performance the king received gifts, payments, and tributes, subsequently distributing a part of this wealth as gifts to the crowd.

The economic aspect of the process can be analyzed as a movement of goods and money toward the center and out of it again, that is, redistribution. It was the main occasion of building up the finances of the royal administration and of distributing cowrie and other imports among the people. It took care of the remuneration of all higher officials to whom valuable rewards of brandy, tobacco, silks, robes, carpets, and other luxuries were dispensed. Foreign traders and businessmen contributed considerable sums to the king's revenue while native administrators, occupying lucrative posts handed a share of their revenue to the king. These payments were not always publicly made, while the royal return gifts were staged with a view to the utmost effect.

Held each year upon the return of the Dahomean army from the wars, the Customs was symbolic of the religious and political unification of the peoples of Dahomey under the Aladoxonu kings. It was the occasion upon which the people did honor to their ancestors and gave thanks for victory in battle. The king was the mediator between the living and the dead, sacrificed large numbers of captives, "watering the graves" of his forebears with the blood of the victims, and recommitting the nation to the care of the ancestral spirits. These observances were repeated on an even vaster scale at the Grand Customs, which marked the period of public mourning following the death of a king of Dahomey and the accession of his successor.

The Customs expressed the core values of Dahomean life. Herskovits writes:

> In the life of every Dahomean, his ancestors stand
> between him and the gods . . . the respect and wor-
> ship of the ancestors may then be thought of as one

of the great unifying forces that, for the Dahomean, give meaning and logic to life.[1]

Snelgrave, with the point of view natural to a trader, asked a high Dahomean military official why the Dahomeans should sacrifice so many captives when these could be sold to good advantage. To which the officer replied:

It had ever been the custom of their Nation, after any Conquest, to offer to their God a certain number of Captives.

Burton says,

Human sacrifice in Dahomey is founded on a purely religious basis. It is a touching instance of the king's filial piety, deplorably mistaken, but perfectly sincere. The Dahomean sovereign must . . . enter Deadland with royal state, accompanied by a ghostly court . . . This is the object of what we have called the "Grand Customs."

And after every military campaign, Burton continues,

decorum exacts that the first fruits of war and that all criminals should be sent as recruits to swell the king's retinue.[2]

Every event in which the king was involved, whether being visited by a white man, or merely moving to another palace, had to be reported to the ancestors by some male or female messenger. No prospect of additional profit through the sale of slaves would induce the king to spare a single victim from the number required.

The Customs was the occasion for a collection and redistribution of goods on a grand scale. All Dahomeans of any note, including all who held office, attended the cere-

[1] Melville J. Herskovits, *Dahomey, an Ancient West African Kingdom*, Vol. I, New York: Augustin, 1938, p. 238.

[2] Captain Sir Richard F. Burton, *A Mission to Gelele, King of Dahome*, Vol. II, London: Tinsley Brothers, 1864, pp. 13–14.

monies in person, bringing gifts to the king. The Europeans in Whydah,[3] as well as emissaries from African sovereigns, were expected to present themselves before him, likewise bearing gifts. During the festivities, which continued for weeks at Abomey, the king himself made disbursements to the population. As many as thirty or forty thousand people might be present. On the platform erected for the king and members of his court, cowries, rum, cloths, and other fine goods were heaped up to be scattered among the crowds by the king or the dignitaries of the court day after day as the ceremonies continued. A great variety of goods were distributed, items coming from as far away as Europe and India, in addition to manufactures such as fine cotton cloths from neighboring countries.

The size of the contributions to the king varied greatly. Lavish gifts were expected and received from the traders on the coast. One of them later complained that he had brought with him the value of his year's profits as gifts for the king.

The captives taken in battle were presented to the king at this time and the king, in turn, gave public recognition to his warriors and officials by making gifts of slaves to those who distinguished themselves. These formal gift exchanges celebrated Dahomey's wealth and power, and reaffirmed the mutual relations and obligations between king and people.

Army

Men and materials of war were collected and distributed by the monarch. Each year after the harvest, the king went to war leading an army into the field estimated at up to fifty thousand, including followers, no less than about one-fourth of the total population. The standing army was composed entirely of women of remarkable physique and

[3] [Whydah was the coastal port through which the slave trade was transacted. Ed.]

fierceness in combat. This contingent was supplemented by annual provincial levies on the male population. A minimum of military training was assured to all young males by assigning to each soldier in the field a young boy as attendant "to be trained up in Hardships from their Youth."[4]

The organization of the army was decentralized. While the general command was exercised by the king's officials, the caboceers, or top officials, of the various towns and regions led their own forces into the field. The caboceers were expected to place their men at the army's disposal for the campaign and some of them, such as the king's traders at Whydah, "owned thousands of slaves and supplied whole regiments for the annual slave hunt." The rank of Ahwangan, or war captain, according to Burton, "includes all officers that can bring ten to a hundred dependents or slaves into the field." While the soldiers were subsisted by their own masters, certain foodstuffs, such as honey, were collected and stored by royal officials for the use of all the troops. The caboceers were entitled to the booty taken by their own soldiers: "The caboceers, whose soldiers captured them, were always considered to be the owners of the slaves taken in the war," the king told Duncan.[5] The Amazons constituted the private army of the king and their booty belonged to him.

The separation of the civil power and the military power provides another example of the institutional divisions in which Dahomey abounded. The army was under civilian command except on the field of battle. The Mingan and the Meu who commanded the right wing and the left wing respectively were the highest ranking civil officers of the kingdom. Under the Mingan was the Gau, the military

---

[4] Captain William Snelgrave, *A New Account of Some Parts of Guinea, and the Slave Trade,* London: J. J. and P. Knapton, 1734, p. 79; quoted in M. J. Herskovits, *Dahomey,* Vol. II, p. 80.

[5] John Duncan, *Travels in Western Africa, in 1845 and 1846,* Vol. II, London: R. Bentley, 1847, p. 264.

commander-in-chief, and corresponding to him on the left wing was the Po-su. The Gau assumed command of the armies in the field, taking precedence even over the king. In civilian life, the king always occupied the highest stool, but on the battlefront the king sat on a low stool, while the Gau sat on a higher one.

A meticulous disposition was made of captives taken in battle. After setting aside a sufficient contingent for the sacrifices to the ancestors, a number of captives were set apart, corresponding exactly to the Dahomeans lost on the field of battle. These were eventually distributed to the royal plantations to replace the losses. The balance of the captives was divided into three parts: one part going to the king for his household; a second to be sold by the king as slaves; and the third to be distributed among the warriors and chiefs as a reward for valor.

Once assigned to the royal plantations, slaves could not be diverted for resale. Snelgrave complained of his unsuccessful attempt to buy additional slaves from the king:

> I understood afterwards the King had no Slaves by him for sale, tho he had great Numbers of captive Negroes, which tilled his Grounds, and did other work. For it seems, after they are once enrolled for that Service, his Majesty never sells them unless they are guilty of very great Crimes.[6]

Economic Administration

While devastating famines are not an infrequent occurrence in the Niger region to the north, there is hardly any record of famine throughout Dahomey's history. We may judge the success of the Dahomean agricultural policy thereby. This fact is especially remarkable because of the toll in manpower and resources exacted by an annual war,

[6] Snelgrave, *A New Account*, pp. 106–107; quoted in Herskovits, *Dahomey*, II, p. 97.

and because the bush stood as a constant threat to the cultivators, encroaching upon the cultivated land as soon as
effort was relaxed.

"The King of Dahomey enforces cultivation over all
his dominions", Duncan writes. And the king himself tells
Duncan "that he had long ago issued orders that all the
spare land in and around the town of Griwhee (Whydah)
should be cultivated with a view of lessening the chances of
epidemic diseases."[7]

In the injunctions to a new village official, delivered
upon the occasion of his ceremonial installation before the
king and his court, the king's policy in regard to the rural
economy is clearly stated:

> The King has said that in Dahomey a chief must see
> to it that everyone holds firmly where his hand
> rests . . .

> The King has said that Dahomey is a vast land, and
> that everyone must confine his work to the place where
> he lives. That is why it is forbidden to any of the
> young men who cultivate the earth to stop work in
> the fields while the grass remains uncut.

> The King has said that a country must be loved by
> its . . . (people) and that is why he has forbidden
> his people to migrate from one part of the country to
> another, since a wanderer can never have a deep love
> for his land.[8]

The permanent administration of agricultural affairs was
in the hands of the "Minister of Agriculture," the Tokpo;
under him were the Xeni, the chief of the "great farmers"
or gletanu, and his assistant. Every important official was a
plantation owner and thus a member of the gletanu. It was
the duty of the agricultural officials to insure a balanced
production of crops and adjust resources to requirements.

[7] Duncan, *Travels*, II, pp. 268–269.
[8] Herskovits, *Dahomey*, I, p. 67.

Principal crops were grown in different areas of the kingdom. For example, in a district not far from Abomey, only millet was grown, in other areas only yams or maize. In the area between Whydah and Allada, maize and manioc were the chief crops. If there was overproduction or underproduction of any crop, the farmers were ordered to shift from one crop to another. As Paul Mercier says, "In economic matters there was a strict control, not only of exported products—palm oil—but also of food crops." If supplies of corn were short, no export of corn was permitted. Pigs, the chief source of meat, were counted and orders might be given banning slaughter or sales for a certain period in order to replenish stocks.

From early times on, conservation measures were undertaken by the king. The output of palm oil was safeguarded by the king's ruling that no palm wine could be made except from the palm trees growing wild in the bush, since the making of palm wine destroyed the young trees under cultivation. During the growing season for crops, the king decreed that all animals should be tied up to keep them from trampling the new crops.

Other products were likewise subject to administrative controls. At Whydah, as we have seen, two quarters in the town were set aside for salt-workers and the output of these workers was supervised by the Viceroy of Whydah and the "salt-officials" of the court. Tradition held that the king wished no revenue from salt since it was a necessity of life, hence the tax-in-kind on salt was smaller than on other products. Moreover, salt had to be sold to anyone who needed it, *even if he could buy only one cowrie's worth*.

The total output of honey went for the use of the army and no private production or sale was permitted. Ginger was regarded as a medicinal product; as with honey, private production or sale was prohibited and distribution was handled by royal officials for medicinal purposes only. Private persons were permitted to grow pepper on a quota basis, each owner of a field being allowed that number of pepper plants which would yield one raffia-sack of pepper for his own use. Certain districts were set aside for the production of pepper for the market, and a tax in cowries was levied on pepper in transit from these districts. Groundnuts could be grown only in quantities sufficient for private use. According to Burton, the cultivation of coffee, sugar cane, rice, and tobacco was banned in the neighborhood of Whydah for what reason we do not know, but probably because these were regarded as undesirable luxuries.

The king's responsibility for the food supply of the kingdom was manifested in the relation of the crown to local markets. The market-place had to be consecrated by human sacrifice, and since none but the king could take human life, the market had to be directly instituted by the crown. All markets were established by authorization of the king, and officials stood in attendance in the market-place to insure order and obedience to the regulations. No food could be purchased except for cowrie in the market, as noted. The distribution of cowries from the royal hand during the Annual Customs was the means of providing the general population with the currency to buy food. Similarly, all visitors to the court were given gifts of cowries by the king, should they wish to buy food in the market over and above that provided by the king's hospitality, and in token of permission to depart, visitors were "passed" with cowries, as the saying went, to enable them to buy food on the return journey.

Census

The redistributive system of the palace economy was linked with a large apparatus of planning and administration. Many of the economic affairs which made their appearance on the agenda of the Annual Customs were the concern of the royal administration throughout the year. The livelihood of the people was a charge upon the mon-

215

arch, and this responsibility extended into every phase of the economy. Much of the machinery of administration was set in motion in preparation for the ensuing Customs.

Immediately after the close of the great rainy season when the harvests had been completed, the king began his preparations for the annual military campaign. This marked the time for undertaking the census, which provided the data on the basis of which levies were made and taxes collected. The census covered population, agricultural and craft production, livestock, and most other products and resources of the kingdom.

Care was given to the manpower resources. A total count was taken of the population and of the numbers of workers in each occupational category: cultivators, weavers, potters, hunters, salt-workers, porters who carried goods, blacksmiths, and also slaves. Following the enumeration of the cultivators, a count was made of the agricultural produce stored in granaries, of palm trees throughout the kingdom, of the number of cattle, sheep, and poultry and the output of the various crafts. After these data were gathered, taxes were assessed on the whole produce of the kingdom: grain, palm oil, salt, and craft products from which provisions were secured for the forthcoming campaign. As each of the village chiefs reported to the king the population figures for his village, he was told to what division of the army his men were to report, and the army went into action shortly thereafter. The data on population gathered during the census were a state secret, known only to the king, and any village or provincial chief who disclosed the figures for his group would have been garroted.

Ingenious administrative devices were employed in the census, which served operationally as substitutes for written records. But the main reason why the country-wide census involved so little bureaucratic harassment was the participation of the population, which internalized the law and responded spontaneously to the rules. The census data then provided the basis for the levies in kind and cowrie, which were the substance of the flow of goods and services to the state under a redistributive pattern.

The census of population[9] was carried out as follows: in the palace, under the charge of a woman official, there were thirteen boxes, each divided into two parts, one part for males, one part for females. As every birth was reported to the king by the village or district chief, a pebble was placed in the proper section, according to the sex of the infant. At the end of each year, all the pebbles were moved up one box, leaving the first box empty, in which to begin again in the recording of births during the coming year. The pebbles in the thirteenth box were thrown out, since the children who had reached the age of fourteen were considered adults and were enumerated in the annual count of adults.

In another room of the palace, the boxes recording deaths were kept, and the count made in a similar manner. Reports of deaths in each district were relayed to the palace, and two army chiefs were charged with the task of reporting the number of men killed in battle.

The counting of slaves and captives was entrusted to two other officials. With their reports made, the total tally could be arrived at. The sacks from each village were placed in four large bags: one each for men, women, boys, and girls, and each sewn with the corresponding symbol—short trunks for men, beads for women, the male sex organ for boys, and a small figure with the female sex organ for girls. In addition there were three other sacks; one in black representing men killed in battle; one in red, representing deaths from illness; and one in white indicating captives.

In taking the count of adult Dahomeans, males were enumerated first. Some ten to twelve days before mobilization, the head of each family group was required to report the number of males over thirteen years of age in his

[9] Cf. Herskovits, *Dahomey*, II, pp. 72 ff., whom we follow closely.

group. The village chief kept a record of the count by placing pebbles in a sack for each male reported to him. On the sack was sewn a symbol indicating the village from which it came. A basket-making village, for instance, might have a basket for its emblem. These sacks were brought to Abomey either by the village chiefs themselves, or by the district chiefs to whom the sacks were turned over by the chiefs of each village. As each chief presented himself before the king, he was told the army corps to which men from his village were to be assigned.

After the army had been assembled, the count of females took place. The commander of each army unit was instructed to ask each of his soldiers the number of women in his family. These were likewise recorded in pebbles, village by village, and sent to the palace. The women belonging to families whose men had not gone to war that year were counted later when a commission of war chiefs received a report from each village on the number of men who had not appeared for the campaign. It was at this time also that a check was made on how well the villages had complied with the call to arms. No military quota was assigned to each village. After the war was over, however, and the army commanders had reported how many men from each village answered the call, this number was checked against the pebbles recording the total male population of each village. Should the soldiers number less than half of the total male population of the village, the village chief was strangled.

The procedure for the economic census and taxation of livestock[10] was as follows: The king initiated the annual census of pigs by calling the three hereditary chiefs of the butchers to report the names of the villages in which they bought their pigs. Thereupon, a message was sent to the village named, summoning the chiefs and all those who had pigs for sale, on the grounds that the king was about

[10] Cf. Herskovits, *Dahomey*, I, pp. 116 ff.

to set a new price for pigs. A count of the number of pigs in each village was taken by the chief of the village before his appearance at court, and this provided a check on the accuracy of the reports made by each villager as to his stock of pigs. A complicated system of controls was then set in motion. First, an order was given to the villagers, banning any slaughter of sows for the next six months. This was intended to keep the number of sows at the current level so that this figure could be taken as a constant in subsequent calculations of the total. Secondly, an order was issued to all toll-posts throughout the kingdom to prevent any pigs from being carried through the gates. And finally, every market official was ordered to bring to the palace the heads of all pigs sold in the market during the next six months. At the end of this six-month period, village chiefs reported the number of male pigs in their villages, and this count, plus the number of heads delivered at the palace during the period, was supposed to be at least as large as the total reported at the beginning of the period. If it were found that too many pigs had been slaughtered and sold, the sale of pork was ordered suspended for a year. The animal tax was based on the data thus collected. Slaughterers were taxed according to the number they had handled, and in addition, everyone who raised pigs was assessed a basic toll of one animal per year.

For other livestock—cattle, sheep, and goats—control was less systematic. A census of these animals was taken only about every three years. On such occasions, an impending "catastrophe" would be announced by a crier in the market-place, perhaps an epidemic among the cattle, a drought, or other calamity invented for the occasion. All owners of cattle would be instructed to bring a cowrie shell for each animal, as an offering to placate the gods, and these shells were collected from all over the kingdom. A female official in the palace set aside a pebble for each cowrie, keeping the piles separate for each type of animal, and placed each set of pebbles into a separate sack, before sending the cowries to the temple. A symbol sewn on each sack indicated the type of animal enumerated therein—a horn for cattle; a beard for goats, weeds and a tongue for sheep; and if pigs were included in this census, a butcher's knife on the sack for pigs. The tax was based on this count, each village giving a certain percentage of its stock to the palace, about 12½% in the case of goats. The count was made by taking five animals out of every forty, or every eighth animal.

Taxation

Sources of royal revenue from outside of the palace and its plantations came from a comprehensive system of taxation, levies and contributions. Taxation in Dahomey was general and was linked to an efficient system of collecting, accounting, and control. Indirect techniques were often used for double-checking on evasion of taxes.[11] Every type of produce of the kingdom was taxed as well as internal trade, and the tax system was linked to various measures of economic planning and control discussed in the following section.

Meat was supplied to the palace by various groups of hunters. Hunting was an important source of meat for the population as a whole. Consumption of the meat of wild animals probably exceeded that of domestic ones and the annual hunt is still a feature of Dahomean life. There were two hunting chiefs at court, one for hunters and one for fishermen, and a chief of the hunt (*dega*) in each village. A count of the hunters was taken annually in the course of ceremonial observances at the shrine of the deity of the hunt near Abomey. On the basis of this count, the *dega* were divided into thirteen groups, four *dega* for each Dahomean month, and each of the thirteen groups was required to furnish meat for the palace during one month.

[11] Cf. Herskovits, *Dahomey,* I, pp. 107 ff.

In addition, the heads of all animals killed were sent to the palace to decorate the entrance. A tax on fishermen was paid in dried fish, and presumably collected by means of procedures similar to those for hunters.

With regard to domestic animals, all who kept pigs were assessed one animal per year. Slaughterers were taxed on the basis of the number of animals they had killed. Cattle, sheep, and goats were taxed every three years, a certain proportion of the animals being taken such as one in eight for goats. The techniques of control and enumeration accompanying these taxes are described below.

Horses, on the other hand, belonged only to certain individuals of high status. A tax of four thousand cowries a year was collected for each horse. Contributions of honey, pepper, and ginger were made by two districts near Abomey devoted to their cultivation. These products were regarded as military stores and their production closely supervised.

The taxation of salt was also based on a close supervision of production. Salt was obtained by the evaporation of sea water, and production was limited to the coastal town of Whydah. The salt-workers, resident in two quarters of Whydah, were required to dig hard-pans where the process of evaporation was carried out, and permission for digging had to be obtained from the king's deputy. From each salt-worker the king required ten sacks of salt (about eight kilograms) each year. These sacks were deposited with the Viceroy of Whydah, who set aside a pebble for each sack received, sending these "salt-pebbles" to Abomey at stated times. At Abomey the pebbles were counted, in sets of ten, to determine the number of salt-workers represented. A separate check on the honesty of the Viceroy was made by sending another official from the court to the salt-workers' quarters at Whydah to count the number of salt-pans set out. This count had to tally with that submitted by the Viceroy, and any discrepancy was a grave offense for which the Viceroy might be punished by being deprived of his revenues of office for the period of a year. From the proceeds of this tax the king supplied his household, perhaps also the army.

The forge was the unit for accounting, taxation, and other administrative measures relating to iron. Twelve forges throughout the country were designated to make hoes, and production of hoes was limited to these forges, each of which was under the watchful eye of an official charged with supervising production. Since no hoes could be sold directly from the forge, all sales had to take place in the market under the supervision of market officials. The market head or his deputy had to witness every sale of hoes, recording the sale by placing a pebble in a box, which was marked with the device of the forge at which the hoe was made. Every forge had its device. It was stamped on the product of the forge, and copies of all the devices were registered with the palace and distributed to all market officials. There were twelve boxes in the keeping of each market head, one for each forge, and as each box was filled, it was sent to Abomey and replaced from the capital. A supplementary count of production was taken by summoning smiths to the palace to determine how many hoes were made at their respective forges. From the total thus reported, the number of hoes sold in the market was deducted, leaving the total number on hand. The tax was based on this count, each iron worker being given a token bar of iron by the king and instructed to return with a specified number of cartridges, more or less in number according to the quantity of unsold hoes remaining at the forge.

Other smithies not engaged in making hoes were enumerated through the priests who served the god of iron (*Gu*). Each forge had its shrine to the deity, and at specified times, the priests were called together to receive from the hand of the king the cocks needed for the annual ceremony to the god. The number of forges in the kingdom was then calculated by deducting the number of cocks given out to the priests from the total number on hand at the palace before the distribution to the priests. In addition, the number of smiths was determined by asking each priest how many men worked at his forge. The weavers and wood cutters were likewise assessed a certain proportion of their product.

Internal trade also was taxed. A "passport" system was used in keeping count of porters who carried goods through toll-houses and in levying the taxes on such trade. There was a toll-house at the entrance to every town, at certain places on the lagoons and at the doors of European trade establishments. During the Annual Customs,

> the public crier was sent to the markets to announce that all porters must declare themselves before a given official . . . As the men reported, each gave his name and, in secret, proffered some kind of sign to constitute his passport. Thus, one might employ a small chain, counting the links, so that there would be one for each tollgate through which he must pass, the other links of the chain being distributed among the keepers of the gates. Another might give a small raffia-cloth . . . replicas of these cloths being also distributed to all officers at the toll-posts. When . . . this porter . . . arrived at a toll-post, he was asked for his "passport" and produced the cloth. This was then compared with the cloth that had already been received by the keeper and if there was even a minor difference between the two, the carrier was bound and sent to prison.[12]

The method of levying the tax was as follows: "A small pebble was set aside at each toll-gate every time a given porter passed through it, and at the end of the year the amount he was assessed was based on the number of trips he had made."[13]

[12] Herskovits, *Dahomey*, I, pp. 130–131.
[13] Ibid., I, p. 131.

Other taxes were facilitated by the enforcement of carrying. Pepper, for example, except for limited quantities, could be produced only in certain districts, which were located at some distance from the market. This enabled a tax in cowrie shells to be levied on the goods in transit.

Taxes-in-kind in local markets were taken in the form of "samples" of each type of produce sold in the market. Forbes remarks, however, that "collectors stationed at all markets . . . receive cowries in number according to the value of the goods carried for sale."[14]

A poll tax on every inhabitant of Dahomey is mentioned by Duncan. For certain individuals this might be very high. For example, each of the Viceroy of Whydah's slaves is reported to have paid an annual head-tax of $4000 in cowries [sic].[15]

The death of an official was accompanied by an inheritance tax levied as follows: First, the possessions of the deceased were brought to the king's palace at Abomey. Then the king decided whether the deceased's son was to assume his father's official position or whether it would be awarded as an honor to someone else such as a soldier who had distinguished himself in battle. Only if the son was reappointed would he inherit his father's wealth. Since the king had over-all title to property and land in Dahomey, the return of his father's property had the status of a gift. At the same time, a portion of the inheritance was retained by the king.[16]

The basic tax was that on all agricultural produce. Each year after the harvest, the "minister of agriculture" the Tokpo and his assistants counted the granaries in the king-

[14] Frederick E. Forbes, *Dahomey and the Dahomans, Being the Journal of Two Missions to the King of Dahomey, and Residence at His Capital in 1849 and 1850,* London: Longmans, Brown, Green and Longmans, 1851, Vol. I, p. 35.

[15] Duncan, *Travels,* I, pp. 122–123.

[16] Herskovits, *Dahomey,* II, p. 6.

dom where the crop was stored, recording separately the supplies of maize, millet, peanuts, beans, and yams. A check was made of the granaries inspected against the number of agricultural workers determined from the census (discussed previously) to see that all had been counted. When all reports were in, the king then fixed the tax of agricultural produce, assessing each village its share of the total as a unit.

A tax existed on grave diggers, related to the number of burials performed. Contributions were also made by the family of the deceased to the palace. These were ear-marked after a year to pay for the burial of princes, chiefs, and foreign captives who had died a natural death and had no family in Dahomey. The fee for certifying the natural death of a slave was 3000 cowries.

Occasional references occur to ransom demanded for prisoners, and some revenue resulted from confiscatory fines and penalties. Other sources of state revenue were the taxes and tribute on subject towns, and the revenue from foreign trade.

Royal Equivalents

Among the duties of the king was that of proclaiming certain of the equivalents that were to prevail during his reign.

There were many equivalents of a customary character in Dahomean life, such as the payments made to the bride's parents at marriage, the ritual fees to priests and various village officials on ceremonial occasions, the precisely calculated gift exchanges between kin groups at funerals, etc. These were customary equivalents, and there is nothing to indicate that they would change from one regime to another.

The equivalents prevailing for imported goods were pro-

225

claimed by the king. Dalzel reports that Adahoonzou "issued a proclamation, that no trader should, at any market pay more than thirty-two cabesses of cowries for a man and twenty-six cabesses for a woman slave . . ." and the king himself bought slaves at this price, "he paying the price which he himself had fixed, in strung cowries, at the gate of the palace."[17] To Commander Wilmot, the king said that his price for a slave was "80 dollars, with 4 dollars custom on each."[18] Port dues also "varied with every reign."[19]

The situation was somewhat different with respect to market prices. While these were usually fixed by local bodies, it was the responsibility of the king to determine the general levels which were to prevail during his reign and to make such changes as might be necessary in response to shortages or abundance of stocks. Eventually, in time of difficulty such as that which apparently prevailed during the regime of Gelele, all equivalents were raised. Indeed, Gelele seems to have instituted a kind of ten-year plan. According to Burton, "It is said that Gelele has resolved to grind the faces of his subjects for ten years of which six are now elapsed. After that time they will be supplied to honest labor, and a man shall live on a cowrie a day, so cheap will provisions become."[20] During these six years, equivalents had been raised fourfold. "Prices have quadrupled during the last six years," Burton says, and again, "The Cankey-ball (Dahomey's quartern loaf) fetched, under the old king, three cowries—is now worth twelve."[21]

Equivalents in Dahomey were monetized, that is to say, expressed in cowries. Their character as proclaimed equiva-

[17] Archibald Dalzel, *History of Dahomey,* London: Author, 1793, pp. 213–215.
[18] Burton, *A Mission to Gelele,* II, p. 249.
[19] Ibid., I, p. 94, n. 1.
[20] Ibid., II, p. 57, n. 1.
[21] Ibid., II, pp. 162–163.

lents, however, was unmistakable. Not only were they officially administered, but they changed relatively infrequently and took on a customary character. This is evident, for example, in the lists of market prices reported by Forbes and others where the price of each item is given as the prevailing price for that time and place. Even the designation of the currency unit may reflect the customary equivalent as in the well-known instance of five strings of cowries being called a "galinha," "because it was the price of a fowl."[22]

Nothing in the nature of an organized labor market existed. ". . . As Mungo Park stated in the last century," Burton observes, "paid service is unknown to the negro. Indeed, African languages ignore the word."[23] At Whydah, in Forbes' time, canoemen and carriers, mostly strangers from other parts of the coast, were "hired out" in work parties by their head men. "The subsistence . . . for carriers and hammockmen . . . is three strings of cowries . . . for men, and two for women, per day."[24] Though reckoned in cowries, the payments were made, at least in part, in goods—cloth, tobacco, and rum.[25] The "load" for carriers was likewise fixed. When one of Duncan's carriers lagged behind in traveling from Abomey to Whydah, a messenger was sent to the Prime Minister in the capital who "immediately sent fresh men with orders to punish the villains who had hung back, as, he said, he had himself examined each of their loads, and found them all considerably under the regulated weight for carriers."[26]

So far as the evidence indicates, there were no substitutive equivalents such as would permit the giving of one kind of goods for another in payment, e.g., in taxes. Taxes

22 Ibid., I, p. 107, n. 1.
23 Ibid., II, pp. 132–133, n. 2.
24 Forbes, *Dahomey and the Dahomans,* II, p. 81.
25 Ibid., I, p. 122.
26 Duncan, *Travels,* II, p. 291.

on agricultural produce were collected in kind, and no provision for substitutions is reported.

Public works were also the concern of the king. Dalzel remarks that "the King summons his Caboceers, and portions out the labour among them, paying their people for their trouble."[27]

The state of the roads is, as we have noted, reviewed at the Annual Customs. Dalzel tells also of the king instructing his caboceers to build a road from Abomey to Whydah, providing each with a piece of string to designate the width of the road."[28]

The king exhibited his concern for the family by his appointment of "public women." There were in Dahomey, Burton says:

> public women, an organized and royal institution, appointed from the palace . . . The present king has appointed a fresh troop of ladies of pleasure, but they have not as yet received permission to practise.

In this instance also the name derives from the equivalent:

> At first the honorarium was twenty cowries; hence the common title "Ko-si", score-wife . . . at the representation of the ministers the solatium was increased to two strings, or fourfold.[29]

The king appointed these women to take up residence throughout the kingdom, "to safeguard the peace of private families." Norris explains that such a precaution is necessary because people of rank engrossed the major part of the women and the penalties for adultery were severe. Dahomean men, moreover, might be required to abstain from sexual contact with their wives for as long as three years after the woman gave birth. Otherwise subsequent children, it was held, would be sickly.[30]

[27] Dalzel, Introduction, *History of Dahomey,* p. xii.
[28] Ibid., pp. 170–171.
[29] Burton, *A Mission to Gelele,* II, p. 148.
[30] Herskovits, *Dahomey,* I, p. 268.

The Palace

The state sphere in Dahomey was closely tied to the royal household and its palace economy. No neat division existed, nor can it in fact be introduced between the revenues and the functions attributable to the palace on the one hand, the state on the other. Their roles were intimately connected. For this reason we have combined them under the heading of the Palace economy.

The king's wives numbered, for instance, according to some estimates, about 2000. Many of these played an important part in the administration of the state. Others were employed at various crafts. These were all resident at the Abomey palace and in the king's palace at Akpueho.

Also resident at the Abomey palace were many members of the Amazons, Dahomey's standing army estimated to number up to 5000 women.[31] Other female residents of the palace included a large number of slaves at the service of the harem and the older women of the household, the latter in charge of the graves of the deceased kings. One of several estimates places the total number of women at the Abomey palace itself including Amazons at 3–4000.[32]

Some of the king's offspring acted as special messengers and performed other duties in the king's service. Burton estimated the royal descendants to have numbered about 2000. Le Herisse gives much higher figures, namely, 12,000.[33]

Dahomey employed an extensive state bureaucracy of ministers, administrators, auditors, toll-collectors, police, and others. The chief functionaries in Abomey, although

[31] Ibid., II, p. 88, n. 3.
[32] Edouard Dunglas, *Contribution à l'histoire du Moyen-Dahomey* (*Royaumes d'Abomey, du Ketou et de Ouidah*), IFAN: Etudes dahoméennes, XIX–XXI (1957–58), p. 92.
[33] A. Le Herisse, *L'ancien Royaume du Dahomey. Mœurs, religion, histoire,* Paris: 1911, p. 257.

living in their own houses, were supplied with food from the king's palace.[34]

The palace itself was an imposing structure. Each monarch erected a gateway of his own that consisted of a gap in the wall closed by rough wooden doors. Before this gate a long shed was built alongside of the wall about twenty feet in breadth and sixty feet high with a sloping thatched roof. Here the monarch would recline on mats to dispense justice and perform his other royal duties, with his court squatting around him.

The king's plantations were one of the sources of royal revenue. These yielded palm oil and other produce. Oil and palm kernels from the king's palace at Akpueho were exported at Whydah. The king's plantations were tended by domestic slaves who had a special status and could not be sold.

Also at the Akpueho palace were located various crafts, such as the making of cloth and pipes. Textiles for the king and other members of the royal household were woven here. Long storage sheds contained maize and other supplies. There were also dye-houses and pottery works, and in all these enterprises the king's wives participated. A minor source of revenue were the elephant hunts of the Amazons. These provided not only food for feasts but bones and skulls for the fetish houses, and eventually tusks and teeth for export at Whydah.

Administration and Duality

The administration of Dahomey attained excellence in the way of honesty, precision, and reliability. Gautier rated its performance as unsurpassed among African states. Almost automatic means of check and control were employed. Operational devices were in use which offered mnemotechnical and arithmetical facilities to master admin-

[34] Duncan, *Travels,* I, p. 257.

istrative detail. As we shall see, institutional checks of a rare effectiveness also were practiced. An original method offered in the difference of the sexes, linking officials of every grade by twos and twos, as male acting official and female controller. As Burton says, "Dahomean officials, male and female, high and low, are always in pairs."[35] In this the initiative came from above and belonged to the state sphere. Another deeper and broader initiative sprang from the non-state sphere and worked as a spontaneous protection of autonomy. Ancestor worship, with its shrines present in every dwelling, crowding around fetish houses and, in even greater profusion, around cult houses present in all sib-compounds, created an atmosphere of faith exerting an anti-bureaucratic pressure. The emotional foundations of the rule of law were thus internalized, making superfluous the governmental apparatus of constraint with the masses of the people.

The startling device of relying on the duality of sexes was carried through with thoroughness. In the royal administrative system everything went by pairs, and even multiple pairs. First of all, every official in the kingdom had his female counterpart, or "mother," resident in the royal compound. Within the palace, then, the king had a complete counterpart of the administrative apparatus throughout the kingdom. These women officials were called *naye*. It was the duty of each woman to know intimately all the administrative affairs of her male counterpart and to keep constant check upon his operations. Herskovits gives an illustration of how it worked:

For example, it may be supposed that one of these *naya* was entrusted with remembering the previous reports of the *Yovoga* who, being in command of the sea districts, controlled all the makers of salt. The particular *naye* to whom the *Yovoga* reported would be spoken of as the *Yovogano,* the "mother of the

[35] Burton, *A Mission to Gelele,* I, p. 33.

Yovoga," and she was always present whenever the question of the production of salt was brought up at court councils. She already had in her possession the report of the independent officers sent by the King to survey the salt industry, and it was her task to see that the *Yovoga's* statement of operations corresponded to this other when he made his accounting . . . It was the stated policy of the King to listen to none of his officials unless he first called for the *naye* who was the "mother" of this chief.[36]

Another group of women, the *kposi,* or "wives of the leopard," were in command of the *naye.* There were likewise two groups of *kposi:* one, consisting of eight women, always present when the king held audience with his counselors; a second group, similarly of eight, which over and above stood in attendance when ministers or priests reported. In this way there existed three sets of witnesses to statements of an important official—his "mother," the eight *kposi* who were always present, and those other eight specialist witnesses called in when particular ministers made their report.

Dual organization existed also throughout the army. The army was divided into two wings, the right and the left, and within each wing into a male and female part. Every male, from the highest ranking officer down to the last soldier, had his female counterpart in the palace. The right wing, for example, was commanded by the Mingan, or Prime Minister of Dahomey, and his counterpart was the "She-Mingan, (who) being within the palace, takes precedence of him."

Forbes says of the army:

Considered as one army, it is in two brigades, the *miegan's* and the *mayo's,* the right and the left . . . In the right, there are two *miegans* and two *agaous,* a male and an amazon; and the same equivalent rank

[36] Herskovits, *Dahomey,* I, p. 181.

is carried down to the private in each brigade, male and female. These relationships in military rank are called father and mother; and . . . the male soldier, when accused, appeals to his "mother" to speak for him.[37]

All visitors to the court at Abomey were assigned a "mother" who looked after their needs during their stay and who was present at all audiences granted to the guest of the king.

The new king, upon his succession to the throne, retained the ministers who served his father, but appointed younger men of high rank as his own representatives. This served the purpose of training the younger men in their duties while at the same time providing a check upon the elder statesmen.

Provinces incorporated into Dahomey were permitted to retain their own administration if they had voluntarily submitted, but a man from the king's court, called a "king's wife," might be sent to reside with the local caboceer and exercise surveillance over his affairs on behalf of the king.

In the house of each minister lives a King's daughter and two officers: these superintend the minister's trade, on which he pays tribute according to their report. If a dispute arises in which the King's interest is at stake, these officers report direct; and if the dispute is serious, the minister is arrested or fined.[38]

There is, of course, a paradox in talking about a reduction of bureaucracy in view of the type of duality that doubled and quadrupled the numbers of officialdom. Yet the fact cannot be gainsaid, that all responsible observers, friendly or otherwise, are agreed in acknowledging the Dahomeans' outstanding efficiency in civilian and military affairs.

One cannot ignore the possibility that a sociological ele-

[37] Ibid., II, p. 84; quoted from Forbes, II, pp. 89–90.
[38] Forbes, Dahomey and the Dahomans, I, pp. 34–35.

ment was at work, namely, a predominance of female characteristics. We refuse to attempt to appraise the relative weight of the physical and the cultural factors that might have been operative. The fact is that in very few communities of state level were women called upon to play so large a part in services vital to functioning of the polity. The gifts of the female sex for absorbing detail, retaining information on facts of everyday life in which common sense is anchored have been tested and not found wanting.

The recognized excellence of administration and the eminent role played in it by females does not seem fully to account for the extent to which Dahomean women were drawn into public life up to its highest levels. This suggests that behind the duality device as such there must have been active some motivation, stemming from a mental attitude that transcended considerations of practical efficiency.

Duality was indeed a pervasive feature of the Dahomean culture. The tissue of officialdom was extended there not only vertically as a hierarchy but also horizontally by additions on the same level. Symmetry, comprising all organs of the state, from the body of the field army down to its least unit, could hardly exist unless it was due to an ingrained culture trait. The predilection for twins left its stamp on the semantics of kinship, the organization of the pantheon, and the order of everyday soothsaying. Such pursuance of a dual notion extending from the cosmos to the microcosm of the community did not stop even at the person of the monarch. Kingship itself was "twin." The king had a double role, as Bush King and as Town King. Burton describes the fact:

> One of the Dahomean monarch's peculiarities is, that he is a double . . . two in one. Gelele, for instance, is King of the city, Adde-kpon, of the "bush"; that is to say, of the farmer folk and the country as opposed to the city.[39]

[39] Burton, *A Mission to Gelele,* II, p. 58.

The Bush King had a duplicate of the environment which existed for the Town King: there was a palace set aside for him only six miles southwest of Abomey, with a corps of officials duplicating those of the Town King: in the army organization, the Bush King had his captains, male and female; the Annual Customs of the Town King were followed by a repetition of the Annual Customs for the Bush King: and there was a "mother" for the Bush King, as well as for the Town King. As Skertchly says,

> whatever is done for the king (Gelele) in public is thrice repeated; first for the Amazons, then for Adde-kpon, and thirdly, for Adde-kpon's Amazons.

Actually, a veritable obsession with the perfection of duality prevailed from the earliest mythological notions of a metaphysical order down to the domestic predilection for twin births. The liking for an ample progeniture may have induced this bent. A statistical frequency of twins might explain the conventional preference attaching to offspring born proximately to twins, whether after, before, or between pairs of twins.

At the head of the Dahomean pantheon there was the dual divinity of *Mawu-Lisa*. "The ideal type of every group in the divine world," Mercier says, "is a pair of twins of opposite sex, or more rarely, of the same sex."[40] He refuses to follow up the cultural interpretation of the androgynous element in the cult of twins, preferring to turn to the sphere of political organization "in which duality is immediately apparent."[41] He obviously has in mind the institution of the Bush King, the *economic* importance of which he was the first to recognize. "The dual monarchy," he says, "did not perpetuate itself, until it was revealed to Geze that the prosperity of Dahomey depended on its revival. Thus Geze installed Gãpke and Gelele, Adde-kpon and

[40] Paul Mercier, "The Fon of Dahomey," in *African Worlds,* D. Forde (ed.), London: Oxford University Press, 1954, p. 231.
[41] Ibid., p. 232.

everything that was done for the one had also to be done for the other."[42] Thus the nineteenth century re-enacted the ancient story of King Akaba and his twin sister Xãgba "who ruled jointly, in accordance with the doctrine that twins must always be treated alike."[43]

We now turn to the question of the economic function of the Bush King with his seat in Kana. In Dalzel's time Kana was a large town, about eight miles from Abomey, numbering some 15,000 inhabitants. Quoting Norris, he wrote: "The king frequently resides here, and has a spacious house which occupies with its appendages almost as much ground as St. James's Park: it is enclosed with a high mud wall, which forms nearly a square."[44] Norris measured one side of it and found it 1700 paces long. From the stature of Mr. Norris, this was nearly as many yards, or about an English mile, the editor of Norris remarks, in a footnote. "Halfway between Kana and Abomey is a country house of the King's called Dawhee the ancient residence of the family and a capital of their little territory, before they emerged from their original obscurity."[45] The countryside of Calmina—an earlier name for Kana—was very fertile and its crops sustained the neighboring towns.

Kana contained a royal burial place and one of the oldest and largest market places of the country. It grew from the family's favorite resort and burial place into the residence of the shadow government and court, as well as into a separate economic capital. Since Dahomey's redistributive economy was transacted in kind, the Bush King's palace had an important function of its own. It was a storage and industrial center, housing a large volume of crops collected as taxes, and distributing them, together with manufactured items.

[42] Ibid.
[43] Ibid.
[44] Dalzel, *History of Dahomey*, pp. 118–119.
[45] Ibid., p. 120.

The separation from the royal court at Abomey of the productive and distributive economic activities focused on Kana may have been a convenient procedure and even necessary from the administrative, the military and technological angles.

At his Dawhee palace, halfway between Abomey and Kana, the king was only an hour's distance by a landscaped and perfectly built road from both his political and his economic capital. Treasure goods were guarded and cared for in the Simbony Palace, i.e., Great House, at Abomey. Such were cowries, iron bars, clothes, arms, ammunition, and some articles of European furniture. Provisions for the king's numerous family were also kept here. Besides, wives for substantial young men against sums of up to 20,000 cowries were delivered at the gates of the treasure-house at the political capital. Raw materials for the blacksmiths who produced arms and tools, payment in kind to a diversity of craftsmen, building materials for fortifications, gates, walls, bridges and strategic highways were distributed. The permanent danger was Oyo. Since 1712 a heavy tribute, the *agban,* at times increased at short notice under threat of a devastating cavalry incursion, was a source of anguish to Dahomey. It was annually delivered at Kana to the Oyo delegation. Several incidents show how unreliable the surrounding tribes were, in spite of the proximity of the capital. Several times the king had to pacify the area to protect the royal cemetery and the peace of the market. Since ancient times a Yoruba settlement had existed in Kana which, after the disastrous defeat of the Dahomeans, acted as an intermediary between Dahomey and the Oyo conquerors in negotiating the tribute. Forty-one cases, containing forty-one guns each, formed part of the *agban.* It was understandable, if the munition at least was kept well away.

10

Ports of Trade in Early Societies

I

This study is intended as a confirmation of the global presence of the economic institution to which, for want of a better word, we have given the name "port of trade."[1]

Previous to modern times, so it appears, the typical organ of overseas trade was an arrangement capable of dealing with the security requirements of trade under early state conditions. The general emergence of price-making markets must be regarded as a later development, characterized by competing groups of buyers and sellers, whose activities are governed by market prices. In the port of trade, [governmental] administration prevailed over the "economic" procedure of competition. Trade between primitive communities, whether expeditionary trade, gift trade, ceremonial beach meeting, or other chieftain's trade must face up to the security aspect of carrying goods over a distance in unpoliced areas. In the desert, on mountains and high seas, robbery and piracy are accepted forms of existence; on land, panyarring or kidnapping are the stranger's risk; coastal sites are threatened from sea and hinterland. The port of trade was often a neutrality device, a derivative of

FROM "Ports of Trade in Early Societies," *The Journal of Economic History,* Vol. XXIII, No. 1, March 1963, pp. 30–45. Reprinted by permission of the editor.
[1] K. Polanyi, C. M. Arensberg and H. W. Pearson (eds.), *Trade and Market in the Early Empires,* Glencoe: Free Press & Falcon's Wing Press, 1957; cited hereafter as *T. & M.* See Chapters II–IV, VII–IX.

silent trade, of the prehistoric Mediterranean low-walled *emporium,* open to the sea, and of the neutralized coastal town. The archaic syndrome comprised a trade carried on at set prices, and by other administrative means. Native inhabitants provided organs for mediation and accountancy, while competition was avoided as a mode of transaction. Where present, it was relegated to the background, or was merely lurking on the periphery.

Ports of trade were in evidence on the north Syrian coast ever since the second millennium B.C., in some Greek city-states of Asia Minor and the Black Sea in the first millennium; in the Negro kingdoms of Whydah and—later—Dahomey on the Upper Guinea coast and of Angola on the Lower Guinea coast; in the Aztec-Maya region of the Gulf of Mexico; in the Indian Ocean on the Malabar Coast,[2] in Madras, Calcutta, Rangoon, Burma, Colombo, Batavia, as well as in China.

Thus we find the port of trade as a universal institution of overseas trade preceding the establishment of international markets. It was, as a rule, situated on coastal or riverain sites, where inlets and extensive lagoons eased transportation by land. A related institution, however, might also be found far inland, on the border of two ecological regions, such as highland and plain, but particularly on the border of the desert, that *alter ego* of the sea. The caravan cities of Palmyra and Petra, Karakorum, Ispahan and Kandahar may be said to have fallen in the category of *quasi* ports of trade.

Even the barest outline of the origins and development of the port of trade confronts us with a number of forms, varying in range and scope as widely as do market institutions to which, in historical retrospect, the port of trade may appear as a functional alternative. Indeed, markets differ as an African bush market does from the New York

---

[2] A. Leeds, "The Port of Trade in Pre-European India and as an Ecological and Evolutionary Type." Paper presented at the Annual Meeting of the American Ethnological Society, 1961.

Stock Exchange, and the international market for capital, freights, and insurance from the slave market in the American South of a century ago, yet all of them are authentic markets. In either case—market-type institution and port of trade—history and anthropology present a bewildering ramification.

Among riverain trading sites of antiquity mention will also have to be made of the Babylonian *kar*. Was it essentially competitive market or administered port of trade? The two patterns, an administration proper and a system of price-making markets, are mutually incompatible, though some of their elements may mix. On the answer to the nature of the Babylonian *kar* important issues in the dating of the civilizations of antiquity may depend.

An appeal to administrative action in the economic field appears to many intrinsically as a relinquishing of rationality since, as Max Weber taught, market behavior was to be regarded as the paradigm of rationality. The great Assyriologist Paul Koschaker showed on this score a mood of resignation in his last study.[3] For him the full-blown market-economy was a tissue of contracts or transactions. This tissue was knit of rational acts and could therefore be resolved logically. Administrative acts, on the other hand, possessed no safeguard of equality of exchange, since such acts were an outflow of power not of a free contract. A Romanist by training, Koschaker had established almost singlehandedly our knowledge of transactional law in Babylonia. In 1942 he published a paper on the governmentally administered economy (*staatliche Verwaltungswirtschaft*) of Larsa, dealing mainly with the revenue of the palace in regard to fish. Reluctantly, he confessed his inability to find a consistent interpretation of the textual evidence in which the transactions between palace and *tamkarum* were laid

[3] P. Koschaker, "Zur staatlichen Wirtschaftsverwaltung in altbabylonischer Zeit, insbesondere nach Urkunden in Larsa," *Zeitschrift für Assyriologie* N. F. Bd. 13 (Bd. 47) (1942), 179–80.

down. Koschaker had justly inferred that the so-called *tamkarum* (traditionally interpreted as a private merchant) was actually "a governmental trade officer, a state-banker."

The situation, so it seemed, lacked rationality. At least partly, it was the result of administrative decisions, not of the free exchanges on which a market system must be based. The fish prices of Larsa—like the wool prices of Sippar—were probably state-fixed,[4] as Koschaker himself had written. Yet he had also stated that "in the Old Babylonian period we should assume the existence of a fully developed system of market exchange, and even one with recorded price fluctuations."[5] This was conclusively evidenced, he asserted, by the manifold terms used to describe prices as attested in the Series *ana ittišu,* 2 III 10 f. Actually, the resolution of the paradox was within his reach. The manifold adjectives attached to prices in *ana ittišu,* which understandably disturbed him, were not conclusive proof of the existence of a "fully developed system of market exchange," for they might well have formed part of a predominantly administered economy such as the early New Deal, or the actual Soviet economy.

In this paper, starting with antiquity and proceeding toward the modern era, the following instances of a port of trade or its antecedents are touched upon: the North Syrian coastal towns; the Greek *emporium* in two distinct meanings, the first being Lehmann-Hartleben's discovery, his prehistoric *emporium* (in its few Norse instances called *wik*),[6] the second the commercial harbor of the classical Greek coastal city which, as a survival from prehistoric times, was a characteristic formation in Greek seaports.[7] Drawn from

[4] Ibid., p. 142.
[5] Ibid., p. 158.
[6] E. Ennen, *Frühgeschichte der europäischen Stadt* (Bonn: Röhrscheid Verlag, 1953).
[7] K. Lehmann-Hartleben, *Die antiken Hafenanlagen des Mittelmeeres* (Leipzig: Klio, Beih. 14, 1923), pp. 4 ff.

more modern times are the Aztec-Maya lagoon towns of Mexico,[8] the Guinea coast of West Africa,[9, 10] as well as the Malabar coast of India,[11] all before the European conquest. To this list is added the Babylonian *kar*,[12] the port-of-trade character of which, as I said before, is controversial.

II

Al-Mina and Ugarit,[13] on the North Syrian coast, may have been among the earliest ports of trade in the Mediterranean. Al-Mina was situated some forty miles north of Ugarit, on a marshy tract, not far from the small inland kingdom of Alalakh[14] (Atchana). Al-Mina itself lay at the mouth of the Orontes, and appears as a small principality of its own. Both coastal towns served as sources of imports to the empires of the hinterland. The Babylonians in the East, the Hittites in the North may have been keen to keep Al-Mina neutral. Egypt in the South felt similarly towards Ugarit.[15] They maintained friendly relations with

[8] A. M. Chapman, "Port of Trade Enclaves in Aztec and Maya Civilizations," in *T. & M.*, pp. 114–53.

[9] R. Arnold, "A Port of Trade: Whydah on the Guinea Coast," in *T. & M.*, pp. 154–76; "Separation of Trade and Market: Great Market of Whydah," in *T. & M.*, pp. 177–87.

[10] K. Polanyi, in collaboration with A. Rotstein, *Dahomey and the Slave Trade* (in preparation).

[11] A. Leeds, "The Port of Trade," cited in ft. 2.

[12] A. L. Oppenheim, "A Bird's-Eye View of Mesopotamian Economic History," in *T. & M.*, pp. 30–31.

[13] R. B. Revere, " 'No Man's Coast': Ports of Trade in the Eastern Mediterranean," in *T. & M.*, pp. 38–63.

[14] K. Polanyi, "Comparative Treatment of Economic Institutions in Antiquity, with Illustrations from Athens, Mycenae and Alalakh," in *City Invincible* (Chicago: Univ. of Chicago Press, 1960), pp. 347–48.

[15] R. B. Revere, "Ports of Trade in the Eastern Mediterranean," pp. 40–43.

the small kingdoms on whose neutrality peaceful access to the ports depended. The excavation of Ugarit[16] by Cl. Schaeffer's French expedition and of Al-Mina[17] by Sir Leonard Woolley's British group produced evidence of warehouses close to the beach. History points toward a broadly independent existence of these ports of trade. Almost a millennium later their neighbors to the south, the Phoenician port towns of Sidon[18] and Tyre[19] replaced Ugarit and Al-Mina as ports of trade.

Lehmann-Hartleben saw in Herodotus' "silent trade" the origins of his prehistoric *emporia,* archaeological vestiges of which he discovered on the Mediterranean coasts. The Carthaginians, according to Herodotus,[20] indulged in a dumb barter with the natives of the African coast, exchanging their goods for gold. Caution impelled the parties to repair, in turn, to a spot near the beach, leaving there an amount of goods and gold, respectively. This was repeated, until the other party was satisfied with the amounts offered, both sides withdrawing then with the purchase sought, never having met their counterparts face to face. Lehmann-Hartleben found remnants of semi-enclosed spots open toward the sea and showing ruins of an altar, separated only by a low stone wall from the background area. The low wall did not by itself offer defense against attack, it merely indicated the area to which the protection of the altar and the "peace" of the *emporium* extended.

In this meaning, introduced by Lehmann-Hartleben, the term *emporium* conveys a meeting place of traders, located outside of the gates of a town, or even on an uninhabited coast.

[16] Ibid., p. 53. Cf. also Cl. Schaeffer, *Ugaritica,* III (Paris, 1956).
[17] Ibid., pp. 53–54. Cf. also Sir Leonard Woolley, *A Forgotten Kingdom* (London: Harmondsworth, 1953).
[18] Ibid., pp. 58–59.
[19] Ibid., pp. 58–59. Cf. Ezekiel 27.
[20] Herod., IV. 196.

It is from the prehistoric *emporium* that in classical Greece another meaning accrued to the word, namely that part or sector of a coastal town which was devoted to foreign commerce. Separated from the rest of the city, it contained its harbor, quay, warehouses, mariners' hostel, administrative buildings. The classical *emporium* as a rule had its own food market.[21]

Monuments, closely resembling Lehmann-Hartleben's *emporia* with their semicircle of low stone walls open towards the river, lake, or sea were found more recently in northern Europe and have been named *wik*.[22] Three are on record: Durstede[23] in the Waal delta of the Rhine, Haithabu[24] on the River Schley in eastern Schleswig, and Birka[25] on the Lake Målar, near Stockholm. They are credibly attributed to roving traders of Norse origin, who erected the walls for protection of their meetings with other overseas traders' caravans that carried or portaged their wares from central and eastern Europe, maybe from as far as southern Russia, or the Near East, including Iran.

Although none of these northern *emporia* subsequently developed into towns, some German economic historians of the 1930s believed that the frequent "wik" or "wich" ending of German and English town names might indicate a Viking origin. This idea was subsequently rejected for

[21] The use of the word *emporium* as denoting a large center of commerce is of later origin.

[22] E. Ennen, *Frühgeschichte*, p. 124. Cf. also W. Vogel, *Wik-Orte und Wikinger*, Hans. Geschichtsbll., 60 (1935). F. Rörig, *Lübeck*, Hans. Geschichtsbll., 67/68 (1942–1943); *Magdeburgs Entstehung und die ältere Handelsgeschichte*, Misc. Akad. Berol. II, i (1950), 103–32. H. Planitz, *Frühgeschichte der deutschen Stadt*, Zschr. Savigny Stiftg., Rechtsgesch., Germ. Abt., 67 (1950).

[23] E. Ennen, *Frühgeschichte*, p. 56.

[24] Ibid., p. 59. Cf. also Jankuhn, *Haithabugrabungen*, 1930–1939.

[25] Ibid.

several reasons.[26] First, German historians on the whole accept Pirenne's view that long-distance traders settling around the cités and bourgs of northwest France started the movement of the revival of towns which then spread east to Germany, reaching her therefore by no means from the North.[27] Second, the "wik" ending was quite obviously derived from "vicus," the common Latin term for an unwalled urban settlement.[28] Third, insofar as the "wik" ending might have had a Nordic derivation, it denoted a bay or bight, which in Scandinavian is called "wick."[29] The fact that a few semicircular walled areas off the coast or the waterways have been found in northern Europe, should be regarded merely as proof that Lehmann-Hartleben's *emporium,* common in the Mediterranean, was not unique to it.[30]

Pirenne's portus theorem should be mentioned in this context on account of the current meaning of "port" as a harbor. It is common knowledge that the revival of the European towns about the eleventh and twelfth centuries was attributed by him to the so-called *portus*[31] development around the towns of northwest France and south Flanders.

[26] F. Rörig, *Lübeck.* Th. Frings, *Wik.* Beiträge zur Geschichte der deutschen Sprache und Literatur, begr. v. Braune–Paul–Sievers. Herausgegeben v. Th. Frings, 65 (1941–1942), 221–26.

[27] F. Rörig, *Magdeburgs Entstehung,* p. 128. H. Planitz, *Die deutsche Stadt im Mittelalter* (1954), p. 54 ff.

[28] E. Ennen, *Frühgeschichte,* p. 130, "Die Autorität von Frings steht hinter der Herleitung von 'vicus'," also n. 202, same page.

[29] K. Polanyi, review of E. Ennen, *Frühgeschichte,* in THE JOURNAL OF ECONOMIC HISTORY XVII, No. 2 (June 1957), 312.

[30] E. Ennen, *Frühgeschichte,* p. 69, "Die Wikingischen Emporien lassen sich allenfalls mit den Emporien vergleichen, die von Lehmann-Hartleben bei vielen antiken Seestädten nachgewiesen wurden."

[31] "a place through which merchandise was carried."

But this development consisted in the actual settlement of traders in the suburbs outside of the walls. The word "portus" itself derived from the Latin *portare,* and denoted places of transshipment or portage where wares were stored and guarded and which offered the traders a chance of settlement. Such spots were mostly located on waterways and attached to towns, outside of which the traders found an abode over the winter. These traders' settlements were credited by Pirenne with eventually contributing to the growth of the town, whether bourg or cité.

These populous settlements had very little, if anything, in common with the *emporia,* which typically were empty locations. The traders of Pirenne's portus became residents in the portus, while our port of trade is inhabited by natives, not by strangers. Medieval law regarded the trader as resident not where he was born or occasionally traded, but where he died, *ubi mercatores moriantur.*

III

During the precolonial era ports of trade, not market places, were the growing points of the world economy.

Anne M. Chapman's eminent paper on pre-Conquest Mesoamerica[32] is to our knowledge the only record of a large geographical region in which small ports of trade were densely located. Between two neighboring trading Mesoamerican empires, Aztec and Maya, an expanse of inland waterways settled by tribal communities existed, in which dozens of villages developed into ports of trade. Traders met there to transact business.

Thus the Mesoamerican ports of trade played a vital part in Aztec-Maya commerce. The close network of waterways—rivers, lakes, and lagoons of the Gulf of Mexico —were the sites of many Nahuatl-[33] as well as some

[32] A. M. Chapman, "Port of Trade Enclaves," in *T. & M.*
[33] Ibid., pp. 117, 138.

Chontal-speaking[34] tribes that served as long-distance meeting places of status traders, Mexican *pochteca*[35] and Mayan *ppolom*.[36] Outstanding was Chicalango[37] in the Laguna de Términos. The area was politically neutralized by the conjoint interest of the powers of the Northwest and the Northeast. The advantages of the site lay in the abundance of waterways, some running parallel to the coast, while the western mountains sent their rivers coastwards, linking the landlocked interior such as Acalán[38] by boats and pirogues with the low-lying lagoons. The port of trade was equipped with warehouses and storage, and a population skilled in the portage and handling of wares. For the long-distance traders of either side were not from among the local people,[39] but were rather leaders, both western and eastern, of caravans trekking from the North. Apart from the superior transportation facilities, there were also plantations growing cacao beans,[40] which served in long-distance trade as current money and that all strangers were keen to acquire. There is evidence of a neutralizing policy of the Mexican empire, which shunned any manifest lordship over Chicalango, presumably so as not to frighten away the hillmen who might fear to be kidnapped by the military on the spot. The coastal area was dotted with tribal villages, the names of which are recorded on the sixteenth-century Spanish maps. These small-scale trade ports possessed no market-places as a rule, and served merely for storage and meeting in long-distance trade. With the Spanish conquest the political organizing centers of long-distance trade were destroyed, and the ports of trade vanished.[41]

[34] Ibid.
[35] Ibid., pp. 120 ff.
[36] Ibid., p. 132.
[37] Ibid., pp. 139–40.
[38] Ibid., pp. 142–45.
[39] Ibid., p. 116.
[40] Ibid., p. 134.
[41] Ibid., p. 119.

On West Africa's Guinea coast, more than a century later, a port of trade appeared that attained world fame: the slave port of Whydah.[42] It was a politically neutral open port, which carried on passive trade with all the European powers by administrative methods. In 1727 Dahomey conquered Whydah and incorporated its territory, subjecting trade to its own administration.

Passing on to precolonial Asia, many highly developed ports of trade meet us on the Malabar coast of India and in other parts of the Indian Ocean. The great majority consists of independent small states. Counting only coastal cities south from Sandabur (formerly Portuguese Goa) to Calicut and Quilon (Kawlam), more than a dozen ports of trade flourished from the fourteenth century onward.[43] The Malabar towns differed in three regards from the ports of trade hitherto cited. No commercial profit of the state was involved; in other words, the town itself did not trade. Its interest was purely fiscal, restricted to customs duties, port fees, and other items of revenue. Second, the administration of trade was not according to a uniform pattern, since it comprised both competitive attitudes and adherence to statutory prices. Third, the motivation of transactions was partly collective, as in guilds, partly individual; in either case the traders' morale, whether Hindu or Muslim, reflected the grounding of their status in religious affiliations.

The ports of trade hitherto mentioned differed in their politico-economic character. They can be distinguished according to whether the port functioned as the organ of an independent small state (Ugarit, Al-Mina, Sidon, Tyre, Whydah in its first stage), or whether it was in the possession of a hinterland empire (Whydah after 1727). Again, the neutrality of the port of trade may have been safeguarded either by the agreement of the hinterland empires

[42] R. Arnold, "A Port of Trade," in *T. & M.*

[43] The Rehla of Ibn Battuta (tr. Mahdi Husain, *Gaekwad's Oriental Series*, CXXII, 1953), map facing p. 176.

(Ugarit and Al-Mina), or by the consensus of the overseas trading powers (Whydah), or by reliance on the port of trade's own naval strength (Tyre). Finally, there is in contrast to the majority of cases in which the port looked to overseas trade, the rarer case in which only inland trade was involved (Chicalango).

A port of trade *sui generis* was, it appears, the Babylonian *kar*. As mentioned before, it was a riverain port, the economic organization of which is still obscure. No archaeological remains whatever have survived, but business documents amply testify to its widespread occurrence. Now that doubts have arisen about the very existence of a market system in ancient Mesopotamia, the *kar* has unexpectedly gained focal interest for the Assyriologist. Also, historians of antiquity have become conscious of the fact that the economic historiography of Greece had been firmly built on the assumption that the institutions of Greek trade derived from the old Orient. If our interpretation proves true to fact, and the Babylonian economy was not grounded on a market system, the question arises: "How, when and where did market trade, fluctuating price, profit and loss accounts, commercial methods of business, commercial classes and all the paraphernalia of a market-organized economy originate? The history of market trade may then be found to have shifted (from Babylonia) by a thousand years downwards, and several degrees of longitude westwards, to the Ionia and Greece of the first millennium B.C."[44]

IV

The traditional assumption, which reached axiomatic status since the discovery of Hammurabi's Code in 1902,

[44] K. Polanyi, "Marketless Trading in Hammurabi's Time," in *T. & M.*, p. 26.

was the commercial character of Babylonian culture and society. The underlying concept was that of an economic life governed by the profit motive. Gain was here made on price differentials, and the economy oriented on fluctuating prices.

Doubts first voiced by Paul Koschaker in 1942[45] were taken up by the end of the 1950s.[46] They focused on the *tamkarum,* the central figure in trade; on the origin and nature of the prices recorded in thousands of clay tablets; on the different moneys and money-uses; finally, on the precise meaning of the Akkadian terms that in various contexts had been rendered as "market" and "market-place."

In a collective work, *Trade and Market in the Early Empires,* 1957, A. Leo Oppenheim of the Oriental Institute of the University of Chicago and I argued in separate essays the absence of market-places within the cities of the ancient Near East. Oppenheim laid down the background of the approach:

> The reaction against the thought patterns evolved in the nineteenth century in the fields of history of religion, linguistics, sociology, etc., have taught us to respect alien civilizations and sharpened our faculties for self-observation in those areas; but this, unfortunately, is not true with regard to economics. There, epistemological discussions, traditional or otherwise, have created an atmosphere in which there is no understanding of any economic pattern beyond that which has grown out of the spectacular economic development of Western Europe since the eighteenth century. The resulting attitude of the economic historians, be their background that of historical materialism or of traditional liberalism, is characterized by a markedly

[45] P. Koschaker, "Zur staatlichen Wirtschaftsverwaltung," p. 179: "Meine Ausführungen schliessen mit Zweifeln und Dissonanzen."
[46] K. Polanyi, "Marketless Trading," pp. 12–26, and A. L. Oppenheim, "A Bird's-Eye View," pp. 27–37, in *T. & M.*

inadequate treatment of the economies of so-called primitive peoples as well as by a complete disregard for the essentials of the economics of the ancient great civilizations.

A new approach to this problem has been opened up by the Interdisciplinary Project at Columbia University, and has been tested in several areas with considerable success.[47]

The basic advantage of this approach is that it provides us with a new set of concepts[48] which can be used to describe large sections of the complex and varied array of data which the Assyriologist culls from the economic texts.[49]

I shall use it here with a view to elucidating the problem of the market and *kar* in Babylonia. Babylonian towns, Oppenheim explains,

. . . consisted of the town proper (u r u), the suburb (u r u . b a r . r a) and the port (k a r). *The absence of a market-place* [my italics, K. P.] *is exactly as reveal-*

[47] Columbia University, Interdisciplinary Project on the Economic Aspects of Institutional Growth, *Selected Memoranda*, 4 vols., 637 pp., 1953–1958 (available at Columbia University, Butler Library, reserved). C. M. Arensberg, "Anthropology as History," in *T. & M.*, pp. 97–113. Paul Bohannan, "The Impact of Money on an African Subsistence Economy," in THE JOURNAL OF ECONOMIC HISTORY, XIX, No. 4 (Dec. 1959), 491–503. Paul Bohannan, *Tiv Trade and Markets* (in preparation). T. K. Hopkins, "Sociology and the Substantive View of the Economy," in *T. & M.*, pp. 271–306. W. C. Neale, "Reciprocity and Redistribution in the Indian Village: Sequel to some Notable Discussions," in *T. & M.*, pp. 218–36. H. W. Pearson, "The Economy has no Surplus: Critique of a Theory of Development," in *T. & M.*, pp. 320–41.

[48] K. Polanyi, "The Economy as Instituted Process," in *T. & M.*, pp. 241–70. Cf. also K. Polanyi, *The Great Transformation* (New York: Rinehart & Co., College edition, 1957) ch. IV, "Societies and Economic Systems," pp. 43–55.

[49] A. L. Oppenheim, "A Bird's-Eye View," pp. 28–29.

ing of the internal economic structure of the city as is the presence of a special extramural district, called the port [*kar*] for intercity economic relations.[50]

I listed some prima facie arguments supporting the view that Babylonia possessed no market system, and apparently practiced risk-free forms of trading in the frame of a redistributive system carried on through administrative methods. I invoked, *inter alia,* a passage from Herodotus which had been practically ignored by economic historians of antiquity. The Greek historian, who had visited Babylon sometime between 470 and 460, was writing after the Persian Wars (490–480). Herodotus intended to highlight the meeting of the hostile worlds, East and West, the clash of which was to be the focus of his nine books. The contentious innovation of the food market was the Athenian topic of the day. He made Cyrus, King of Kings, pointedly choose that subject, when meeting the Spartan embassy in Sardis, that was delivering a protest against his interference in the affairs of the Hellenes of Ionia. Cyrus turned on them:

> I have never yet been afraid of any men, who have a set place in the middle of their city, where they come together to cheat each other and forswear themselves.

Cyrus meant these words, so Herodotus comments,

> . . . as a reproach against *all* the Greeks, because of their having market-places where they buy and sell, which is a custom unknown to the Persians, who never make purchases in open marts, and indeed have in their whole country not a single (paràpan) market-place.[51]

Herodotus, as we know, saw the fate of empires in terms of the *hybris* of their rulers. The Persians were indulging

---

[50] Ibid., pp. 30–31.
[51] Herod., I. 153 (tr. Rawlinson).

in chauvinistic war propaganda and Cyrus' successors paid on the battlefield for having underrated the morale of the polis.

As to market-squares, I pointed to the archaeological proof of the almost complete absence of open spaces in the walled towns of ancient Palestine,[52] as well as to the marketless layout of Babylon, attested by the finds in the library of Assur-banipal. In a separate study of the translations of the "Cappadocian" tablets available to me, I developed a conjectural sketch of the administrative functions of the *tamkar;* of non-market trade; of the riskless forms of administered foreign commerce and other requisites of treaty-trade, which appeared compatible with the postulate of non-market methods and with some known uncontentious data.[53]

As early as 1925, in the very first analysis of the "Cappadocian" tablets, B. Landsberger noted the peculiar fact that only gains, not losses were being referred to. Also, in *ana ittišu* he called the *tamkarum* a public trustee (*Treuhänder*).[54] Later on, Koschaker also judged the *tamkarum* not to have been, in Larsa, a private merchant, but a trade officer, a state-banker.[55] Moreover, he wondered, might not fish prices in Larsa have been state-fixed prices rather than market prices.[56]

Eventually, F. W. Leemans moved significantly closer to this position. In his *Old Babylonian Merchant* (1950), he still had upheld all the way the private-businessman view

[52] A.-G. Barrois, *Manuel d'archéologie biblique* (Paris: Picard, 1939), I, 291–92.
[53] K. Polanyi, "Marketless Trading in Hammurabi's Time," in *T. & M.*, pp. 12–26.
[54] B. Landsberger, *Materialien zum Summerischen Lexikon,* I. Die Serie *ana ittišu* (1937), p. 115.
[55] P. Koschaker, "Zur staatlichen Wirtschaftsverwaltung," p. 164.
[56] Ibid., pp. 158–59.

of the *tamkarum*.[57] But in his *Foreign Trade in the Old Babylonian Period* (1960), he professed:

> . . . if the word "market" is used, one must realize that there is no evidence that a market in our sense of the word was held in the ancient cities of Southern Mesopotamia, or, that there was a "market-square." There is not even a word for it in fact. (Cf. K. Polanyi and A. L. Oppenheim, in chapters II and III of *Trade and Market in the Early Empires* [1957].)[58]

There was also a hint that Leemans himself was in the course of revising his previous views about the "activity of the tamkarum."[59] Meanwhile, R. F. G. Sweet, in his doctoral thesis, "Moneys and Money Uses in the Old Babylonian Period,"[60] sponsored by A. L. Oppenheim, surveyed all available tablets—approximately twenty-five hundred. The results confirmed my hypotheses on special-purpose moneys: barley for payment, silver for a standard, and other equivalenced staples as means of exchange. Gardin and Garelli,[61] in a recent study on the "Cappadocian" tablets, described the *tamkarum* as engaged in assisting the traders in their dealings, deriving his own revenue *not* from gains on the transactions in hand but from commission fees. Thus the trend of expert opinion appeared to run in favor of my views critical of the traditional marketing interpretation of the Babylonian economy.

It is at this point that our story reverts to the *kar*.

[57] F. W. Leemans, *The Old-Babylonian Merchant*. Studia et Documenta, III (Leiden: E. J. Brill, 1950), ch. IV, "Conclusions," pp. 36 ff.

[58] F. W. Leemans, *Foreign Trade in the Old Babylonian Period*. Studia et Documenta, IV (Leiden: E. J. Brill, 1960), p. 1, n. 1.

[59] Ibid., preface, p. vii.

[60] Oriental Institute, University of Chicago.

[61] G.-C. Gardin and P. Garelli, "Études des établissements Assyriens en Cappadoce par ordinateur," *Annales*, 16ᵉ année, No. 5 (Sept.–Oct. 1961).

V

An important controversy as to the nature of the *kar* has arisen. Leemans[62] followed up his declaration about the absence of an Akkadian word for "market" in these unexpected terms:

> On the other hand, there is evidence that business was often carried out on the quay, which is in accordance with the fact that the waterways were the principal means of transport. The quay, the *karum, seems to have served the same function as a market in lower Mesopotamia* [my italics, K. P.]. So the price of the quay (kima karum ibaššu, etc.) is what we call, and therefore translate, as the "market price."[63]

Leemans, referring to Koschaker (ZA, 1942, p. 159), added that such a price would be a market price even if it were fixed by the government. F. M. Heichelheim, a classicist, concurred with Leemans on the nature of the *kar* as a market, a view already foreshadowed by Leemans in almost identical terms in his 1958 review of *Trade and Market in the Early Empires.*[64]

The now-admitted absence of market-places and of the market habit, indeed of even so much as a word for "market" in the Akkadian language must raise many questions for Assyriology. The new role suggested by Leemans for the *kar* offers prima facie a clue in the case of the lost market. But apart from there being no supporting evidence, there are also grave objections to his market interpretation of the *kar*. On early markets, whether anthropologi-

[62] F. W. Leemans, *Foreign Trade in the Old Babylonian Period*, p. 1, n. 1.

[63] Ibid., pp. 1–2, n. 1.

[64] F. W. Leemans, "Economische gegevens in Summerische en Akkadische texten, en hun problemen," *Jaarbericht* No. 15, Ex Oriente Lux (1957–1958), pp. 203–4.

cally or historically conceived, we find the distribution of fresh food for general consumption to be their vital function. Among other things, this involves the holding of markets on fixed days, the availability of money in small denominations, such as cowrie shells, gold dust, or fractions of obols, the role of women in the regular preparation of food for sale, popular barter or cash transactions, ceremonial, juridical and ritual customs, gods and altars guarding the peace of the market and strictly delimiting its borders, also market personnel and rules for the settling of disputes. Such matters belong to the most penetrating everyday items of culture, items that leave their mark on religion, law, literature, and common speech. They cannot go unnoticed. Yet Leemans adduces no evidence of this kind. Evidence, such as it is, points rather towards intercity transportation of staples in bulk, under supervision of governmental officers responsible for finance.

The *kar* as an organ of external trade undoubtedly has much in common with authentic ports of trade on the Malabar Coast and in the Maldive Archipelago studied by Ibn Batutah. The fourteenth-century Malabar Coast counted about a dozen coastal states where trade was administered by the Sultan and his body of officers. In at least one case, the Sultan of Fakhanar,[65] a fleet of thirty warships insured that no foreign merchantman passed the town without stopping at the harbor and submitting to its far-reaching customs procedure, the *bandar*.[66] The customs officers were empowered to seize an indeterminate part of the cargo against payment at prices set by themselves, which could be lower than its value. The goods were then resold by the treasury, which benefited from the revenue thus accruing to it. On the other hand, very considerable expenses caused by the lavish hospitality exercised by the port of trade were borne by the *bandar*. The term carried

[65] Ibn Battuta, *The Rehla*, p. 184.
[66] Ibid., p. 184, n. 6.

both the meanings of quay or harbor, and of treasury, customs duty and storehouse. The *two* meanings, however, were fused. The authenticity of the law of the *bandar* is attested by Ibn Battutah,[67] who sojourned for a year and a half in the Maldives, on the chief island of Malan, where he was in office. A troop of mercenaries to the number of one thousand, he wrote, was in the queen's service. They presented themselves daily at her palace, and once a month made a brief appearance requesting their pay, which was thereupon issued to them in rice from the stores of the *bandar.* The etymology[68] of the word—Persian: quay or harbor; Sanskrit (*bhandāra*): treasury, storehouse, tool-shed, magazine—conclusively supports the view of the administrative functions of the *bandar* within the frame of a port of trade.

The importance of the *kar* controversy for Greek classical scholarship is very great. It has been long accepted as unwritten law that the business life of the Hellenes inherited its practices by way of the Lydians and the Phoenicians from the ancient Orient, which was identified with the chrematistic urge attributed to Tyre and, since the discovery of Hammurabi's Code, to the whole of Babylonia. In regard to Greece, G. E. M. de Ste. Croix[69] strongly disagreed with my admittedly late date for the first beginnings of Greek market trade; he seems, however, greatly to favor some of the conceptual innovations of the new approach. The disestablishment of some Western preconceptions concerning the culture of the ancient Orient must deprive the West of its belief in having its roots in a civilization of early Greek market trade; second, on a more scholarly level, of the traditional ready-made answers to the actual development of Greco-Roman market trade from an alleged Cunei-

[67] Ibid., p. 201.
[68] Ibid., p. 200, n. 5.
[69] G. E. M. de Ste. Croix, review of *T. & M.* in *The Economic History Review,* 2nd Series, XII, No. 3 (April 1960), 510.

form mercantile civilization of millennial age. Hence the close interweaving of Assyriologist and classicist reactions to the *kar* controversy[70] follows naturally. In a review, to-

[70] This compels me to try and unravel the interlocking criticisms which F. M. Heichelheim has leveled against my several contributions to *Trade and Market in the Early Empires*, 1957 (in his review of that work in *Journal of the Economic and Social History of the Orient*, III, Pt. I [April 1960], 108–10). Unfortunately, the conceptual system developed in that work had, as he avowed, no interest for him.

Heichelheim's impatience with my voicing of any doubts concerning the dominance of a market system in the ancient Orient antedated Leemans' partial concurrence (1961) with my views on the matter. Heichelheim asked, had I "in fact, never heard of the 'market'-prices at the quays?" It was precisely the suitability of such all-too-often-used terms, that the new conceptual tool box was designed to probe. As a result, trade and market were not only sharply distinguished, but up to a point contrasted in the archaic empires. Heichelheim, having ignored theory, employed "trade" and "market" interchangeably. Since the actual links between market and trade institutions were in question, his insistence on employing the term "market trade" in disregard of the significance attaching to this technical term in the work was anything but helpful.

Still another instance of Heichelheim's practice of "no theory" should perhaps be adduced. The methodological device of transcending time-bound institutions through the introducing of generalized terms was applied by me throughout the work. In order to avoid the marketing connotation of "price" where inappropriate, a new term—"equivalency"—was introduced by me as well as by Oppenheim, which would apply irrespective of the pattern of integration under which the figures denoting the rate occurred. "Thus price systems," I argued, "may have an institutional history of their own in terms of the types of equivalencies that entered into their making." For an historical illustration of the principle, I quoted Max Weber's remark that "for lack of a costing basis Western capitalism would not have been possible but for the Medieval network of statuated and regulated prices, customary rents, etc., a legacy of guild and manor." Heichelheim, in his disregard of the theoretical argument, mistook the long-run history of different types of equivalencies to which I was referring for the history of the actual prices themselves. The legendary thirty pieces of silver received

ether with R. F. G. Sweet, of Leemans' *Foreign Trade*

by Judas as the "price of a man," which typologically appear in the New Testament as a "close variant" of the "equivalency" of a slave as set out in Hammurabi's Code eighteen hundred years earlier, were badly misconstrued by Heichelheim. He assumed I was arguing the derivation of an actual slave price of the first century A.D. in Jerusalem from Hammurabi's Code, which would have been indeed, as he put it, "a howler." As it was, his risky practice of "no theory" boomeranged.

Twice Heichelheim in his review appealed expressly to his authority "as an Ancient Historian and Classical scholar."

First, my reference to Herodotus I. 153—no market places in the city of Babylon—drew from him this answer: "We do not have here probably a Herodotean statement before us, but an interpolation by some post-Classical copyist who was under the influence of Stoic anthropological theory. Cp. here J. E. Powell, *Herodotus Translated* I, (1949), p. IV, 78." Actually, J. E. Powell's preface to his translation contains no reference that bears out Heichelheim's statement about a post-Classical interpolation or Stoic influences. On the contrary, Powell's italics in the Herodotean passage on p. 78 signify both the interest he feels should be attached to Herodotus' comment, and his belief in its authenticity. Cf. Powell's statement of intent (p. v), which leaves no doubt as to his typographical practice. Nor does the critical text of Karl Hude contain any expression of doubt. The same is true of any of the translators, including Rawlinson, who remarked on Herodotus' statement on no market places in Persia. Heichelheim's treatment of Herodotus I. 53 is, to put it mildly, unclear.

Second, Heichelheim's reference to "primary evidence" in the three volumes of *Hesperia* (1953, 1956, 1958) containing the monographs by W. K. Pritchett, A. Pippin, and A. Amyx on "The Attic Stelai" is misleading. They contain exclusively the famous lists of auction prices of the grafitti pottery. No reference to "primary evidence" about market prices is to be found here. Heichelheim has neglected the warnings of the authors not to draw conclusions in regard to "a scheme of prices for actually extant vases," referring to the "many pitfalls" (Vol. XXVII [1958], 278).

Heichelheim's dismissal of *Trade and Market in the Early Empires* as a "most regrettable book" adds nothing to the issue of the port of trade in general, discussed there in several chapters, nor to the subject of the Babylonian *kar,* raised in this paper as an issue of the port of trade.

in the Old Babylonian Period (1960),[71] I expressed the opinion that the perspectives opened up by the *kar* controversy are of a comprehensive interest and merit further research.

[71] THE JOURNAL OF ECONOMIC HISTORY, XXII, No. 1 (March 1962), 116–17.

260

11

Sortings and "Ounce Trade" in the West African Slave Trade

1. African and European Trading

The records of trading between Africans and Europeans on the Guinea Coast[1] since antiquity raise issues the practical resolution of which has never ceased to occupy economic historians. The Herodotean inadequacies of dumb "barter"[2] in Carthaginian goods and in gold dust were fully resolved only at the time of the eighteenth-century slave trade. In Senegambia and even on the Windward Coast, as we now know, the Royal African Company[3] had still to go without an effective profit-and-loss accountancy. With the advent of the regular slave trade two new commercial devices had to be introduced by the Europeans. Both the "sorting" and the "ounce trade" sprang from the vital need for adjustment between the radically different trading methods of Europeans and Africans. And it was not so much a case of mutual adjustment, for of the two systems only one, the European, adjusted.

FROM "Sortings and 'Ounce Trade' in the West African Slave Trade," *The Journal of African History*, Vol. V, No. 3, 1964, pp. 381–393. Reprinted by permission of the editor of the *Journal of African History*, and of the Cambridge University Press.

[1] I am indebted to Mr. Abraham Rotstein, Lecturer in Economics, University of Toronto, for substantial help in resolving some of the problems of Slave Coast economics.

[2] Herodotus, iv, 196.

[3] K. G. Davies, *The Royal African Company* (1957); H. A. Wyndham, *The Atlantic and Slavery* (1935).

In essence, European and African trade could hardly have differed more. The African trade was an *import*-aimed activity of acquiring definite staples from a distance by bartering them against domestic staples at a simple rate of unit for unit, i.e. 1:1, "sometimes 2:1," in Cà da Mosto's phrase (1455). In contrast, European trade was overseas *exporting* of varied manufactures, aimed at the highest price and directed towards monetary gain. Motives, as well as goods and personnel, were different. African goods were standardized staples, exchanged "in kind" by status traders whose income did not derive from the deal in hand. Carrying, guarding, and negotiating were entrusted to the particular institution of caravans, which traveled from one inland seat to the other, at times calling at fairs, their regular meeting places. Business was transacted by the functionaries of the caravans and by those of the local African administration.

If this kind of trading is described as a type of "administered trade,"[4] its very different European counterpart can be designated as "market trading," bent on making a monetary profit on price differentials. Hence the absolute requirement of monetization to secure a profit-and-loss accounting, and of a manifold of export wares valued in a single currency.

The traditional international trade carried on by Africans had, then, three closely related characteristics. Its motive was the need of acquiring staples from a distance. This involved two-way carrying, not necessarily with the intervention of money. The rates at which the staples were traded were set by fixed equivalents, leaving no room for elastic adjustment. In an emergency simple multiples of the rates, like 2:1 or 2½:1 occurred. There were two broad instances of this traditional African trade: the beach trade

---

[4] Cf. K. Polanyi, "The economy as an instituted process," in K. Polanyi, C. M. Arensberg and H. W. Pearson (eds.), *Trade and Market in the Early Empires* (Glencoe, Ill., 1957), 263.

with the Europeans, and the trans-Saharan caravan routes of the Sudan.

These requirements of African trading were, in fact, interlocking. Carrying over very long distances required compensation for the transportation and payment for the goods. In the circumstances, if trade there was to be, the burden of adjustment had to be borne by the European. He could, and up to a point did, meet the Africans' requirement of bartering at set equivalents. Nevertheless, he could not forgo profit-and-loss accountancy, yet it was not possible to fit this into the African trading system of gainless barter. For this latter, the principle of exchange of equivalents was fundamental.

As K. G. Davies has pointedly summarized, the conditions in which the Guinea trade was carried on were dominated by the Africans' ways and needs. Indeed, not only did the Europeans' trade follow the Africans' pattern of staple trading and of employing staples as conventional standards, but whenever African and European standards were to be related, as a rule, the African standard prevailed. In Senegal, for instance, the European goods were rated in hides, slaves—an African good—in bars of iron, but between these two standards, the European and the African, a rate existed of one bar of iron equal to eight hides, i.e., the African good served as the common standard.

England was "on gold" and, in buying gold with trade goods, the cost of which in gold was known, the balance of the venture should have been evident. One would think therefore that the gold trade was accompanied by a natural advance towards accountancy. Yet Davies explicitly lists the Gold Coast along with Senegambia, and asserts that "the ledgers surviving from both regions gave an incomplete and probably misleading record of profit and loss."[5]

Only the slave trade at its height in the administered port of Whydah brought a breakthrough to monetization.

[5] Davies, op. cit. 238.

263

With accountancy came not only a growing variety of manufactured export goods, but also a built-in profit margin. This was worked through the introduction of the assortment of trade goods called a sorting, and of the fictitious money unit of the ounce trade.

2. Sortings

Slaves were indivisible and of high relative value compared to the single pieces of goods for which they were bartered. In spite of this stark fact, their sale and transport were carried on in the same way as that of all other trade goods—salt, oil, the precious metals, iron, copper, and cloths. All these were handled as staples, i.e., for similar motives and by similar techniques of exchanging them in kind. Various commodities had to be offered in different assortments conjointly before they were equivalent to a slave. A monetized accountancy therefore called for methods of payment that would overcome the limitations of a strict staple exchange, while at the same time fitting into the African pattern of trading in units of 1:1.

An artificial trade unit was evolved by the Europeans that allowed accountancy to extend to variegated trade items by their being added up and equated to a slave. This was the sorting, a bundle of trade goods totaling several ounces of gold. It first made its appearance, to our knowledge, in offshore ship-trade engaged in purchasing single slaves, sometimes two or at the most three of them. But sortings gained real importance only later in large-scale slave trading.

Two distinct institutions were fused in the sorting, historically and geographically. Trade on the Bar (or Windward) Coast contributed the local unit, the bar; the gold trade on the Gold Coast added to this the unit of the gold weight, the ounce (480 grains). Each sorting had a total value in ounces, expressed in ackies, i.e., sixteenth parts of an "ounce gold," while its composition varied according to changes in domestic prices. How many items of a staple added up to a bar depended on the staple and on the coastal region. Over and above this, it was subject to policy decisions at the head office of the Royal African Company. The bar did not form part of the gold weight system, a fact that allowed an elastic handling of the sorting as a unit of trade.

Trade in sortings had its peculiarities. Sortings were carefully selected to meet the needs and tastes of the slave-exporting "hands." A trait that could not be ignored by the European trader was the African's conservatism. A mis-selected assortment could not be sold by reducing the price. This is not to say that the interlopers' undercutting of the Royal African Company by as much as 25 to 30% failed to attract the Africans; slighter price reductions, however, went unheeded. Barbot denies any price competition of European traders among themselves, and asserts that the mode of payment—what part cowrie, what part other goods —was the only matter of contention between African and foreigner. Over a period of more than a century, under the rule of several kings and with a number of European countries participating and hundreds of cargoes of slaves dispatched, no troubles arising from "rates of trade" are on record. Prices were "traditional" and accepted as unchangeable, with the king taking note rather than negotiating them. The French Governor Gourg said that prices never changed, except for iron bars, corals, and Indian silks. The former were, of course, a standard, the latter two subject to quality. Change was mainly inhibited by the rule of the previous ship's rates being valid. We must assume that arrangements were made for the recording of the actual rates and particularly for the admittance of new goods into the sortings, which we know to have usually caused a month's delay. We cannot be sure whether and to what extent the "rates" of the items in the sorting may have been subject to confidential bargaining. The few instances in Angola and the Calabars that speak of lengthy negotiations are rather vague.

The sorting was, then, a device of extending to the indivisible trade-good "slave" the principle of trading in units of 1:1. If defects in a particular slave made compensation of the buyer necessary, operational devices were employed that maintained the principle of transaction in kind and thereby reinforced, rather than weakened, the institution of the sorting. Isert gives the male and female adult Negro's height as 4 feet 4 inches and 4 feet, respectively. "The amount by which they fell short of this measure is reckoned at 8 risdallers per inch. For the absence of a tooth 2 risdallers, if there are larger defects such as the loss of an eye, a finger or other limbs, the deduction is greater."[6] But how was the compensation to be defrayed? The sorting had to remain intact. It was the seller of the slave on whom it fell to compensate the buyer, whose payment was not reduced. To reduce the sorting would have left it to the European trader which item to remove from the assortment, thereby permitting him to rearrange the sorting. This would have constituted an infringement of the principle of trading in kind, and interfered with the sorting as an operational device.

Another device speaks for itself. James Barbot, Jr., in listing age groups and appraising them, starts with "the Black from fifteen to twenty-five years of age" as the standard age. He continues: "from eight to fifteen and from twenty-five to thirty-five, *three pass for two;* below eight and from thirty-five to forty-five *two pass for one . . . .*"[7] The deficiency of being under-age or over-age was here operationally ironed out by a counting device, which compensated the buyer without interfering with the sorting.

[6] P. E. Isert, *Voyages en Guinée et dans les îles caraïbes en Amérique* (Paris, 1792), 110–11.

[7] James Barbot, Jr., *Churchill's Voyages,* v (London, 1746).

If slave trading through sortings adhered to the African principle of bartering 1:1 in kind, it also left room for the trader's commercial skill in adjustment, in introducing new products and offering the trade goods most profitable to him. Though the amounts of the goods that were in some places laid down as equivalent to a bar were fixed permanently in kind, the selecting among these of the goods that happened to be cheapest at home was the prerogative of the European trader.

This still left over a vital requirement of organized European trading. Sortings introduced the feature of monetary gain into the trading transaction, but did not per se contain the element of a built-in profit.

7. The "ounce trade" and the French "once"

Incipient monetization may be seen in the use the Africans made of their trading staples, which they employed as a standard, a practice essentially followed by the Royal African Company in Senegambia and on the Bar Coast. The prominent case was the use of the iron bar in the Company's exports. But this sub-monetary employment of the iron bar did not ensure a margin of profit to the European. Already in the initial decade of the Company's trading, no less than 150 European goods were, according to Bosman,[8] traded in units of various dimensions—brandy and gunpowder by volume, iron bars and guns by the piece, cloths by lengths, cowries by tale, weight, and volume. How in a trade carried on in kind were the Europeans to avoid transactions leading to financial losses? Or, more exactly, how was trading to be planned to secure a profit and how was that profit to be realized? This was eventually done in the slave trade by combining the sorting with the monetary innovation of the ounce trade.

[8] W. Bosman, "A New and Accurate Description of the Coast of Guinea," in J. Pinkerton (ed.), *Voyages and Travels* London, 1814), XVI.

The initial but misleading success of the iron bar in the Company's exports was mainly prompted from the demand side, i.e., the cultural bias of the Africans toward the use of iron. But the value of iron bars in terms of gold was fluctuating, besides being different in the several regions of the coast. Prior to the slave rush the marking up of the iron bar could serve locally as a commonsense precaution against losses on the Gold Coast. In 1694 Captain Thomas Phillips bought his iron bars at 3s. 6d. in London and sold them for gold at Bassam on the Gold Coast at 7s. 6d. This was an early mark-up of slightly more than 100% in the gold trade, which was to be prophetic. It set the pace for the "average 100%" mark-up which was to become the rationale of the ounce trade (as well as of the French once). With the spread of this unit of accountancy the Europeans gained both the chance of a variety of exports in principle unlimited, and a built-in margin of profit. The device of the ounce trade simply consisted in paying in variably in kind for the gold ounces that the European owed the Africans for slaves, but valuing their own goods in ounce trade, i.e., with an average 100% mark-up.

The historiography of the ounce trade is obscured by our inadequate sources for business data, which, for understandable reasons, were withheld from the contemporary public. Witnesses did not wish to appear as discounting the substantial profits accruing to the national economy from the slave trade, while claiming also—at least by inference—that occasionally English slavers were made to pay excessive prices, and to that extent were to be sympathized with by the Parliamentary bodies. Bosman had left a blank in the text of his published correspondence skipping the figure of the actual prices of the slaves and leaving a conspicuous dash instead.

The relation of mark-up to ounce trade was not unaf

[9] Th. Phillips, "A Journal of a Voyage to Africa and Barbadoes," *Churchill's Voyages* (London, 1746), VI, p. 211.

ected by such reticence. Witnesses of high standng would offer elliptic information for reasons of tact, preferring rather to disappoint latter-day economic historians than to occasion doubts, however unjustified, of their personal honesty in the minds of their contemporary African business partners. Nonetheless, ample evidence of the existence and justification of the ounce trade—no less relevant to the French *once*—has survived.

For analytical purposes it is useful to distinguish between the three different aspects of the mark-up. First, the practice of marking-up of staples *ex ante* in order to secure a profit margin; second, the varying levels of realized profits *ex post;* finally, the fictitious monetary unit, the ounce trade (or the French *once*), both equally rated at 16,000 cowries, as distinct from the ounce gold which, before and after, was rated at 32,000 cowries.

The vagueness of the witnesses on these facts has had lasting effects. Wyndham and Davies make no mention of the ounce trade. Until recently, it has been ignored by historians of the slave trade, and even in the latest literature there are signs of uncertainty in discussing the issues involved. C. W. Newbury writes:

> The price of slaves cannot be accurately determined
> except in terms of the trade 'ounce'; and this unit of
> account was made up of assorted European goods—
> cloths, cowries, beads, guns, powder, rum, tobacco and
> iron bars—valued locally in ounces, but varying greatly
> in their original purchase price.[10]

The reference is obviously to the novel practice of payment in sortings. It does not even attempt to do justice to the distinction between ounce gold and ounce trade, a distinction firmly established by Dalzel's and Isert's time.

The Parliamentary Committee of 1789 on the Slave Trade enquired into the mode of payment practiced in the

[10] C. W. Newbury, *The Western Slave Coast and its Rulers* Oxford, 1961), 22.

West African trade. The answer emphatically was: "N payment; nothing but barter." Further questions con firmed the meaning of barter to be that payment wa invariably in goods. Governor Dalzel, a man of authority added that the payment amounted to only "about half" th price of the slave. Another witness said: "A pound sterlin would cost the European 10s."[11] Atkins, "a gentlema from Suffolk," who had joined a slave ship's complemen as a surgeon, was more explicit. He wrote that in the slav trade at Cape Apollonia slaves were rated in ounces at ounces each. "Allowing 100 per cent in Goods," he wrote "they cost at a medium 8 pounds Sterling."[12] That is slaves rated at 4 ounces were paid for in goods costing i England only £8 sterling, while 4 ounces gold amounte to £16 sterling. Put differently, the Europeans paid th ounces owed by them, in goods marked up 100%. Th ounce they paid was what later authorities such as Dalze idiomatically referred to as ounce, trade, when its valu was formally recognized at half the ounce gold, or £2.

It has been stressed by us that the 100% mark-up b understood as *an average*. The actual mark-up varied fo every good, and even for every transaction. Yet the trade could hope to secure *ex post* "at a medium" or "about such a mark-up from his trade. Admittedly, individua transactions, or even whole cargoes, yielded a much lowe profit.

In Whydah, the 100% mark-up was known at an earl date and was noted by both Barbot[13] and Bosman.[1 Writing in 1680 of his purchases in the coastal market place, Barbot informs us that chickens cost "about six

[11] A. Dalzel, in *Parliamentary Papers* (1789).

[12] J. Atkins, *Voyages to Guinea, Brasil and the West Indie* (London, 1737), 74.

[13] John A. Barbot, "A Description of the Coasts of Nort and South Guinea," *Churchill's Voyages* (London, 1746), v 330.

[14] Bosman, 503.

pence apiece, if bought for goods, which is threepence prime cost." In estimating the amount of customs fees paid at Whydah, he remarked that the customs—these were paid in goods—"amount to *about* 100 pounds in "Guinea value," as the goods must yield there."

The ounce trade was, then, a fictitious unit used by the Europeans in the settling of their gold debts with the Africans. Among themselves the Europeans called it the Guinea value of the goods (Barbot) or, according to Wyndham, settling in "coast money." The King of Whydah had hitherto ignored a treaty with the slaver companies (6 September 1704)[15] which implicitly recognized payment for slaves in sortings, by barring the King from insisting on payment in *one* kind only.[16] This left payment in more than one kind, i.e., the sorting, as the sole recognized mode of payment for the Europeans in the slave trade. It seems probable that Davies' confidential "articles" almost simultaneously "entered into" by the French, English and Dutch chartered companies' agents in Whydah (1704–5) committed them amongst themselves to the practice of an average *ex ante* mark-up of 100%. For the *ex post* mark-up the qualifying terms quoted above, such as "at a medium," "almost" or "average," are never omitted in our sources. Yet the English ounce trade, as recorded in Governor Dalzel's table of cowrie values, gives its value, as we have said, at an unqualified £2.[17] M'Leod called it 40s.[18] Isert throughout follows the same practice. Dalzel always cautious, however, shifted to the Editor (J.F.) the responsibility for inclusion of this item into the "table." As a witness before the Parliamentary Committee he was per-

[15] Cf. pp. 392–3.

[16] Fr. J. B. Labat, *Voyage du Chevalier Des Marchais En Guinée* (Amsterdam, 1731), II, 91.

[17] A. Dalzel, *A History of Dahomey* (London, 1793), 135.

[18] J. M'Leod, *A Voyage to Africa with some Account of the Manners and Customs of the Dahomian People* (London, 1820), 90.

sonally vague on the price of a slave in Whydah, and spoke of the "average slave" as costing 5 ounces (trade), equal to £10, equal to 40 iron bars, while a "prime slave" was given by him "when supply was low," as "little short of £30."[19]

The prices of trade goods, whether slaves or iron bars, were fluctuating, yet the cowrie rate of gold at 32,000, as well as the gold value of the fictitious ounce trade at 16,000 cowries were entirely stable.

A survey of the ounce trade requires also an account of its French parallel, the *once*.

For the facts we must rely on Simone Berbain's monograph on the *compagnie* slaver *Dahomet* (1772);[20] for interpretation we will have to remember what we have found to be the case for the English ounce trade, of which the French *once* was a later, independently developed variant.

The facts themselves, which research reveals, are simple. The *once* was, in Berbain's emphatic phrase, "a fictitious money of account, subdivided into sixteen livres."

A typical entry in the *Dahomet's* papers runs as follows:

1 woman at 8 onces *purchased from Bouillon*

	onces
3 barrels of brandy	3
123 lb. weight of cowries at 41 lb. to the *once*	3
2 pieces of handkerchief stuff	1
8 platilles (a closely folded white fabric)	1
	8

The sorting included besides the usual trade goods—brandy, platilles, handkerchiefs—also a considerable amount of cowries. The total of 8 *onces* added up the 5 *once* units of trade goods and the 3 *once* units of cowries, each unit

[19] 1789 Committee, 191.
[20] S. Berbain, *Le comptoir français de Juda (Ouidah) au XVIIIe siècle,* Mémoires de IFAN, No. 3 (Paris, 1942).

of cowries given by weight as 41 lb. The repeated speci-
fication of 41 lb. weight to the *once* is of vital importance.
As Berbain herself emphasizes, it represents the weight of
16,000 cowries. She omits to add that this identifies her
once with the English ounce trade, which she ignores.

On a closer view of Berbain's presentation of the *once*,
a comparative treatment of the English and the French
fictitious ounces raises a number of questions. Like the
English scholars, she reveals the limitations under which
her research was carried out. As the title of Berbain's essay—*Le comptoir français de Juda (Ouidah) au XVIII*
siècle—says, its subject was the functioning of the Whydah
office of the French slave trade. Its theme was to be restricted to the French slave trade as focused on Whydah.
Important consequences followed. Both the slave trade in
the French Antilles and the Whydensian slave trade *other*
than French remained outside the scope of her work. The
twin establishment of the English in Whydah was not considered, and the even older English ounce trade was left
unmentioned. This logically made the French monetary
system the frame of reference for the treatment of the
once, which again resulted in her never mentioning but
merely tacitly implying the fundamental distinction between the English and the French monetary systems of the
period. The basic role of gold in the English currency system (£ *s. d.*) contrasted with the independence of the
French livre from gold. In actual fact, the independence
from gold, which left the livre a fluctuating currency, for
historical reasons *did not extend to Whydah and its French*
establishment. Yet for circumstances inherent in the slave
rush, the French could not avoid—as little as could the
English—trading by sortings with their built-in mark-up, as
well as the setting-up of a fictitious unit of account. The
English, with their gold currency, naturally anchored this
fictitious unit in gold. *Neither could the French in Whydah*
avoid doing so. Hence the presentational paradox which
confused Berbain's picture: the French *once* was to main-

273

tain a stable cowrie value. The fact that by virtue of this it was *indirectly* linked to gold remained obscured. No less artificial was the avoidance of any mention of the ounce gold, of which the West African ounce equaling 8 Arab mitkhals was the traditional unit. Hence also the device of giving throughout the French *once* by weight of cowrie, instead of giving its equivalent of 16,000 cowries by tale. It may be symptomatic that her voluminous tract has a reference to the figure 16,000, "i.e., 4 cabess at 4000 cowries each" and that the printer intervened by misspelling the figure as 1,600 (p. 69). The well-known figure of 16,000 occurs correctly, however, in a second passage (p. 124) where it is said that "41 liv. (weight) bouges (cowries) ou 16,000 valent une once ou 4 cabèches." Another revealing remark of the author, this time an indirect reference to gold, is equally significant: "Exclusively on the Slave Coast was the value of the cowries maintained after the Dutch started importing them." Actually, this geographical limitation lacks validity, yet it implies that admission that *the Whydensian livre was "on gold."* Since direct reference to gold was barred to Berbain, indirect reference to it was made by stressing the stability of cowries, the gold value of which was recognized as being absolutely stable.

In all this semantic hide-and-seek, history played its part: France, as Berbain occasionally admits, was the only power that had had *no gold trade on the Guinea Coast.*

4. The controversial slave Treaty of 1704

Focusing on the slave port of Whydah, in about forty years the monetary system underwent three institutional changes. In Petley Weybourne's time, the end of the 1680s, two monetary standards, iron bars for European goods and cowries for slaves, were current side by side in Whydah, which still formed part of the kingdom of Ardra. Then in 1703–4 the King of Whydah proclaimed himself sovereign, and foreign traders had to pay the customs to him. Iron bars and cowries were replaced as a standard by the much larger unit of the slave. On the other hand, sortings had become general. Finally, in 1727 Dahomey seized Whydah, and from that time on cowries, the Dahomean currency, dominated, and the stability of gold in precise numerical terms of cowries became a symbol of Dahomean overlordship.

A unilateral introduction of a fictitious money unit into the commerce established between two civilizations—European and African—was bound to cause disturbances. The vagaries of the price of slaves come to the fore. Broadly, the reaction of the Africans to the Europeans' ounce trade was a massive raising of the slave price in terms of the traditional gold ounce. To quote K. G. Davies: "In the 'seventies and 'eighties the conventional price of an African slave was £3, this being the rate at which Petley Weybourne [of the Royal African Company] contracted to supply negroes at Whydah in 1687."[21] Davies continues:

In 1693 the African Company's captains were instructed to buy what Gold Coast negroes they could at up to £5 a head. After 1702, there were further increases, though possibly less marked at Whydah than elsewhere. Soon negroes at the Gold Coast were costing £10, £11 and £12 apiece, and in 1712 as much as £16 and £17 was being paid. Thus in the course of little more than twenty years the price of a slave had risen almost five-fold.[22]

In point of fact, some time in the eighteenth century the European traders informally created in Whydah a new unit of account, specifically for purposes of the slave trade, the fictitious unit of the ounce trade, worth in English terms half an ounce of gold. The French *compagnie* slaver *Dahomet* employed in its sortings this very standard, call-

---

[21] Davies, op. cit. 236–7.
[22] Davies, ibid. 237.

ing it *once* (1772). Captain John Johnston's *Swallow* (1791–2), presumably an English boat,[23] kept its accounts entirely in *values of ounce trade,* marked *Vozt.* But already a century earlier Captain Thomas Phillips of the *Hannibal,* trading off the Gold Coast (1693), marked-up iron bars a little over 100%, as we have noted. Items of daily necessities, such as sixpenny fowls, were purchased even earlier by Bosman in the coastal markets on the Gold Coast by bartering English threepenny goods at a 100% mark-up. We cannot set a date for the ounce trade entering the slave trade. Only in 1793 is there found an official confirmation of an English ounce of that denomination, in Governor Dalzel's *History of Dahomey.*

Our historians, like K. G. Davies, have attempted to explain the steep rise of slave prices around the turn of the century by referring to the competition of the French and of the interlopers, without any mention of the ounce trade. The obscurities which confront us when consulting the English Parliamentary Committees' Reports, turn mainly on the manner in which the English slaver made payment for the gold debts which he incurred in purchasing slaves from the Africans. The English witnesses at the 1789 hearings were anything but eager to clarify the price movements and currency turbulences in the slave trade, merely insisting that the terms of payment were very favorable to the English purchaser. That sometimes during the transaction the European slaver found himself induced to compensate the African seller for what obviously was an excessive mark-up may account for Mr. Matthews' cryptic evidence before the Parliamentary Committee: "We gave them salt, some manufactures. £15, to £18 are paid over and above the invoice prices. . . ." This passage raises further doubts about Davies' footnote:[24] "So far as I have been able to

[23] *Proceedings of the American Antiquarian Society,* new series, XXXIX (1929), 379 ff.

[24] Davies, op. cit. 236.

discover, all prices of slaves quoted represent the invoice value of the goods with which they were purchased. In most cases this invoice value was the same as the price which the company had paid in England, with no allowance made for cost of transport." We have already noted that his book makes no mention of the ounce trade, any more than do the Minutes of the Parliamentary Committees. Hence the sudden rise in slave prices remained unaccountable.

The ounce trade necessarily acted on two levels: one institutional, the other "economic." Analytically distinct, these two strands of change were interacting. Larger sortings and ounce trade amounted prima facie to a one-sided revision of the rates of trade to the advantage of the Europeans. Nothing shows a change in the Africans' own gold units that would correspond to the European practice of paying in ounce trade. We hold that the Africans' reaction was a raising of slave prices in gold ounces at £4 an ounce. The aboriginal African way of 1:1 long-distance staple trading in kind proved its elastic quality. In accepting, in spite of the massive mark-up, a sorting, even though an enlarged one, for a slave, African trade smoothly absorbed the European fictitious money unit of the ounce trade. The squaring of the circle was accomplished in attaching the adjective "trade" to the 100% marked-up European ounce, while retaining the unqualified ounce as the Africans' money unit in pricing slaves. The traditional gold ounce at 32,000 cowries would still run in the gold trade, while in the slave trade the new ounce of one-half of the cowrie value of the former was employed.

This article partly relies on the ships' papers of an English and of a French slaver, but above all on the text of a Treaty made available by French sources. The political validity of the Treaty was not accepted by English historians. It was a French diplomatic success. The document itself, made out in one copy, was retained by the King of Whydah. Not only the validity of the instrument but also the authenticity of the text proved by the Chevalier Desmarchais, an alleged co-signatory, was contentious. Yet Dunglas, the French historian, does not doubt it.[25]

In the light of the story of the fictitious monetary units of account, the figures given in the Appendix of the Treaty offer conclusive internal evidence of the authenticity of the text.

The Appendix declares in a solemn Preamble the purpose of the Treaty to be the establishment of a

> grand union (*une grande union*) for the purchasing of slaves in order to transport them from Africa to the islands and mainland of America with intent to set off to advantage the productive assets there established. In view of this sole purpose of the traffic it is appropriate to make known the quantity and quality of the trade goods to be given in exchange per head of slave.

More than a dozen different equivalents for a slave are listed. Of these we shall here concentrate on barrels of brandy, platilles (folded white linen), and cowries, the trade goods expressly mentioned by Berbain as necessary and sufficient for slave trading in Whydah. The Appendix gives the price of a male slave at "4 to 5 onces," being equal to "4 to 5 barrels of brandy," or "40 to 50 platilles," or "180 lb weight of cowries." Precision is added to the last: "To attain the price of a slave, depending on the market, 18 to 20 cabess are required, i.e., 70,000 to 80,000 cowries, the weight of which is put at 180 livre of Paris." The latter figure gives precisely 5 *onces* at 16,000 cowries each. The cabess is given at "20 galinhas equal to 4000 cowries." The papers of the *Dahomet* give the slave price in *onces,* the *once* at 41 lb. weight of cowrie. The *once* is uniformly reckoned at 1 barrel of brandy, or 10 platilles,

[25] E. Dunglas, "Contribution à l'histoire du Moyen-Dahomey" (Royaumes d'Abomey, de Ketou et de Ouidah), *Etudes Dahoméennes,* XIX–XXI, IFAN (Porto Novo, 1957), 137.

or 41 lb. weight of cowries. Berbain herself quotes the *once* at 16,000 cowries. Some ambiguity may be thought to be introduced through the phrase "depending on the market," also through the fact that the treaty of 1704 differs from the *Dahomet* papers of 1772 by referring to 16,000 cowries as weighing 40 lb., not 41 lb. Considering the time span and the lack of uniformity in cowries as a medium of payment by weight, the slight disparity cannot affect the internal evidence supporting the authenticity of the text. Indeed, the Treaty of 6 September 1704 was the occasion for the Africans to adjust slave prices to the monetary changes occurring in the West African slave trade in the first decade of the eighteenth century. Our sources bear this out. The 1704 slave price of 80,000 cowries, equal to 5 *onces* at 16,000 cowries, amounts to £10 sterling, which amounts to a doubling of the slave price of £5 sterling, quoted by K. G. Davies for 1702. In whatever staples prices were expressed in the Treaty, the Africans' adjustment later on certainly tended to overcompensate the instituted changes in the currency.

Archaic Economic Institutions: Cowrie Money

Societal Functions of Archaic Money

Our analytical sketch deals with a West African instance of the manner in which the process of livelihood may be embedded in archaic economic institutions. Of the three exchange institutions, archaic variants of [external] trade and [local] markets have been already presented. Money, however, the stability of which was a singular attainment of the Dahomean economy, has hardly been touched upon. What keeps the value of native moneys regionally stable and how are the equivalents maintained without any appropriate mechanism?

The answer, we suggest, is to be sought in the societal functions of money and their effects on the social structure. Take the variant of money here represented by the cowrie currency, and as a substitute for a market system look to the solidity of the structures that make up archaic society.

We shall call "archaic" such economic institutions as are absent in "primitive," kinship organized society and only emerge in state societies, but fade again when money as a means of exchange becomes widespread. Economic institutions, then, that make their appearance in state societies fall roughly into two groups: those such as the taking of interest, mortgage, or business partnership which, once established, continue into modern times, and others, like

FROM Chapter XI, "Archaic Economic Institutions," of Karl Polanyi, *Dahomey and the Slave Trade,* Seattle: The University of Washington Press for the American Ethnological Society, 1966. Reprinted by permission of the publisher.

voluntary work teams, the pawning of children, or the entailing of fruit trees, which eventually recede into insignificance or disappear altogether. Only these latter, which are restricted to early state societies, deserve to be called specifically archaic economic institutions. They number several dozen; a few shall be listed: The antichretic pledge served a purpose akin to the taking of interest. The object given as a surety, whether land, cattle or slave, was not only handed over to the creditor, as usual with pledged objects, but the creditor was also entitled to use it until the debtor had paid up. In parts of the Sudan sales were regularly done through brokers and even auctioneers were employed who often were also the brokers. Sales could thus be ensured even in the absence of markets. Equivalents were established for almost all staples in what we have called "staple finance," particularly in the operation of redistributing and household accountancy.

Exchange institutions such as trade, market, and money possessed their archaic variants. Notably this was the case in "administered" trade, involving the status trader, or the port of trade; "isolated" markets with a compulsory money-use; and last but not least archaic variants of money, of which the cowrie currency of Dahomey was an outstanding instance.

In general terms, money is a semantic system similar to speech, writing, or weights and measures. Of these it most resembles speech without which humans would not be what they are, neither in the individual, nor in the societal sphere. This holds good of all three money-uses—i.e., for payment, as a standard, and as a means of exchange. Now, archaic money has the singular effect of solidifying the social structure. Institutions tend to be strengthened by the quantitative identification of obligations and rights resulting from the introduction of numerals. Sociological features to which institutions attach, are mainly status and state-building. Archaic economic institutions were as a rule mediated through links to these two. Status is confirmed and

281

the state is consolidated in the course of the development of such institutions, which, on the other hand, rely for support on interests benefiting groups and classes.

Apart from their economic role, societal functions also attach therefore to archaic economic institutions. Ibn Batutah is to be credited with the discovery of the thin and thick copper wires as status money in the fourteenth-century Niger empires. Thin wires, in which wages were paid, bought only firewood and coarse millet, while the thick ones bought anything, not excluding elite goods. Limitations of consumption were thus set up for the poor, while the higher standard of life of the leisure classes was automatically safeguarded. Without unfairness one can here speak of *"poor man's money"* as an instrument of maintaining upper-class privileges. But status connotations of a deliberate welfare intent were also on record. In the sixteenth-century Near East a "poor man's ell" existed, in Basra, for the purchase of cheaper sorts of cloth. It was longer by a fifth than the regular ell, with which the expensive cloths were bought. Mention was already made of millet, with which everything could be bought at a lower price in the Sudanese markets.

The opposite bias prevailed in the "elite circulation" of Homeric Greece, in reciprocating gifts of treasure. In West Africa elite circulation was a principle of trade. Horses, ivory, skilled slaves, precious metals, jewelry, and treasure objects could be acquired only in exchange for items within this sphere of elite goods. In the ancient Near East status differentiations attaching to archaic moneys may serve as a key to some cuneiform economic riddles. According to the Code of Hammurabi loans repaid in silver carried an interest of 20%, while if the loan was repaid in barley, the rate was 33⅓%. Yet the mode of repayment was apparently left to the free choice of the debtor, which would certainly seem odd. If, however, as there is reason to assume, silver loans were accorded *only* to nobles, while the common man could expect *only* a barley loan, status

282

would account for the apparent absurdity. It is evident that archaic money was in various ways connected with status, which would create powerful invisible links in the social tissue.

Cowrie and Gold

Separate currencies operated in each of the three neighboring countries of Dahomey, Ashanti, and Whydah. In Dahomey units of cowrie shells were issued by the monarch; in Ashanti gold alone was current; in the port of trade of Whydah the English slavers developed the money unit of the "ounce trade" as a money of account, the French used the no less fictitious *once,* and the Dutch and Danish the "rixdaller monnaie."

If the international gold standard of the nineteenth century rested on the pound sterling as the firmly established artificial money unit, on most of the Guinea Coast this function fell to the Dahomean stringed cowrie. It was issued regularly in peace and war, remaining stable in terms both of the domestic price level and of foreign exchange between cowrie and gold.

The comparison of the roles of gold and cowrie, however, must not be strained. In the West gold served as a backing for bank notes, and, through the foreign exchange rates, also as a regulator of the mechanism of external trade. No such integrative tasks attached to the shells. On the other hand, Dahomey possessed no merchant fleet and carried on no active trade; and the shells, which were its sole money, originated on distant coral reefs, whence traders could export them as ballast at a very slight expense to themselves.

As was the case with gold, however, the problems that related to the non-obvious advantages and disadvantages of cowrie money largely turned on detail. Hence a more adequate acquaintance with the physical properties of these shells is required than is commonly possessed.

During the last three quarters of a century, intensive research was carried out on the uses of cowrie, both as an ornament and as money. Conchology, geography, cultural anthropology, archaeology, and economic history contributed.

The occurrence of single cowrie shells, just a few of them, is prehistoric and was almost general, as J. W. Jackson ascertained. He found Cypraeidae of a great number of varieties ornamentally, ceremonially, and magically used in almost all continents, certainly in Europe, Asia, and America.

Archaeology, anthropology, and history agree that the monetary use of cowrie is recorded only in historical times, but, on a careful check, the money-use is found to be by no means coincident with the prehistoric sites. Between prehistory and history a gulf is evident. Historical cowries are only of the monetary type, namely, *Cypraea moneta* and *Cypraea annulus*. The heavier and larger *Cypraea annulus* with its bluish-grayish shade and yellow-ringed body was usually mixed with the milk-white, dainty *Cypraea moneta*. The place of origin of annulus was the east coast of Africa, opposite Zanzibar. This second-rate cowrie reached Dahomey mainly by sea and had to compete with the much handier and also neater *C. moneta*. Anyway, cowrie currencies nowhere show dependence on prehistoric finds in the same areas. Also, there is in historical times, including antiquity, an absence of cowrie money in the Near and Middle East in contrast to most of West Africa and part of the Far East.

Currencies, with their institutional features, are a phenomenon far removed from the merely ornamental aspects of cowrie as a culture trait. This gives to the study of cowrie money that conceptual definiteness that lends its fascination to economic history. J. W. Jackson[1] recorded the total

[1] *The use of Cowry-Shells for the Purposes of Currency, Amulets and Charms.* Manchester Memoirs, Vol. LX, No. 13, 1915–16.

range of the prehistoric spread of cowrie. Only exceptionally were specimens of the two money cowries found: others of the numerous species of Cypraeidae were preferred by early man as more ornamental or more stirring to the sexual imagination. Passing from prehistory to early historical times, when over wide areas iron, copper, and the precious metals were used as money, cowrie appeared alongside of the metals, but very rarely, if ever, as the sole currency.

A warning against the ethnocentric bias is in order that so easily takes hold of us on economic subjects that arise outside of our own Western culture. Over many centuries silver and gold, on the one hand, cowrie on the other, were in competition. Although in the Near East for at least two millennia silver had been ahead of gold, eventually modern man in his sophistication ranked gold as the winner. We will here disregard silver and restrict the comparison to gold and cowrie.

A rough balance between the native qualities of gold and cowrie that enhanced or reduced their respective suitability as units of currency, may be appropriate. Among the indisputable advantages of shells over gold is their existence in recognizable units, the latter having no such units—it is measured by weight, while no acceptable units of gold weight exist; another advantage of the shells is their minute unit-value, which brings the vital item of primitive life, the mouthful of food, within popular reach, where gold with its elite connotation may be at a disadvantage, specks of gold dust in the Whydahsian market notwithstanding. On the other hand, in its "industrial" use gold possessed an alternative employment of great economic importance which derived from a highly elastic demand. The ornamental demand for cowrie is inelastic, and even within its limited range not of comparable economic significance to that of the "industrial" use of the precious metals. When it comes to the stability of a gold currency, the essential role of the industrial uses of gold are too well known to be stressed here.

But, to return to the virtues of cowrie—it cannot be counterfeited, while gold dust and gold bars are frequently adulterated by admixtures of brass dust, and gold coins are subject to clipping. Still another policy aspect recommends cowrie: it reveals hoarded wealth through its bulk. The Spartans, aware that their leaders could not resist the lure of bribes, had to forbid the import of gold, favoring iron instead. King Gezo of Dahomey is quoted by Burton as saying that, although there is gold in the neighboring Kong mountains, he prefers cowrie for two reasons, because it cannot be counterfeited, and because no man can become secretly rich.[2] A physical quality of cowrie plays a part in its ambivalent fluidity. Cowrie shells can be poured, sacked, shoveled, hoarded in heaps, kept buried in the soil and chuted like gravel—they remain clean, dainty, stainless, polished, and milk-white. They are transportable in their tens of millions, which tends rather to impede the successful operation of a cowrie currency and, indeed, to cause already established cowrie currencies not infrequently to disappear again.

We are used to ranging cowrie with the other shells as a sample of primitive money in a supposed evolutional perspective of the "origins and development of money." Historical research removes this evolutionary bias. Cowrie currencies emerged on the Middle and Upper reaches of the Niger at a time when metal currencies and indeed coined money were long established in the Mediterranean heartlands. This is the background against which the emergence of a new non-metallic currency in Islamic West Africa should be viewed. It will then not be erroneously regarded as part of a general evolution of money, but rather

[2] Captain Sir Richard F. Burton, *A Mission to Gelele, King of Dahome,* Vol. I, London: Tinsley Brothers, 1864, p. 117, n. 3.

as a feature in the spread both of centralized government and of food markets in the early Negro empires, which left its imprint on the local history of money.

In the Dahomean area gold dust and cowrie happened to be in close competition for the money role in food markets. The river Volta provided ample gold dust, and cowrie was available whether it had entered via the Guinea Coast in the south or the Niger region in the north. Gold also was found, as we know, in the mountains of north Dahomey. But gold dust could not be employed by males in the market, unless a fine balance (usually carried as in Ashanti by an attendant) was at hand. The Ashanti also used various non-standardized, personal gold weights without common units. Whydah women were reputed to distinguish the qualities of gold dust and identify even a minute speck with their fingertips. This, however, could hardly compare with the discrete units of small change offered by the shells. In the food market cowrie won any time over gold. Moreover, it could be measured both by weight and by volume, not to mention count by tale. What proved in the long run its weakness, its extreme cheapness and volatility, was not fatal under archaic conditions. Cowrie easily held its own against European coins, and succumbed eventually to the advantages of gold only under the conditions of international finance, for which it was utterly unsuited.

Cowrie from North and South

Black and White met in West Africa on two fronts, well before Dahomey came into being. The story of cowrie in Africa should then reveal some of the modalities of that meeting, first on the Middle Niger and, a century later, on the Guinea Coast. When, where, and how did cowrie shells penetrate West Africa? And by what agency was cowrie established as a currency system?

Dahomey was situated between the Guinea Coast and

the vast Niger Bend. On the beaches of the Bight of Benin and on the Middle Niger, respectively, cowrie was infused by two different sets of traders—Berber Tuareg and later Arab on the one hand, Portuguese on the other. Their zonal fronts were, however, separated by more than a thousand miles, the distance between Timbuktu and Gogo, where the Venetians were dispatching the Maldive cowrie by Tuareg caravans, and the Portuguese in the south in Benin and Ardra, those outposts of Yorubean culture.

The earliest date at which cowrie can be presumed to have reached West Africa from the north is the departure of Marco Polo from Venice for his voyage to the Far East, about 1290. He did not feign surprise when in a detailed account he described his meeting with cowrie money in southwestern China's province of Yünnan. His story reflects the thrill of a sensational experience. Our sources name Venice, Marco Polo's home, and the domicile of the family business, as the agency that transmitted the cowries from the Persian Sea to the Niger, in order to purchase its gold for those exotic shells. This narrows the time range from 1290 to the spring of 1352, when Ibn Batutah found cowrie money in use at Gogo, on the Middle Niger, where the river sharply turned south. By all indications, in the empire of Malli, cowrie was along with gold bars and copper wire a regular currency, the gold rate of which Ibn Batutah unhesitatingly quoted by tale. He had been, like Marco Polo before him in Yünnan, much astonished at meeting with cowrie in the Far East, although unlike Polo he was thoroughly conversant with it and its use as money. He was struck to find that its value was as high as 1150 to a mitkhal, or gold ducat, which in the Maldives would fetch no less than 400,000 cowries, if not three times as much, i.e., 1,200,000, which also happened. Their exchange rate in Gogo was mentioned by him with assurance. And Cà da Mosto, who had never seen cowrie, described in 1455 *Cypraea moneta* correctly from hearsay and added specific information about their traject from the Persian

Sea to Venice and from Venice by the desert route of the Western Sahara to the Niger.

The later date, when cowrie entered West Africa from the south is almost as definite, though the medium of transportation by which this happened is much less certain. The Arab traders of the north represented the eleventh-century world movement of Islam (its seventh century irruption had been quite brief and superficial). They were now keen to tap the sources of the gold that was flowing since Roman times from the Upper Niger toward Carthage and Lybia. Their cultural influence on the Upper and Middle Niger was paramount and cowrie with which they were familiar from Arabia and India was current in Malli, at least as far as Gogo in the east. The Arab trader was bred to the use of the mitkhal and its fractions, besides gold and silver dinars and dirhems, and not limited, like the "unbelievers," to damba beans and takus for their gold weights. When in the fifteenth and sixteenth centuries he was faced with the Europeans on the coast, his mullahs felt they were equals in trade, if not their superiors.

Fifteenth-century Portuguese trade in Benin was a somewhat different proposition in the Arabs' eyes, who deemed it an intrusion into their inland beat. The Portuguese first established themselves on the Gold Coast where they traded in the African staple, gold, for a limited number of European goods: cloths, guns and powder, used sheets, hardware such as basins and knives, but mostly iron bars and rings of copper. Neither caravan slaves nor cowrie did yet enter into the picture. And with the opening of the sea route to India, in 1497, Portuguese commerce changed direction. Based on the islands of Fernando Po and St. Thomé, the Bight of Benin was turned by them into a Portuguese lake. Their purchases from the natives were now intended for use in their local island plantations of sugar and for coastal trading. This brings us back to the two regions where the Portuguese penetrated to some extent into cowrie-using areas: Benin and Ardra.

The insalubrious beaches from which Benin and Ardra themselves withdrew were not favored for settlement by the Portuguese either. They preferred the islands off the coast or inland fairs that lay about sixty or seventy miles from the sea. They induced the inland natives to trade the goods they had to offer, including slaves. But the superior civilization of Benin, heir to the religion, art, and statecraft of Ile-Ife, set narrow limits to Portuguese cultural expansion. Besides, the Arab traders from the far north would meet them there and bar further entry.

On Ardrasian matters, however, the Portuguese exerted a formative influence. The king himself had been brought up in a Christian monastery on St. Thomé. A momentous feature of the cowrie currency resulted. The numerical denominations of that system, for example, the designation of the smallest stringed unit of 40, the toque; the five toques of 200 shells, the galinha; the 20 galinhas of 4000 shells, the cabess all carry Portuguese designations. Important culture symbols like the *fetish* have Portuguese names, as well as the administrative heads of any group or bearers of any port of importance, the *cabosseros*. It must be noted, that the vernacular for the various cowrie units was also current in Dahomey. Yet the Portuguese terms were employed over the whole area of stringed cowrie money, including Dahomey itself.

Within a reasonably narrow span, sometime between the end of the thirteenth and the middle of the fourteenth centuries, cowrie then reached the Middle Niger; in the last quarter of the fifteenth century the Portuguese may also have found it in inland Benin. While on the Middle Niger it came undoubtedly from the Mediterranean by way of the northern desert route, its presence in Benin may have been due to seepage by Negro or Arab traders from the Niger in the north. In any case, this influx was later to be amply reinforced from overseas, rounding the Cape. The trickle of cowrie shells from the east coast by way of the valleys of the Congo can be ignored.

Our question regarding the origins of the cowrie currency in Africa, consisting of loose shells at first, probably mixed moneta and annulus, can now be partly answered. The when and where of its arrival renders it a certainty that Dahomey was *not* the originator of the cowrie currency system, although it soon incorporated it and became its protagonist. Of this crucial initial phase of a stringed cowrie currency in Dahomey we know, however, next to nothing, except that Whydah stringed its cowrie even before the Dahomean conquest. Naturally, we do not have here in mind the mere monetary use of loose cowrie shells, but that organized system of cowrie as a currency which, once it struck roots in Dahomey, became so notable an instrument of its national existence and of the regional economic organization over a wide area of the Guinea Coast.

Reference to a more authentic episode of economic history may be of interest. The Portuguese square cloth money stamped in Lisbon with the royal arms of Portugal may have stimulated the monetary imagination of the new inland rulers of the Guinea Coast. Barbot's nephew, James Barbot, Jr., gave an intriguing on-the-spot report of Angola, printed as a supplement to his uncle's work about the Guinea Coast. Angola's secession from the empire of the Congo gave the Capuchin monks a chance of converting the natives and introducing an economic organization with domicile in Lisbon. A comprehensive taxation system was based on the local administration, which again was put in the care of a privileged native stratum, the Sonassen. The monetary systems of Angola were regionalized and were partly made into a royal monopoly. The shells current as money, the inferior simbos (*Olivetta nana*) were only partly of domestic origin, others were imported from Brazil. Of the domestic simbos those of *Loanda provenience* were valued most for their beautiful color. These favorite simbos were carried by native servants in straw sacks, which held a load of sixty-four pounds, to the Congo to be there exchanged for slaves and square cloths of different sizes, made of the bark of a native tree. All things in Congo, James Barbot wrote, are bought with these shells, even gold, silver and provisions, adding that the use "of coin, either of gold or any other metal is suppressed and forbid in all Congo, as it is in some other parts of Africa."[3] The Portuguese government in Lisbon, however, combined tax-farming with the monopoly of the issuance of fiat money stamped in Lisbon and thence introduced into Angola at an excessive profit to the tax farmer and fiscal monopolist of this royal "mint." The official value of the marked clouts (cloth money) was four times the value of the unmarked ones, the double marked clouts being worth five to six times the unmarked clouts. Except for fourth century B.C. and ninth century A.D. Chinese experiments with paper money, no such ambitious schemes are anywhere on record on an empire scale. The intellectual influence of the Portuguese on Dahomean state finance should then not be underrated. The daring Guinean enterprise of regionally stable moneys may have originated from previous Angolan experiments. From the Niger empires of the North, greatly antedating Dahomey, no hint of such a sophisticated currency has reached us.

We must confess to ignorance of a more elementary kind, namely, how in the first place these shells came to be moved physically in the mass from their homes along such vast trajects. Traditionally, the migration of the cowrie was traced by ethnographers with confidence to the Indian merchants' interest in monetary gain. But trade is no explanation, since it needs itself an explanation in terms of demand. Admittedly, the profit, in Ibn Batutah's authentic terms, was in the possible range of 100,000%. This, however, leaves the mainspring of the transaction untouched, namely, why specifically for currency purposes cowrie was so much in demand in Africa. Nor does it answer the

[3] James Barbot, Jr., *Churchill's Voyages,* London: 1746, p. 518.

question, whence the purchasing power was forthcoming, capable and willing to be spent on a large scale in such a manner.

The economist is indeed at a loss to account for the emergence in an early society of an effective demand of first magnitude for a means of currency as such. The notion that economic developments are mainly referable to what we have become used to calling "economic interests" is apt to be misleading. Rather, weighty events in the sphere of state-building and of economic organization may have accounted for the introducing of currency systems in West Africa. Such may have been the source of the demand for money objects to be used as currency and consequently of the finance capable of supplying the purchasing power for their acquisition. The economic historian might have to seek for an explanation in the rise of new empires, or even in the need for a popular currency which would facilitate the functioning of local food markets. Cowrie legend seems to point in this direction.

Cowrie Legend

Native legend on the coming to Dahomey of cowrie and of food markets connects the two events. The natives' changeover from hunting to a settled life may have left them without a place either in the kinship or the village organization. The distribution of food to the dislocated new subjects must have raised a problem for the Niger empires in the north, as it did later for the new bush and savanna kingdoms in the south. The latter may, up to a point, have followed the northern example. Perhaps some anachronistic reminiscences of such distressing conditions passed down to us in folklore.

One of the legends concerning Te Agbanli (1688–1729), brother of Hwegbadja, the first king of Dahomey, tells of the circumstances of his settling in the Porto Novo area. One particular incident points to a close connection

293

between money and markets. The narrator, recalling the time when there was no money, goes on to say that Te Agbanli "invented" a market:

> In those days there was no money. If you wanted to buy something, and you had salt and another man had corn, you gave him some salt and he gave you some corn. If you wanted fish and I had pepper, I would give you pepper and you would give me fish. In those days there was only exchange. No money. Each gave what he had to the other, and got from him what he needed.
> Now, as Te Agbanli was a stranger, he said to the people of Akono, "I see you have no market here. I want to invent a market for you."
> There was an Akono man there, who said, "Why should one give everything to a stranger? We gave him a place to live, and now he is asking for land for a market."[4]

The unfortunate Akono man who raised these objections became the human sacrifice to consecrate the market.

At about the same time, Te Agbanli's brother Hwegbadja, the founder of the dynasty of the Alladoxonu kings of Dahomey was engaged in a dramatic contest for power with Agwa-Gede, king of an autochthonous people, the Gedevi, on the southern reaches of the Abomey Plateau. The two kings vied in the realm of magic and social innovations.

Hwegbadja introduced a new code of laws, spinning and weaving of cotton cloths, burial of the dead in the earth rather than putting them in trees, and payment in perpetuity by each succeeding monarch for the right to use the land for burials. "The people liked this very much. They said, 'all right. We like you. We will make you King for all time.' "[5]

---

[4] Melville J. and Frances S. Herskovits, *Dahomean Narrative*, Evanston: Northwestern University Press, 1958, p. 364.
[5] Ibid., p. 361.

But though Hwegbadja won in the end, he lost out in the short run to Agwa-Gede. The latter king produced rain in a drought, "magic charm" locusts that ate the crops, a further charm to make the locust plague cease, produced the peanut from the earth, and also cowrie money. The latter two events were intended as verification of his rightful status as king:

> There was an herb called *tengbwe*. It sprang up at the moment. He (Agwa-Gede) said again, "If the earth is truly my father's, then when I pull up this weed, a peanut will be pulled up with it." He pulled up the weed, and a peanut was there.
> The people cried out. They put their hands over their mouths and acclaimed him.
> He said again, "If the earth truly belongs to my father, if I pull up an herb, I shall see cowries." He did this, and there were cowries.
> People now found food to eat, and no longer exchanged articles. They had money . . .
> The people hurried to Agwa-Gede and declared, "You are our King. We have no other . . ."
> And so the people refused to recognize Hwegbadja, and it was only after the death of Agwa-Gede that Hwegbadja began to reign.[6]

Cowrie money thus appears in the legend as an innovation of an autochthonous king. And the result—"people now found food to eat and no longer exchanged articles"—suggests a close connection in their minds between money and markets. Actually, as we know, Dahomean markets were food markets in which—a notable fact—cowrie payment was enforced.

The acting force that shaped and organized the economy was the state, in the person of the king. Food, money, and market are all state-made. The Hegelian concept of a state as contrasted with the economic society (*bürgerliche Gesellschaft*) of which it is only a function, is inapplicable

[6] Ibid., pp. 366–367.

to the early state. From Pharaonic Egypt and Babylon to the empires of the Niger the state-building drive makes its appearance as a secular force within the sphere of economic organization. The factors that doubtless pressed toward statehood as such are a different matter. Together with the military factors they belonged to the economic prehistory of the state. But once set on the course of state-building, the monarchy was engaged in the organizing of an army and its provisioning "in kind"; the launching of a currency as an instrument of taxation, and the creating of markets and of small change for the distribution of the food. This again involved state-made "equivalents," which determined the rate at which staples could be substituted for one another in the payment of taxes and in rationing. These performances of government concerning the economy are here recalled from previous chapters to provide a more realistic approach to the origins and functioning of the cowrie currency which was strung by the king's wives in Dahomey for the provisioning of the conquered peoples in the local food markets.

Cowrie and the State

Primitive society does not know centrally issued shells for money-use; nor have these survived in societies where money is common as a means of exchange. Indeed, Dahomean stringed cowrie may strike us as an impressive archaic institution, because the modern mind still grapples with some comparable technicalities of monetary policy. While cowries had vital welfare functions to perform, it happened that they were exceptionally hard to stabilize. Grave obstacles had to be overcome in achieving stability on a national and, indeed, an international scale.

Somewhat misleadingly the dilemma might have claimed a distant resemblance to modern alternatives of welfare versus inflation. Owing to their infinitesimally small value, cowrie were over centuries the money of the poor. Therefore in India and later, if to a lesser extent, in the Western Sudan, they actually served as an element of the welfare state, while their fluidity—lack of viscosity—made the maintenance of a formal exchange rate in terms of the precious metals as good as impossible. Nonetheless, in Whydah and the whole of the Dahomean range, a perfect stability of cowrie in terms of gold was achieved under the complex conditions of an international port frequented by a number of trading countries practicing accountancy in gold or silver.

India's currency problems long preceded those of West Africa. The Moghul Empire visited by Ibn Batutah in the second quarter of the fourteenth century displayed the utter extremes of rich and poor, and also what latter-day civilizations would have described as an interest of rulers in the livelihood of the masses. Ibn Batutah, having been appointed to a high municipal post in Delhi, had to shoulder, during a famine, the maintenance of five hundred poor, as a private man. In the circumstances, cowrie formed in India a part of the Islamic-Hindu state's welfare economy. In Africa, under the Moorish administration on the Niger some four centuries later conditions were not very different, except that—apart from Timbuktu where cowrie were still current—shells had been replaced by millet as the money of the poor. A reflex of the archaic popularity of the cowrie in the north might be seen in the Dahomean legend of the hunter's praise for the founding king who dispensed the threefold gift of peanuts, cowrie, and foodmarket, all in one. Yet we have no knowledge whatever of the forces that moved the Fon dynasty of Dahomey to embrace cowrie money as a vehicle of empire building.

After Ibn Batutah had been in an important post for three years in Malan, the biggest of the Maldive Islands, he took his leave and was presented with a very large sum of cowrie by the king. He refused to accept the gift, as useless to him, in spite of the king's insistence that he could buy rice with it in Bengal to where he was going on his way to

China. Batutah at first was inclined to agree, on condition that the king's officers accompany him and manage the deal. Eventually, the king gave him a sum in gold. Other accounts also tell of cowrie as the money for which the poor could buy their daily rice, but which, even by the shipload, would not buy gold.

On the Malabar Coast, which he had also visited, gold and silver were the money of commerce, but in the inland towns of the subcontinent cowrie was in use as the money of the poor. Cowrie was employed loose and by no means subdivided into conventional denominations as in the Dahomean system. It is difficult to ascertain at what rate it exchanged against coined dirhems, and, if such exchanges existed at all, when and how the rate fluctuated. After all, even in the Maldives with its highly developed government that rate appears to have been extremely unstable, as Batutah recalled in relating his experiences in Gogo.

The contemporary West African empires began to import cowrie not later than the beginning of the fourteenth century. It was a novelty on the Middle Niger and, although extremely cheap in India, by no means valueless in Gogo, where Batutah personally found it much appraised. Yet the Berber traders, who carried it one way on the beat across the Western Sahara, insisted on payment in gold for carrying anything the other way. In the neighboring Central Sudan cowrie was unknown, and during the famine the Moorish king distributed millet to the poor, which, besides being edible, bought everything in the market at a lower price than any other currency. Cowrie money certainly had been a vital feature of welfare policy in the early state.

Technologically, Dahomey's cowrie was by no means primitive money. Paradoxically, it differed from the shell moneys of Oceania by being closer to the state of nature than the moneys of "savage" peoples, which are all artifacts. The cowrie that was strung on threads was otherwise unworked and still in its natural condition as when it was "harvested" on the coral reefs of the Maldives. The shells of the primitives were polished, cut, carved with skill and perseverance, often by strenuous communal labor. Hence the "scarcity" of the natives' money. Its value derived both from that scarcity and from the emotional response to the human effort that went into its making. Cowrie, on the other hand, gained the status of a currency by virtue of state policy, which regulated its use and guarded against its proliferation by preventing shiploads from being freely imported. Neither in primitive society, nor later under modern conditions was such a handling of cowrie possible, though for different reasons. Bornu, in 1848, faced great difficulties in setting up a cowrie currency. Eventually, cowrie as a currency disappeared in Dahomey itself with the coming of the French administration, the introduction of metallic currencies, and the general use of money as a means of exchange.

In our terms, then, the cowrie currency was emphatically an archaic economic institution. Its functioning deserves to be closely followed. The Dahomean rate of the seventeenth and eighteenth centuries was precisely 32,000 cowries for an ounce of gold (equal 8 Arab mitkhals), while in the Sudanese region rates quoted by Heinrich Barth, O. Lenz, and S. Nachtigal in the middle nineteenth century fluctuated within 3500 and 4000 for a mitkhal (i.e., still very close to the standard). Nearer its origin in the Indian Ocean, it was almost without value except by the shipload. Before the second half of the nineteenth century the sheltering that was accorded by the great geographical distance from the place of origin operated against disastrous fluctuations of the rate.

All the more noteworthy were the lacunae in its occurrence in West Africa. The dispersion of archaic money was quite different from that of primitive money, which, like culture traits in general, tended to be pervasive, spreading in all directions. The areas of West Africa in which cowrie was at any time simultaneously current as money, were circumscribed. Cowrie-using areas and areas where it was not accepted for payment, were as if their boundaries had been drawn by administrative authority. Admittedly, we are ignorant of the operational side of this "ecology of cowrie money," as one might call the phenomenon, which surprisingly comprised a rigid exchange rate between gold and cowrie often in fragmented but distinct areas. Hence the limited value of the attempts of mapping the areas of cowrie in West Africa in terms of a west-east boundary line dividing north and south: it was rarely found extensively employed in other than (to some degree) organized areas *and* along the trade routes. This again is explained by the nature of a caravan that possessed a traveling extraterritoriality as a semipolitical body, similar to the early state. For an evidence of fragmentation: The city of Timbuktu, center of the gold trade, is known to have always been an enclave of cowrie money, lying between the non-cowrie areas of the Sahara and the broad area of the northern Niger Bend. Farther west, again, cowrie stopped short of the Atlantic coast region. Nor did the area of its currency spread from the Niger toward the east into the Hausa states until much later. Binger, having passed through the cowrie belt of the southern part of the Niger Bend and the trade center of Bonduku in the Upper Volta on the way to Ashanti, with the gold dust currency, noted that the village of Aouabou was the last spot where cowrie still ran and that the next village to the south refused it.

Only under early state conditions, as in Dahomey, or in the caravans connecting state and state could the cowrie shell's excessive fluidity be neutralized. But outside of the historical empires of Malli and Songhay, which antedated Dahomey, the vast areas of the valley and bend of the Niger had nowhere reached a level of statehood comparable to Dahomey. Hence the patchiness and the fluctuations, none of which existed in the realm of the cowrie currency of Dahomey, where it was an archaic economic institution. With the breakthrough of the world market, the fluidity of the shell caused its supply to get out of control again.

When these slick shells poured forth from the holds of oceangoing ships literally by tens of millions, cowrie had become a nightmare to the colonial administrator. After Bornu, in 1848, decided to introduce it, cowrie exports from Liverpool amounted, in 1848 and 1849, to 60 and 300 tons, respectively, i.e., together to 7200 cwt; twenty years later, in 1868–70 its imports to Lagos amounted to no less than 172,000 cwt, equal, at the rate of about 380 cowries to the pound, to more than 7 billion cowries over the three years.

In Uganda the British administration took action.

> In 1896, cowries were exchanged for about 200 for the rupee, but by 1901 the exchange rate rose to 800. After 31st March, 1901, cowries ceased to be acceptable in payment of taxes. At the same time the government placed an embargo on the import of cowries . . . having received information that large amounts were being imported from German East Africa. The Government's own stock was eventually burnt for lime. It was estimated that in 1902 after the destruction of the Government's stock there were still some three hundred million shells in circulation in Uganda.[7]

In the Sudan the French were fighting a losing battle against the maldistribution of the supply of cowries: "At Segou the French authorities accumulated at one time over twenty million cowries . . . At Djenne (a distance of some hundred and fifty miles) . . . the Administrator did not accumulate any." To relieve local shortage of cash in three villages, four million cowries had to be spent urgently in

---

[7] Harold Bekan Thomas and Robert Scott, *Uganda*, London: Oxford University Press, 1935, p. 231, quoted in Paul Einzig, *Primitive Money in Its Ethnological, Historical and Economical Aspects,* London: Eyre and Spottiswoode, 1949, p. 134.

those communities by the French. Again, distribution was the issue.

By the end of the nineteenth century, cowrie depreciated in Hausaland. C. H. Robinson's expedition had to sell a horse that fell ill and needed a few days' rest.

> The trouble is, that we cannot sell it, as its value in cowries would require fifteen extra porters to carry, to whom we should have to pay all the money they carried, and a great deal more besides . . .[8]

The cowries had ceased to form part of an archaic economic institution, without, however, becoming a commodity distributed by a market system that was not yet ready to take over. What, then, were the specific qualities of *archaic money* which produced societal effects that accounted for the near-perfect regional currency system of the eighteenth-century Guinea coast?

Status and State-Building

Recent anthropological and historical studies have broadened our horizon in regard to primitive money. In the place of the museum exhibits of exotic objects, attention is now directed to the institutions that invest the objects with the functions of money. Insight into the ranking of moneys on ethical grounds, as presented by Paul Bohannan, bring the status-building function of moneys in primitive society to the fore.[9] This aspect of primitive currencies gains in importance under the early state, along with their novel function of contributing to the creation of the state.

[8] Charles Henry Robinson, *Hausaland*, London: S. Low, Marston and Company, 1896, p. 46; quoted in Paul Einzig, *Primitive Money*, p. 148.

[9] Paul Bohannan, "Some Principles of Exchange and Investment among the Tiv," *American Anthropologist*, Vol. 57, No. 1, February 1955, pp. 60–70.

Archaic money was in effect closely linked with the evolving state structure. Mrs. Quiggin has shown how in primitive society the ceremonial presentation of staples by visiting tribes in the way of gift offerings to chiefs and kings endowed the objects with *mana*.[10] Utilitarian goods gained rank and dignity through their display as dues, tribute, or gifts of honor, and their acceptance by the head of the community. Such impressive public dealings invested the goods with the prestige quality of money, the uses of which stood under manifold rules. She deemed this to be one of the institutional sources of currencies, which, as we might add, introduce a quantitative connotation into rights and obligations, a fact which contributed decisively to the solidity of the social structure. It became more resistant to the wear and tear of time, and also to the internal tensions that are inseparable from stratified state society.

A number of archaic transactions assumed the existence of statutory or customary equivalents, *as a moral safeguard against any, even though involuntary, profiteering.* The Jewish Mishnah showed a veritable obsession with the possibility of committing "usury," i.e., profiting through exchange. This again lent support to a legal casuistry in the Mishnah that distinguished pedantically between money and goods in all cases of sale-purchase, a procedure, which, in principle, would exclude the purchase of money with money. Mrs. Quiggin has empirically established her thesis that money is not, in primitive society, primarily a means of exchange. But neither was it primarily a means of exchange in early state society, where indeed it ranks among the building stones of the early state and its solid social structure.

Indeed, money as a means of exchange presupposes status-free money. Economic transactions, such as sale-purchase or renting-hiring, are here as a rule still accessory

[10] A. H. Quiggin, *A Survey of Primitive Money,* London: Methuen & Co., 1949.

to status transactions, that is, goods follow the fate of persons. The appropriation by individuals of land, cattle, and slaves is linked with changes of status, such as adoption or marriage. The transfer of use only, instead of that of property, is frequent, including even the mutual exchange of use, (the property being retained by the families as in the *ditenutu* of the Nuzi of Babylonia). Also as a matter of status, land grants are linked to priestly, military, or trading posts. Thus under archaic economic institutions, economic integration and status structure may be interdependent. The rights and obligations that flow from status can have integrative effects insofar as the privileges of some persons correspond to the negative status of others. Conversely, forms of economic integration may channel status effects reinforcing them at the same time. This clearly holds good of redistribution, reciprocity, and householding, in regard to their state-building and status links.

Exchange is no exception. Archaic variants of trade produce the status trader, whether the status is of kinship origin or by appointment. The port of trade is another such archaic institution. Women's status is still another, derived from the archaic variant of food markets. In this sequence the cowrie currency of Dahomey moved into focus.

Alongside of status, the early state also belongs to the archaic world of institutions in the organizing of the economy. The economy of the state sphere and its administrative contacts with the state-free sphere shape the economic process as a whole. Again, also where exchange forms of integration are present, the state plays a formative part. Equivalents in regard to rates of substitution and to the setting of prices; administrative ports of trade for imports and exports; compulsory money-use in the local food markets are typical archaic economic institutions, which, at least peripherally, rely upon governmental functions. The peeling-off of economic transactions from the status transactions to which they originally adhered, happens in the frame of statute law evolved in the state sphere. The dual focus of state and status thus shapes the development of archaic economic institutions. Hence that close organization of society which is justly regarded as a source of archaic economic strength.

13

On the Comparative Treatment of Economic Institutions in Antiquity with Illustrations from Athens, Mycenae, and Alalakh

Tools of Analysis

A broad indication of the different ways in which we find the economic process institutionalized in society may, eventually, throw some light on the role of the economy in the territorial spread of the cultures that may or may not accompany the process of social growth. No frontal attack on the problem of size appears as yet promising.

Two features of the economy have been selected for inquiry: the relations between the economic and the political system in society, and the manner in which the uses of money are instituted, primarily in palace economies. In either case some random reflections on territorial expansion seem possible, yet the main emphasis must lie not on these reflections but rather on the conceptual tools employed in the comparative treatment of economies as we meet them in history.

The economy, then, in our reading, is an institutionalized process[1]—a sequence of functional movements that are em-

FROM Karl Polanyi, "On the Comparative Treatment of Economic Institutions in Antiquity with Illustrations from Athens, Mycenae, and Alalakh," pp. 329–350 in C. H. Kraeling and R. M. Adams (eds.), *City Invincible: A Symposium on Urbanization and Cultural Development in the Ancient Near East,* Chicago: University of Chicago Press, 1960. Reprinted by permission of the publisher.

[1] Karl Polanyi, Conrad M. Arensberg, and Harry W. Pearson (eds.), *Trade and Market in the Early Empires,* Glencoe: 1957.

bedded in social relations. The function of the movements is to supply a group of individuals with a flow of material goods; the social relations in which the process is embedded invest it with a measure of unity and stability. The movements are either locational or appropriational or both. That is, the things move either in relation to other things, which movements include production and transportation, or in relation to the persons who need them or dispose of them.

Process and institutions together form the economy. Some students stress the material resources and equipment —the ecology and technology—which make up the process; others, like myself, prefer to point to the institutions through which the economy is organized. Again, in inquiring into the institutions one can choose between values and motives on the one hand and physical operations on the other—either of which can be regarded as linking the social relations with the process. Perhaps because I happen to be more familiar with the institutional and operational aspect of man's livelihood, I prefer to deal with the economy primarily as a matter of organization and to define organization in terms of the operations characteristic of the working of the institutions.

I am conscious of the inherent limitations of such a treatment particularly from the point of view of general sociology. For the process is embedded not in "economic" institutions alone—a matter of degree, anyway—but in political and religious ones as well; nor do physical operations exhaust the range of relevant human behavior, either. But it helps roughly to disentangle the economy from other subsystems in society, such as the political and the religious, and thereby make reasonably sure that we know what we mean when we so confidently talk about "the economy."

In the first approximation, economies form a going concern mainly by virtue of a few patterns of integration, namely reciprocity, redistribution, and exchange. An historically important fourth pattern might be seen in house-

307

holding, that is, the manner in which a peasant economy or a manorial estate is run, though formally this is actually redistribution on a smaller scale. By itself, or together with the others, each of the three patterns is capable of integrating the economy, ensuring its stability and unity. Whether or not integration raises technological problems, mainly of physical communication, or rather organizational problems such as the merging of smaller groups into bigger ones, size may be the essence of the matter; typically such merging occurs whenever peasant economies link up to form a larger society.

In early societies integration happens, as a rule, through the redistribution of goods from a center or through reciprocation between the corresponding members of symmetrical groups. The goods may be appropriated for distribution by peasant or chief, by temple or palace, by lord or village headman, through physical storage or through the mere collecting of rights of disposal of the goods. Both the deliveries to, and the awards from, the center are largely assessed as a function of a person's status, and the actual allocation happens through administrative decision. Reciprocity, as between kin or neighborhood groups, may link individual partners or comprise a whole sequence of symmetrical situations "in turn." Numerous combinations of reciprocity and redistribution occur. A third way of integrating the economy is by exchange or barter. To have an integrative effect, this pattern needs the instrumentality of price-making markets, as in nineteenth-century society where a supply-demand-price mechanism produced integrative prices. The mere presence of market elements or even of non-price-making markets in a peasants' and craftsmen's society does not produce an exchange-patterned economy.

No "stages theory" is here implied; a pattern may appear, disappear, and recur again at a later phase of the society's growth. Admittedly, exchange resulting in an integrative effect only appeared with the self-regulating system of competitive markets inaugurated in the nineteenth century. Where prices are "set," "fixed," or otherwise administered, they are produced not by the market but by administrative action. Redistribution was regularly practiced in primitive tribes at the hunting and collecting stage; eventually it became a function of archaic administration, while in modern times it is a feature of industrial planned economies. Reciprocity was widespread among kinship-organized societies and still survives as the *raison d'être* of Christmas trade of Western cultures. Only integration through price-making markets, as we have said, was unknown until recent times.

These patterns do not—and this should be stressed—supply us with a classification of economic systems as a whole; rather the coexistence of patterns notably of reciprocity and redistribution is common. Also markets, which do not integrate the economy, may fit into either pattern. And any of the patterns may predominate, reflect the movements through which land, labor, and the production and distribution of food are merged into the economy. But other patterns may obtain alongside the dominant one in the various sectors of the economy and at varying levels of its organization.

In the second approximation, patterns of integration are necessarily accompanied by the institutions through which the economy is organized. No complete theory of economic institutions is here intended. Some institutions are inherent in the pattern itself, such as a symmetrical structure for reciprocity or a degree of centralization for redistribution or price-making markets for integration through exchange. And already at this level institutional variants offer, for instance, temple or palace as a redistributive center. In addition, the patterns are, as a rule, accompanied by characteristic institutions, such as the drawing of lots for the division of booty or for the assignment of land or the allocation of burdens "in turn" under a reciprocity pattern.

Storage arrangements, rations, and equivalents go with redistributive patterns. Less important institutional traits, of which there are many variants, tend structurally to adjust to these "characteristic" ones.

It must be apparent that just as the economy forms only a part of society, so the economy itself consists of differently patterned parts, each of which may have its characteristic institutions combined with a variety of traits.

Hence there is need for circumspection before one attempts the task of mapping the changing place of concrete economies in actual societies. One should distinguish between the society as a whole in which the economic, political, and religious spheres meet, the economic sphere itself, which sometimes combines several patterns of integration, the institutions characteristic of those patterns, and finally, variants of other institutional traits. The inquiry may thus come closer to the attainment of more ambitious aims, such as systematically relating the territorial spread of cultures to the economy. At any rate, it should point to some of the potentialities—and limitations—of the economic historian at the present stage of our knowledge.

The two problem groups that follow will serve to illustrate what we call the institutional analysis of economies. To simplify matters, we have selected examples from the economic history of ancient Greece, with references to Alalakh. The first group connects subsystem to subsystem, economy to polity; the second treats of palace economies from the angle of money uses.

Classical Athens offers an example of interaction between economy and polity. By the beginning of the fifth century the agora, in the sense of a market place, had become part of the economic organization of the Athenian polis, as magistracies and other offices and bodies were parts of her political constitution. Both the Athenian city-state's strength of resistance in an emergency and its incapacity to expand territorially sprang from this conjunction

310

of agora and polis government. The agora was not, as our market system is, an open supply-demand price mechanism disciplined through competition and interdependence with other markets. It was (in modern terms) an artificial construct of limited access and dependent for supply, rates of currency, and price control upon the sanctions provided by the polity. The power of the democratic jurisdiction formed a frame of authority, which alone enabled the agora to function but at the same time marred the chances of its expansion by limiting its scope to the confines of the polis. And, conversely, the agora was the mainstay of the democracy, which was the driving force of territorial expansion, yet the self-same agora time and again frustrated such endeavors through its jealous nativism. These mutually restrictive features of economic structure and polis constitution accounted for many of the vicissitudes of the Hellenistic polis. Neither the polis as such, nor its agora, had aptitude for growth. Hellenism was essentially polis-culture of empire size gradually spreading over the Near East by virtue of the "barbarian" government of the countryside, the *chora* (see below).

The palace economies of Mycenae and Alalakh are relatively new additions to our knowledge. For a comparative study of antiquity, the mesh of our patterns offers no more than a rough orientation. In order to study institutional structures, we require a finer texture. At least one further determinant should be added to the economy, namely the dimension of quantitativity. Statements that ignore the quantitative connotation of the movements that make up the economic process are inadequate. This implies that the development of the monetary sphere, in the widest sense, should offer a heuristic avenue to the analysis of economic institutions in early societies. A "monetary" approach of this kind will be attempted here in the comparison of Mycenae and Alalakh. On such a sharpening of our conceptual tools hinges, as will appear, the separation of submonetary devices from money proper in Mycenae, as well as the differentiation of Western Asian palace economies in terms of money uses, as shown by Alalakh.

Economy and Polity: Agora, Polis, Chora

The Athenian agora may well have been the earliest market in the West which might be called a "city market." Yet such use of the term is slightly anachronistic. For the agora was historically not primarily a market place, but a site for meetings, and the Greek polis was not a city in the modern sense, but a state.

First, the agora. From about the end of the sixth century Attica apparently possessed in the town of Athens some kind of market place where food was retailed. Previously only Sardis, the capital of Lydia, seems to have been credited with such an open space, which was crossed by the gold-bearing Pactolus. Gold dust presumably was employed there for the purchase of prepared foods, while coins of electron were used for trade. In Athens, where gold was absent, small denominations of silver coins served the purpose of retailing. Without some such monetary device, distribution of food throughout the market would not have been practicable. Hot meals offered in the inn, cuts of tepid meat and snacks to consume in the alley, foodstuffs to take home for the kitchen were the province of the *kapelos* (of authentically Lydian origin), to whose lowly figure was owed much of the famous ease of Athenian life. In the wake of the downfall of the tyrannis and its palace economy the agora eventually filled up with a variety of figures, male and female, selling mostly their own produce, self-raised or self-made. They rarely acted as middlemen, with the important exception of the grain trade, in which wheat imports were sold by supervised retailers.

Second, the polis. Athens the town had no resemblance to our medieval towns with their privileged citizenry lording it over the *banlieue*. True, the acropolis was an impregnable rock that overawed the flatland for a full day's ride. But the town of Athens had nevertheless no territory of its own, no legal or constitutional status, no juridical personality, no autonomy. Its agora could be put out of bounds to the unfriendly neighbor, but neither voters nor office-holders derived rights from their domicile in Athens. The privilege of keeping a stall in the agora was probably most of the time reserved for citizens, that is, citizens of Attica or Athens, not persons residing in Athens. Hence our hesitation to speak of the agora as a city market.

In what manner, then, did the agora assist the Athenian city-state in its political rise, while at the same time hampering its territorial expansion? And, conversely, how far was the polis constitution favorable to the growth of the market habit, while forming an obstacle to its expansion into a market system reaching beyond the state boundaries?

The agora, even from its beginnings, was an asset to the state. Solon's reforms would hardly have prevented debt bondage from becoming a normal part of the labor structure but for the timely emergence of the market habit. The edge of debt sharpened by the recent spread of currency was blunted by the market. There the farmer could turn some of his produce into money, and the citizen-artisan could find food to keep body and soul together by picking up a job away from home. The chance of selling part of his crop in the market would save the indigent peasant from having to work off his debt; the possibility of getting food at the cookshop would rescue him from bondage to a neighbor to whom he otherwise would have to turn for bread in late winter. The market relieved the pressure of unemployment once foreign beaches began to be closed to overseas colonists; it helped to carry the floating population which provided the nerve of the navy in wartime. Thus the domestic peace for which Attica was famed and which made her eventually feared abroad owed much to the agora.

But the reverse was true as well. The market, which bolstered domestic solidarity and stimulated the forces of a maritime democracy, was also a source of parochialism. Market-fostered popular feeling, which defeated on the battlefield the organizing capacity of the redistributive empire of Persia and acquired a thalassocracy for Attica, was haunted by a xenophobia which denied even the semblance of equity to allies and associates and thereby undermined the military strength of that very empire which patriotism had helped create. Yet nativism was inborn to the agora. To keep a stall in the agora was just as much a citizen's prerogative as was his claim to jury fees. The market place offered modest but easy earnings to the poorer part of a necessarily small citizenry, a feature that was to prove a fateful handicap to a polis way of life in its attempt to conquer the Oriental monarchies.

Let us now view the problem from the opposite angle and regard the growth of the agora as a function of the polity. Again, the two subsystems were out of step.

The agora formed part of the popular platform and was favored by the democratic faction. Cimon, the aristocratic leader, preferred to pamper the conservative voter by offering the genteel poor modest hospitality at his table. Pericles, as the chief of the democratic party, supported the novel market habit; an Alcmaeonid himself, he gave it a fashionable coloring by personally shopping for his large and distinguished household. Democratic policies included daily fees paid from the treasury to citizens for jury and other public services, so that no one would be prevented by poverty from availing himself of his rights and performing his duties as a citizen. This policy fitted well with the practice of having food retailed cheaply in the market. The navy's popularity with the democratic faction reinforced the demand for an opportunity of spending oarsmen's pay on ready-made provisions. Plutarch's account of Pericles' and Cimon's contention spotlights the agoraphil line of policy followed by the friends and partisans of democracy.

By the first decade of the Peloponnesian War this trend was so popular that even Aristophanes—assuredly no democrat—had to moderate his sallies against the market. After the war, polis management of this meeting place of commerce became pervasive. The currency was closely supervised; contact with the piraeus was under check and control; prices were watched; retailers' profit was limited; the time and place of dealing was set out publicly; grain continued altogether under administrative control; the activity of the money changer (the trapezite slave squatting behind his bench), was closely policed. Credit transactions in regard to foreign trade had to conform to rule and regulation. The resident alien was still barred from the acquisition of land and consequently from lending on urban property. Implicit in all this was the principle underlying the existence of the agora: he who appeared in the market must obey the law without hesitancy or reservation. There was no room here for our modern concept of the "laws of the market" as contrasted to the "laws on the statute book." Nor was there any sign of the medieval distinction between the "law of merchants" (*ius mercatorum*) and the "laws of the market place" (*ius fori*). Not the merchant's privileges but the authorities' ordinances were binding. The sanction of the market place was engraved on the heart of the citizens, a word that spelt loyalty to the common gods, not to the invisible god of the Persians nor even to the gods of the Hellenes, whose seat was on high Olympus, but to the local deity whose statue stood in the temple and whose aura maintained the identity of the polis. The boundaries of the market were as immovable as the gods.

It is worthy of notice that these results did not come about through the economic effects of the agora on the standard of life. Only indirectly—through its social effects—did the positive contributions of the agora and, perhaps even more, its negative ones affect the fate of the polis. Material welfare was but slightly influenced by its working. Neither the intense patriotism nor the monopolistic exclusiveness generated in the populace can be said to have greatly added to, or detracted from, the resources or supplies of the country. The market-induced attitudes were felt directly in the life of the community as forces of *anomie* as well as of social cohesion, the balance of which may well have determined the course of national history without any significant change in the national product having been registered.

As a wealth-creating organ the agora was not a determining factor of growth. Producers' goods were not on sale; metals, marble, timber, pitch, flax were not among the commodities available; wholesaling was barred; deals in land were made indoors and were announced by the public herald. Farmers and craftsmen as such were the sellers; the general public with their small daily needs were the buyers. Most manufactures bypassed the market. Many were designed for use in public works, while others went through private contractors to the armament industries or directly to the manorial hall or the exporter, as did the big jars for oil. Bankers were not engaged in financing market purchases and no documents were issued to testify to such deals. Business was in cash. The rich man had his money carried by his servant; the poor who had no cash turned even for small sums to Theophrastus' petty usurer who made the rounds collecting his mites of interest. Payment for market purchases was not to be postponed. Even neighboring markets were unconnected. There was no arbitrage. When Cleomenes of Naukratis began to practice it in the interest of the Egyptian state, an outcry was raised in Athens.

The far-reaching consequences of the agora were, therefore, in the social and political field. Together with the introduction of coinage, it worked for equality of status and a self-reliant type of personality. The husbandman did not have to tremble for fear his landed creditor would auction him off to foreign parts as a defaulter. Similarly to Berber markets in Northwest Africa and the multitudes of small markets in the central and western Sudan,[2] the market place was primarily a social and political institution providing facilities for the people's livelihood.

The market mechanism as such did not create the well-known "economic" obstacles to welfare, which are summed up under protectionism. Domestic producers apparently did not insist on tariffs; no farmer's pressure for higher prices is on record; foreign competition only seldom aroused hard feelings, thus forcing the government's hand in its dealings with allies, and no awkward effects of a competitive price mechanism interfered with national policies. If the demands of businessmen proved a hurdle to a successful empire policy, it was less on account of monopolists' interests than those of a majority of the small men. For at the mere threat of an increase in the population, opposition rallied, particularly if the threat stemmed from a policy of enfranchisement. Parochialism would paralyze any welcoming gesture to immigrants and freeze any influx of new citizens, even from the ranks of the allies. Not market forces, but deep-seated fears of ethnic and religious dilution seem to have been at work. Herodotus, Thucydides, Plato, Aristotle, the pseudo-Aristotelian *Oeconomica One*—none of them elaborate on the economic advantages or disadvantages of the agora. Even the Xenophontian praise of Athenian affluence refers to the Piraeus rather than to the agora. Plutarch, almost five hundred years later, still dramatized the role of the agora in Athenian politics without so much as mentioning the part it played in the economy. The Funeral Oration, an emphatically Athenian pronouncement, takes the agora for granted, as do the Viennese their coffee-houses. Pericles obviously included the agora among the scenes of liberal thought and social amenity and of that blossoming of a free and easy way of life that earned Attica the name of the "Education of

2 Rosemary Arnold, "A Port of Trade: Whydah on the Guinea Coast," and Francisco Benet, "Explosive Markets: The Berber highlands," ibid., pp. 154–75 and 188–213 respectively.

Greece." Antedating the Funeral Oration, Herodotus in hi
history of the Persian Wars (i.153) prophetically elevate
the uncommercial understanding of the agora into a crite
rion of the enlightened mind. And even Cyrus the Grea
his hero among "barbarians," fell down on the test.

The division that eventually established itself between th
Greek and the Persian parts of the Empire was to Rostov
tzeff's penetrating mind among the sources of the disturb
ance in the Successor states of Alexander the Great. An
he added this enlightening comment:

> The main difficulty with which the Successors were
> faced did not lie in their Oriental territories. There
> they had inherited a solid and reliable system of ad-
> ministration, taxation, and economic organization
> from Alexander, who in his turn had taken it over, at
> least in part, from the Persian kings. *Their real diffi-
> culty lay with their Greek subjects in the East.* (Italics
> mine.)[3]

The *poleis* of Asia Minor were dissatisfied with their rigor
ous treatment at the hands of Lysimachus and Ptolemy an
even with the much more liberal regimes of Antigonus an
Demetrius. Eternally struggling to regain their freedom
"the leading Greek cities shifted their support from on
pretender to another, so that stability in this respect wa
never attained." In vain did the Successors create or re
create federations or leagues of cities as "a device directe
against the isolation, political, social, and economic, of th
single cities." The same is true of the synoecisms, "the at
tempts of many of the Successors to merge several smal
cities into a larger, richer, and more reliable State. . .
Synoecism was carried out on a very large scale by Ly
simachus in the case of Ephesus, Colophon, and Lebedus.
The synoecisms, we assume, were carried out particularl
in order to ease the economic and financial plight of "smal

[3] M. Rostovtzeff, *Social & Economic History of the Hellen
istic World,* Oxford: 1941, I, 152 f.

cities with small territories and a restricted population" overloaded with debt and burdening their own people with liturgies and compulsory loans—permanent sources of civil wars, lawsuits, and wars with neighbors.

The incurable particularism of these minute subdivisions "endeavouring to live in economic self-sufficiency" was to Rostovtzeff the canker of the polis system:

> The rulers believed that one of the main reasons why the cities were poor and in distress was that there were too many of them. . . . They therefore tried to convince the cities of the merits of their remedy and to induce them of their own will and decision to carry out a union with their neighbours. In this they mostly failed, and thereupon *had recourse to compulsion, under the cloak of benevolent guidance.* (Italics mine.)

Only through compulsion, then, could the polis be induced to give up its individuality. . . . Nevertheless Rostovtzeff put the blame for what he regarded as the unpardonable political and economic non-co-operativeness of the Greek coastal strip in Asia Minor squarely on the polis.

This judgment sprang, in our view, from a one-sided approach to the economic nature of the polis. The agora, which today is falsely regarded as the germ of an institution capable of linking up with similar entities to form a market system of limitless scope, was in its origin nothing of the sort. It was a creation of the polis, which territorially walled it in. It was not born out of random transactions of unattached individuals whose collective attitudes eventually merged in the market as an institution in its own rights. Such a germination of markets, as anthropologists and sociologists have taught us, is unhistorical. Rather, markets were the result of deliberate policies of a kind of authority that even in bush and jungle enters into the shaping of all structured human behavior. To expect the polis to relinquish its individuality implies among other things the abandoning of the agora which was its organ of breath-

319

ing and nutrition. On the other hand, to expect the agora to expand in a way that some fifteen centuries later the local market was capable of would imply that an institution can transcend its given structural limitations.

Rostovtzeff himself may have felt this contradiction, for he introduced his argument with a well-nigh invalidating admission. "The Successors," he wrote, "tried in various ways to get rid of . . . the particularly unsound and mischievous" elements in the polis tradition, *"though they never attempted to change the type of economic system established in the Greek city-states."* (Italics mine.)[4] Yet short of that nothing could avail.

This concludes our discussion of economy and polity in classical Greece. In justice to two eminent minds who, separated by two millenniums, dealt in their own way with the subject of polis and *chora,* it is meet to remark on the depths of this still unresolved controversy.

Rostovtzeff, in his appreciation of the pseudo-Aristotelian *Oeconomica One* summed up:

> . . . at this time two types of economic and political organization balanced each other in the ancient world; that of the Oriental monarchies, represented by Persia and that of the Greek city-states. Each had behind it a long and glorious evolution, longer in the East, shorter in the West . . . *Each endeavoured to extend its form of economic life to the rest of the ancient world.* (Italics mine.)[5]

Rostovtzeff, it would appear, was at this point very near to penetrating the historical issue of polis and *chora.*

Aristotle's encomium of the small polis has been under a shadow in modern times. He appeared to lavish praise on the irretrievable past at the very dawn of the great empires. But the polis, far from fading out, as modern critics appear to postulate, persisted for several centuries in the

[4] See ibid., p. 154.
[5] Ibid., p. 75.

expanding Hellenistic universe, unchanged and, indeed, unchangeable as Aristotle had upheld with so much conviction, while the ancient empires readjusted their own methods at the hands of the new Hellenic rulers who continued to pour forth from the training centers of the polis.

If Aristotle failed to give the *chora* its due, he at least did not underrate the staying power of the classical polis, provided it did not grow in size.

PALACE ECONOMIES FROM THE ANGLE
OF MONEY USES

Submonetary Devices in Mycenae

Michael Ventris, the decipherer of Linear B, has asserted the absence of money in the palace economy of Mycenaean Greece.[6] The term "Mycenaean Greece" derives from the earliest excavation of Mycenae, and comprises that site and Pylos, in the Peloponnese, together with Knossos, in Crete.

Mycenae, as we shall briefly call all of Mycenaean Greece, flourished in the thirteenth century. Its palace economy was of an extreme type. For it may well be the only case on record in which a literate community eschewed the employment of money for accountancy. Mycenae is, then, of singular interest to the student of early monetary institutions. In the absence of "anything approaching currency,"[7] the actual means of accountancy employed in the Mycenaean palace economy may offer a clue to a very early phase in the development of money.

The economic historian of antiquity cannot make use of the concepts of money, price, etc., inherited from

---

[6] Michael Ventris and John Chadwick, *Documents in Mycenaean Greek,* Cambridge: 1956, p. 198.

[7] Ibid., p. 198.

nineteenth-century market economies without a considerable refinement of these terms. "Money," it is suggested, should be defined as "fungible things in definite uses, namely payment, standard, and exchange," while "price" should be replaced by the broader term "equivalence," which transcends markets.

Operational definitions of money take their start from a particular use to which fungibles may be put. Under Roman Law, *res fungibiles* are things *quae numero, pondere ac mensura consistunt*. In terms perhaps more acceptable to the economist, they are durable objects that are quantifiable, whether by counting or by measuring. The payment, standard, and exchange uses of such objects are defined in a manner that avoids any implicit concept of money creeping into the formulations. This requires *sociologically* defined situations in which the fungible objects are put to any one of those three uses in an *operationally* defined fashion. "Payment" is defined as a handing-over of fungibles with the effect of ending an obligation (always on the assumption that more than one kind of obligation can be ended by the handing-over of one kind of fungible.) In their "standard" use fungibles serve as numerical referents; two different kinds of fungibles, like apples and pears, that are "tagged" to the standard can then be added up. In their "exchange" use fungibles are handled as middle terms (B) in indirect exchange, where C is acquired for A through the medium of B. "Being under an obligation," "adding up apples and pears," and "exchanging indirectly" are thus sociologically defined situations, while the manipulations of "handing-over," "referring to" or "tagging," and "exchanging twice over" are operationally defined. To state that money was absent in Mycenae strictly means that none of the staples were handled in a situation and manner that would amount to their use as payment, standard, or exchange. Not even metaphorically, as in regard to the attractive brides of the epics, are cattle named as a standard of appreciation in the Mycenaean tablets. Apart from a list

322

of small weights of gold, the precious metals are hardly mentioned, though small uniform objects of gold similar to Egyptian units of treasure were found in the Mycenaean Acropolis. Silver—the term *chrysos* we are told is of Semitic derivation—hardly occurs in the tablets at all. Bronze is repeatedly mentioned as a raw material for weapons weighed out to the smiths from the palace but otherwise occurs only once and then not in a valuational context; prestige goods such as tripods serving as elite tool-money in the epics are absent in our accounts, as are also ornamental shells or beads. As to staples more commonly employed as money, such as barley in Sumer and Babylon or cacao in pre-Conquest Mexico, Ventris' unqualified negative settles the point. On the face of it, all this is surprising indeed. Yet its full implications can be gauged only if the scope of the accountancy is considered.

The authentic core of the Mycenaean economy was the palace household with its storage rooms and its administration which listed goods and personnel, land-ownings and small cattle, assessed deliveries in wheat or barley, oil, olives, figs, and a number of other staples, (largely unidentified) and handed out rations. The rest is conjectural: Homer's nine towns that belonged to the king of Pylos have been found, surrounded by a considerable number of villages with their common land and peasant holdings. There were slaves, a class of dependent laborers, also soldiers and oarsmen, who were sometimes recipients of rations, which, however mostly went to women and children. Manufactures were carried on by craftsmen and artisans, many belonging to the palace and others only supplied with raw materials from there. The products may have been partly employed in trading for the palace. Yet the outstanding fact about the inventory and the accounts is and remains the complete absence of money. One kind of goods could never be equated with, or substituted for, an amount of goods of a different kind. Accounts were strictly separate for each kind.

But how, then, was the palace's administration main tained over an economy of the extent of a good-size city-state? The answer lies in devices that up to a poin could be substituted for money and thus make possibl staple finance which allowed an elementary form of taxa tion without the intervention of money.

Staple finance is the dealing with staples on a large scale involving inventories and accountancy, for the purpose o budgeting, balancing, controlling, and checking. As a rul —and this must be clearly understood—staple finance re quires the use of money. This comes about with the help o equivalencies that are set up between the staples and by th use of one or another of them as a standard, which thereb acts as money. Staple finance is, then, always in kind whether its accountancy makes use of money or not, bu the absence of equivalencies necessarily reduces the han dling of staples to a moneyless "finance." Only within on kind of staple is budgeting, balancing, control, and check ing then possible. The vital operation of collecting good at a center through the device of taxation is performe almost blindly. The accounts fail to show the total burde that is put on the contributing unit, whether individual o village. It is not possible to say by how much its burde would be increased or diminished by changes made in an one kind. Neither is there a measure at hand by which t raise the taxes proportionately to an increase in populatio or to maintain equity in the burdens imposed on bigger an smaller communities.

A fairly obvious remedy, still on a submonetary leve obtains as long as the taxation in kind happens within a ecologically homogeneous region. A composite unit can b there formed consisting always of the same main staple in definite unchangeable physical proportions for purpose of taxation. Tax is then assessed according to the size o each village in multiples of this unit. The physical propor tions which obtain between the goods in no way mean tha the staples can be substituted one for another in thos proportions and that the taxpayer is permitted to deliver one kind of staple instead of another. Nothing of the sort is involved. But the totaling of each kind of revenue is made much easier by the composite unit, as is the adjustment of the tax to changes in population. Moreover, and this should not be forgotten—some serious disadvantages of monetization are avoided. The chief requirement of a balance in kind is certainly that at any given moment rations and other obligations that are due are actually available in kind. But any equivalency that has been accepted as a standard may act as an inducement for the substitution of one staple for another, whether in delivery or in handing out, and thereby frustrate that basic requirement. Any assurance of "effective liquidity" would be gone. A composite tax unit avoids this danger.

Linear B, the script in which Mycenaean accountancy was done, shows proof of just such a device. In two cases we have explicit statements of the physical proportions in which the composite tax contained the staples. One is shown in the Pylos *Ma-* tablets:

> . . . A number of townships are put down for a contribution of six different commodities, mostly so far unidentified. The scale of the total contribution varies for each town, but the mutual proportions of the six commodities remain constant at $7:7:2:3:1\frac{1}{2}:150$.[8]

The other occurs in the Knossos *Mc-* tablets, which

> . . . contain lists of four commodities, one of which Evans identified as the horns of *agrimi* goats for making composite bows. Their amounts conform, with rather wider variations than on the Pylos *Ma-* tablets, to a ratio of $5:3:2:4$.[9]

Yet, we repeat, nowhere is there an equivalency, nor anything approaching a standard, and, a fortiori, money.

[8] Ibid., p. 118.
[9] Ibid., p. 119.

A submonetary device acts in a purely operational fashion. Complex arithmetical results, which in the economic
sphere are usually gained through calculations in monetary
terms, appear to have been attained in early society by
means of operational devices without intervention either of
money or of reckoning. In the light of these considerations
we shall try to penetrate further into the earliest history of
money.

From time immemorial wheat has been distributed in
the Indian village community[10] to the various claimants-
tillers, craftsmen belonging to their respective castes, village officials, and last but not least, the landlord and the
prince—by the simple means of handing out grain from
the heap in a certain sequence which combines portions of
absolute amounts with a number of unit measures that go
to each in turn. The traditional sequence is extremely intricate. Yet the method is of utmost simplicity. There is no
need to know how many units the heap contains, nor to
how many units each claimant has a right, nor how much
he actually gets, for once the heap is gone such questions
are rather pointless in view of the certainty that each received his due, neither more nor less. No money and no
reckoning enter into the operation.

Another submonetary device, this time regarding trade
and very different from that of the grain heap, is indicated
in passages from Ezekiel, chapter 27, and some 250 years
later in Aristotle's *Politics*. The Old Testament prophet
describes the many-sided foreign trade carried on by Tyre
Queen of the Seas, while Aristotle offers an analysis of the
role played by monetary objects in long-distance trade.
Ezekiel speaks of the traders as "reckoning" one another's
goods in their own, while Aristotle says that money sets the
limit and the pace to trading. They both appear to have
had the same operational image before them. He who sells

[10] Walter C. Neale, "Reciprocity and Redistribution in the
Indian village," in *Trade and Market in the Early Empires*
pp. 224–27.

a cargo of grain from his ship's bottom, sheep from the corral, or oil from the store beneath the temple makes his ware come forth from the stock—unit by unit—and makes his trading partner move his goods at the same pace in the opposite direction—unit for unit—until one or the other stock is exhausted. Again the method could not be simpler. There is no need for any knowledge of how many units of goods either of them possesses, nor—if the rate happens not to be 1 : 1—of how many units of the other's goods each of them is supposed to receive, nor even of how many each actually receives, as long as the rate at which the operation progresses is the agreed one, since both necessarily have received the right amount at whatever moment the transaction is discontinued. And, as in the former case, neither money nor calculation is required.

These two instances of submonetary devices stem from very different situations. The one may have been common in Pharaonic Egypt with its storage economy, the other in the Fertile Crescent, which could not survive without extended long-distance trade. The one belongs in the realm of redistribution, the other in that of exchange.

Surely it is more than a coincidence that Linear B deviated from the original Linear A precisely at a point which mirrors in a striking fashion this type of difference. Linear A was a fairly primitive script of the Minoan-speaking natives of Crete (whose language is still unknown to us). It was continued and developed by the invading Greeks in Linear B, for the purpose of writing their own language and with a greater wealth of syllabic signs and ideograms. These changes were accompanied by just one other innovation, which can be hardly unconnected with the shifting from the native Minoan economy to that of the Greek newcomers, namely, a different notation of fractions. While Linear A used numerical notation akin to that of the Egyptians, Linear B changed to the wholly different system of fractional measures, used exclusively in the Fertile Crescent. The numerical notation employed figures, such

327

as ½, ¼, ⅓, ⅙, ⅔, while the fractional measures carried names comparable with modern hundredweights, pounds, and ounces or bushels, gallons, quarts, and pints. The simultaneous changeover to the Greek language and to fractional measures happened about the middle of the second millennium B.C. at a time when redistribution of grain from Pharaonic stores was dominant in Egypt, while between mainland Greece and Western Asia trade was on the rise.[11] It seems obvious that the Greek seafarers were more interested in trade with the East than were the Minoan-speaking natives whose script they borrowed and whose economy resembled that of Egypt.

For an analytical study of early money the disentangling of fractional measures in Linear B by Emmett L. Bennett, Jr.,[12] should therefore prove a most promising beginning. It may, as he suggests throw light on the early history of the Mycenaean Greeks. It certainly seems to prove that among the multiple origins of money we must also list manipulations of an elementary character, which do not assume any arithmetical operations whatsoever, not even counting. The composite tax unit that is present in traces in the Mycenaean tablets seems to be such a submonetary device.

The Prestige Sphere in Staple Finance

The first to call for a comparison of Mycenae with the palace economies of West Asia was Michael Ventris himself. Again and again he named those of Sumer, Ur, Babylon, Assur, the Hittites, and Ugarit as parallel instances, not omitting Alalakh from the list. Our own survey of Alalakh, restricted to secondary sources, is in line with

[11] See W. F. Albright, "Some Oriental Glosses on the Homeric Problem," *American Journal of Archaeology* LIV (1950), 162.

[12] "Fractional Quantities in Minoan Bookkeeping," *American Journal of Archaeology* LIV, 204–22.

that suggestion. To our surprise we found that the differences between Mycenae and Alalakh in regard to money-uses were at least as worthy of note as the general similarities between these two palace economies. Ventris naturally centered on the redistributive character common to palace economies, since the role of money had not yet moved into the over-all picture. Otherwise he could not but have remarked on the singularity of Mycenae, which did not know money (a fact he was first to state) in contrast to the West Asian civilizations, which employed money in more than one way.

Still another surprise was in store. Alalakh, which at first glance seemed monetized as much as its Mesopotamian partners, on a closer view turned out to resemble moneyless Mycenae with its Greek culture and Minoan script, a thousand miles away, rather than its own eastern neighbors, whose cuneiform writing and Akkadian official language were first cousins to those of Alalakh.

Several questions arise. Was the original assumption of Alalakh's monetized accountancy well grounded? And, if not, how should the evidence, which seemed to point in that direction, be interpreted? Secondly, how then, did its palace economy function? If Mycenae's hidden strength lay in submonetary devices, what lesson could be drawn from Alalakh?

Alalakh was a small but long-lived North Syrian kingdom, whose external relations from both the political and the economic angle were far from simple. Its economy and even more its finance reflected up to a point the complexity of these conditions.

Sir Leonard Woolley, the excavator of Alalakh, tells us how the city lay in that crowded stretch of the Fertile Crescent where in the second half of the second millennium B.C. the Hittite and Egyptian great powers met. The Hittites had once raided Babylon and eventually defeated Egypt in the battle of Kadesh, on the Orontes. A fourth power, Mitanni, with its mainly Hurrian population, was mostly

wedged between the land of the Hittites and Babylonia
Alalakh was in the eighteenth century B.C. closely depend
ent upon the city of Aleppo. (In the fifteenth century
Alalakh appeared as a semi-independent state.) The key to
the over-all situation, in which Alalakh benefited from the
balance between the great powers, was its geographical lo
cation. It formed the hinterland to the port of al-Mina, a
the mouth of the Orontes, which together with its southern
neighbor on the coast, the port of Ugarit, represented a
vital access to the Mediterranean for the inland empires
whether Hittite, Babylonian, or Mitannian. Ugarit was
moreover, Egypt's maritime point of access to the caravan
routes of the Fertile Crescent. This configuration resulted
in a coastal area of relative peacefulness in the middle of
the second millennium. The inland empires traditionally
avoided conquest of the coast for fear that the "riches of
the sea" would cease to flow through militarily occupied
ports;[13] they preferred most of the time to exert but mild
pressure in the direction of the sea, agreeing to keep the
coast unoccupied and the caravan roads to it open or
maybe even tacitly arranging for zones of influence. Such
an arrangement might, for instance, have left southerly
Ugarit in the Egyptian zone and northerly al-Mina in the
Hittite zone, while allowing the eastern powers, Mitanni
and Babylon, transit to either. Hence there may have been
a network of international treaties by which a militarily
weak and semi-dependent Alalakh secured its position in
the midst of rival empires.

In regard to staple finance and trade the situation of
Alalakh was, then, in all probability more complex than
that of the Mycenaean cities of Pylos, Knossos, or Mycenae
itself. Records show a flow of silver during the eighteenth
century, large amounts of annual regional revenue collected
in silver and passed on to higher administrative authorities;

[13] Cf. Anne M. Chapman, "Trade Enclaves in Aztec and
Maya Civilizations," *Trade and Market in the Early Empires*,
pp. 114–46.

royal visits, betrothals, and other ceremonial occasions requiring a display of valuables; a drain on precious metals exerted by the temples; sums paid out as awards within the related ruling families; expenses of the local prince, particularly for raw materials to the "goldsmiths" (mostly dealing with silver); numerous other requirements of diplomacy and etiquette; purchases of land tracts comprising many villages in the course of adjustments involving exchanges of territory between contiguous administrations; caravan trade in transit, apparently requiring the military protection of nomadic chiefs. All these factors involved a movement of precious metals, whether acquired from foreign mine-owning rulers or indirectly through tributes and taxes. Such was the eighteenth-century picture to which our data refer.

We are here concerned, of course, not so much with the economic as with the financial aspect of Alalakh. According to D. J. Wiseman[14] the silver shekel was in the eighteenth century "a true currency" and "the principal medium of exchange." It seems very doubtful to us, however, that the level of accountancy in Alalakh was actually much higher than that of Mycenae, where money was altogether absent. Only in the prestige sphere, apparently, was silver widely employed for payment and certainly established as a standard of account. Outside that sphere accountancy was "in kind," each species of commodity being totaled separately (as in Mycenae). But the evidence seems to point to an intermediate state of affairs in which a prestige sphere, accounted in silver, formed the core of the staple finance while the subsistence sphere was accounted in kind without the intervention of money.

The sixty to seventy texts mentioning silver shekels would then appear to be satisfactorily explained by the concept of prestige goods. Silver, being treasure, was em-

[14] *The Alalakh Tablets,* Occasional Publications of the British Institute of Archaeology at Ankara, No. 2, London: 1953, pp. 13–14.

ployed for uses that befit prestige goods, and expenditures made for such purposes were accounted in silver shekels. In other words, since the prestige sphere—sacral, royal, diplomatic, or relating to top-ranking civil and military bureaucracy—was the traditional field for the use of treasure, accountancy in silver shekels was the given form of bookkeeping in this sphere. The frequent mention of silver accounts merely proves the presence of important hoards of silver in the possession of king, temple, or treasury and of a rigorous accountancy in regard to it.

Admittedly, much is still unexplained. The use of silver shekels as money of account in the prestige sphere would seem to imply the existence of some silver equivalencies in that sphere. Yet, with a very few unimportant exceptions (see below), no equivalencies in silver are indicated, nor can such be implied. The main group of transfers of silver represents physical amounts of silver given either by weight or as objects for which the silver served as raw material and which are listed by weight in terms of shekels. There follow yearly totals of tribute amounting to over one thousand and over two thousand talents respectively, that is several millions of shekels each. (These two items are from fifteenth-century tablets.) The third group comprises shares in the great king's booty, in royal inheritances, in awards between royal relatives; a fourth large group of items are plain gifts to gods, sovereigns, and other important persons, with no counterpart in evidence. The fifth group consists of the prices of villages and territories bought from neighboring sovereigns. In striking contrast to all these massive transfers of silver without any equivalencies, there are small conventional items such as tips to servants, perhaps according to their master's rank, a day's provisions to a messenger or the fodder for his mount, and similar trivial expenses. The origin of these not too impressive equivalencies is obscure. They seem, however, to derive largely from the equivalency of 1 shekel of silver to 1 *PA* of grain, to which we shall return presently. Finally, there is a group of silver items, which appear to belong not to the treasury but to the household of the palace itself. An amount of 10 shekels goes as a "loan" to craftsmen and artisans engaging them for lifelong service in the palace; employment in the palace seems to have conferred status, in a modest way. Distinctly larger loans of 20, 30, and 60 shekels apparently go to persons of higher status, distinguished by mention of their patronymic, "family," or sons' names. In still other cases either apprenticeship or supervision of training appears to be involved; in these "middle-class" loans there is a curious practice of lending a round sum plus 1, such as 21 or 31 shekels.

All this referred to silver accounts. But by far the largest number of items concerned staple finance in kind, such as deliveries to the palace and rations handed out from there. Nevertheless, no equivalencies either for the various staples or for silver can be traced, with the following exceptions: 1 shekel of silver : 1 pot of best beer : 2 *parisi* of emmer[15] and 1 shekel of silver : 1 *PA* of grain. The latter is of course the oldest and best-known equivalency of the cuneiform civilizations of Mesopotamia. In the light of what has been said above, it might not be too rash to infer that it expressed the status relations of two potential currencies, namely, a currency of the prestige sphere of the ruling classes (silver) and one of the subsistence sphere of the common people (grain).

Indeed, it seems entirely possible that, similarly to the *prestige* function of treasure, which introduces the silver shekel into all records of *prestige* activities, the fact of *status* (another building stone of archaic society) may enter into broad sectors of economic life as a quantifying factor. In Aristotle's time—fifteen centuries later—it was still possible to argue the just price in terms of producer's status. Some quantitative facts of the Alalakh economy bear traces of such a connection. That both deliveries and ra-

15 Ibid., pp. 93 f., No. 324*b*.

tions reflect status seems to us in the nature of things. So may some equivalencies reflect social stratification, in a customary way.

In conclusion we might suggest the notion of a cultural continuum of monetary uses ranging from the zero point of Mycenae to the near saturation point of the Mesopotamian empires of the middle of the first millennium. Palace economies, big and small, Asiatic, Egyptian, and European, may be found to have possessed organizations that were distinguished mainly by the manner in which the various monetary uses were institutionalized.[16]

[16] Thoughts on the operational character of premonetary devices developed here owe much to conversations carried on with my colleagues Harry W. Pearson, Bennington College, and Paul Bohannan, Northwestern University.

The survey of money uses employed in this paper was prepared with the assistance of Mr. Emmett Mulvaney of the University of Manitoba.

The Mycenaean and Alalakh data were compiled with the help of Mrs. Mary S. Winch, B.Sc. (Econ.), London, England, as Research Assistant.

The preparatory study underlying this essay was done partly with the support of the Wenner-Gren Foundation, New York, the Social Science Research Council, New York, and the American Philosophical Society, Philadelphia, Pa.

Index

335